YEATS'S HEROIC FIGURES

YEATS'S HEROIC FIGURES

Wilde, Parnell, Swift, Casement

Michael Steinman

State University of New York Press
Albany

First published in U.S.A by
State University of New York Press, Albany

For information, address State University of New York Press,
State University Plaza, Albany, NY 12246

Printed in Hong Kong

Library of Congress Cataloging in Publication Data

Steinman, Michael (Michael A.)
Yeats's heroic figures.
Based on the author's thesis (Ph. D.)—State
University of New York at Stony Brook.
Includes index.
1. Yeats, W. B. (William Butler), 1865–1939—
Characters—Heroes.   2. Yeats, W. B. (William
Butler), 1865–1939—Sources.   3. Heroes in
literature.   4. Myth in literature.   5. Ireland—
Biography.   I. Title
821'.8   82–19157
ISBN 0–87395–698–2
ISBN 0–87395–699–0 (pbk.)

To
My Mother and Father

If one remembers the men who have dominated Ireland for the last hundred and fifty years, one understands that it is strength of personality, the individualising quality in a man, that stirs Irish imagination most deeply in the end. There is scarcely a man who has led the Irish people, at any time, who may not give some day to a great writer precisely that symbol he may require for the expression of himself.

W.B. YEATS, 1904

You have given us the most important part of history, its lies. Nature notes a fact and gets rid of it as quickly as possible, that is how she lures us. I don't believe that events have been shaped so much by the facts as by the lies that people believed about them.

W.B. YEATS to Lady Gregory,
after she had read him the
chapter of her autobiography on
the Easter Rising

History seems to me a human drama . . . the drama has its plot, and this plot ordains character and passions and exists for their sake.

W.B. YEATS, 1930

Contents

Acknowledgements

This book grew out of a doctoral dissertation done at the State University of New York at Stony Brook and I am grateful to Thomas Flanagan and Jack Ludwig, who read the manuscript and offered advice and encouragement. Special thanks are due Paul Dolan, a perceptive reader, teacher, and friend. I am also grateful to Narayan Hegde and the staff of the William Butler Yeats Archives at Stony Brook for making unpublished material available which contributed greatly to my understanding of Yeats. For permission to quote from that unpublished material, I thank Michael and Anne Yeats.

Many Yeats scholars gave generously of their time, energy, and ideas. David R. Clark was always a model for original approaches to Yeats; Donald T. Torchiana patiently corresponded and made invaluable letters available to me. I thank Richard Ellmann, Edward Engelberg, Augustine Martin, and William Martin Murphy for their kind answers to my questions. I am also indebted to the Reference Department of the Hofstra University Library, who eagerly found the unavailable, and to Nora J. Quinlan, of the Kenneth Spencer Research Library of the University of Kansas.

My friends and colleagues at Stony Brook and Hofstra who offered encouragement and tangible help are many, but I must thank Barbara and Dennis Bengels, Joann Krieg, Carol Levenstein, Hyman Lichtenstein, Jennifer Randisi, and Bob, Laurie, and Charles Rozakis. I am most indebted to Maureen Murphy, of Hofstra and the American Committee for Irish Studies, who first taught me Yeats and read the manuscript in innumerable versions. Her wise guidance and friendship never faltered, and, without her, this book would never have existed. My greatest debt outside the circle of friends and scholars is, of course, noted in my dedication.

The author and publisher wish to thank the following who have kindly given permission for the use of copyright material: A.P. Watt, Ltd., Michael Yeats, Anne Yeats, and the Macmillan

Publishing Co., for the extracts from William Butler Yeats, *Mythologies* (©Mrs W. B. Yeats, 1959), *Essays and Introductions* (©Mrs W. B. Yeats, 1961), *The Variorum Edition of the Poems of W. B. Yeats,* ed Peter Allt and Russell K. Alspach (©the Macmillan Publishing Co., Inc., 1957), *The Variorum Edition of the Plays of W. B. Yeats,* ed. Russell K. Alspach (©Russell K. Alspach and Bertha Georgie Yeats, 1966, ©Macmillan and Co., Ltd., 1965), *The Autobiography of William Butler Yeats* (©1916, 1936 by Macmillan Publishing Co., Inc., ©1944, 1964 by Bertha Georgie Yeats), *The Letters of W. B. Yeats,* ed. Allan Wade (©1953, 1954 by Anne Butler Yeats), *Explorations* (©Mrs W. B. Yeats, 1962), *A Vision* (©1937 by W. B. Yeats, renewed 1965 by Bertha Georgie Yeats and Anne Butler Yeats), *Collected Plays* (©1934, 1952 by Macmillan Publishing Co., Inc.) and *Collected Poems* (©1912, 1916, 1918, 1919, 1924, 1928, 1933, 1934 by Macmillan Publishing Co., Inc., renewed 1940, 1944, 1946, 1947, 1952, 1956, 1961, 1962 by Bertha Georgie Yeats, ©1940 by Georgie Yeats, renewed 1968 by Bertha Georgie Yeats, Michael Butler Yeats and Anne Yeats); Cornell University Press, for the extracts from William Martin Murphy, *Prodigal Father: the Life of John Butler Yeats (1839 – 1922),* (©Cornell University Press, 1978); Littlefield, Adams, and Company, and the Macmillan Press, Ltd., for E. H. Mikhail, ed., *W. B. Yeats: Interviews and Recollections,* (©E. H. Mikhail, 1977); Oxford University Press, for the extracts from William Butler Yeats, *The Oxford Book Of Modern Verse, 1892 – 1935,* (©Oxford University Press, 1935); Random House, Inc., for the extracts from Oscar Wilde, *The Artist as Critic: Critical Writings of Oscar Wilde,* ed. Richard Ellmann, (©Richard Ellmann, 1968, 1969); A. P. Watt, Ltd., for the extracts from William Butler Yeats, *Memoirs,* ed. Denis Donoghue (©Denis Donoghue, M. B. Yeats, and Anne Yeats, 1972); and Columbia University Press, for the extracts from *Uncollected Prose by W. B. Yeats,* vol. I, ed. John P. Frayne (©John P. Frayne and Michael Yeats, 1970) and *Uncollected Prose by W. B. Yeats,* vol. II, ed. John P. Frayne and Colton Johnson (©John P. Frayne, Colton Johnson, and Michael Yeats, 1975, 1976).

1 Introduction

When William Butler Yeats described Blake as ". . . crying out for a mythology, and trying to make one because he could not find one to his hand", he described himself.[1] Separated from traditional national heroes and an orthodox religious mythology by sensitive skepticism, Yeats made a personal mythology of four heroic figures: Oscar Wilde, Charles Stewart Parnell, Jonathan Swift, and Roger Casement. These four were essential, rather than others he celebrated, because they resembled Yeats's heroic conception of himself, and in the artistic ways he chose to re-create their images. They were all distinguished by singular personality, which often approached idiosyncracy or eccentricity. It usually revealed itself in aristocratic pride, their disdain for the common, as they defined themselves outside the accepted social, artistic, or political laws, creating worlds to suit themselves. This defiance of common expectations often led to their ruin, an inevitable result of their heroic conceptions of themselves. When facing their tormentors, they were proud and gallant: Wilde on trial, Parnell in Committee Room Fifteen, Swift as the Drapier, Casement's mad audacity. All had almost conquered England: Wilde, art's prophet, Parnell, Ireland's uncrowned King, Swift as the man whose arrest would require ten thousand men, and Casement, ready to free Ireland by force. Like Yeats, they were born in Ireland and did their work in English, constituting an Anglo-Irish Protestant lineage of intellectual freedom, an answer to Douglas Hyde's Gaelic Irish heroes. They battled an often ignorant and conservative Catholicism, and Yeats invoked them as allies against the "Paudeens", William Martin Murphy, or the Abbey rioters.

A corollary to their heroism was their martyrdom at the hands of the many, for their heroic singularity made the mob hate, fear, and crucify them. Yeats celebrated them in decline; paradoxically, their heroism was most vivid when they were attacked, even defeated. Wilde, Parnell, and Casement had been destroyed by *hysterica passio*,

1

collective irrational rage and envy. Although Swift's suffering was different, Yeats may have thought of Thackeray's "So great a man he seems to me, that thinking of him is like thinking of an empire falling."[2] These models for public heroism were also destroyed by the rage against their private lives: whether apparently or actually homosexual, adulterous, or celibate, they endured the public's moral outrage.

Although their lives shared certain similarities, their strong personalities made them individual variations on the heroic theme. Wilde came to the young Yeats as a heroic image almost by chance, but he was a necessary model, a man who glorified the life lived for art's sake, fulfilling one's self and also making one famous, rich, admired. No matter that their friendship faded as Yeats's critical acuity sharpened, Wilde was always Yeats's first model for the artistic man. His martyrdom intensified his image, for Wilde, once the Irish king of London, remained when Yeats had outgrown Wilde's art. His image, however, was incomplete, for Yeats needed a more authentically Irish hero to satisfy his yearning to be a poet and leader of the Irish people, and he found him in Parnell, after Parnell's fall. Another Irish king destroyed by a repressive church and state, Parnell became Wilde's countertruth, having devoted himself to a national ideal as Wilde had to art. Spurred by Henry Harrison's *Parnell Vindicated* many years later, Yeats wrote passionately of him as a victim of English evil and Irish provincialism. Briefly, Roger Casement became another image of that same martyrdom, reflecting the Parnell principle of a great man destroyed by the unworthy because of his private life.

Wilde and Parnell temporarily balanced art and politics, but Yeats found a completed symbol in Swift, poet and patriot too: the Drapier, a heroic thinker, passionate sufferer – and Swift's verse was the source of his "later manner". He was also a warning to Yeats, not merely of civilization's degeneration, but that a magnificent mind and *saeva indignatio* could not halt the body's decay; weakness and madness could end the noblest life. In his image, however, Yeats found the resolution of the contraries of private aestheticism and public nationalism that T.S. Eliot praised:

> Born into a world in which the doctrine of "Art for Art's sake" was generally accepted, and living on into one in which art has been asked to be instrumental to social purposes, he held firmly to

the right view which is between these, though not in any way a compromise between them, and showed that an artist, by serving his art with entire integrity, is at the same time rendering the greatest service he can to his own nation and the whole world.[3]

Yeats's constant transformation of historical men into myth was as essential as his perception of them as heroes. As static figures, they could not reconcile the contraries; as the artist of his own life, he had to change their shapes, remaking himself in the process. Like his father, he became ". . . the painter who scrapes out every day what he painted the day before".[4] His changes resembled inconsistency, the careless inaccuracy of a poor memory, but they were conscious artistic recreation, as he transcended history to create heroes who were true to character, not fact. Attempting to understand men acting in history's drama, he came to understand himself and the art, politics, and Ireland they shared.

2 Wilde: ". . . Oscar ruled the table"

Yeats remembered "little of childhood but its pain", ". . . that toil of growing up; / The ignominy of boyhood; the distress of boyhood changing into man".[1] Shy and painfully self-aware, he envied the graceful yet despaired of attaining their ease. Childhood and adolescence were also intellectually unrewarding; he was "bored by an Irish Protestant point of view that suggested by its blank abstraction chloride of lime".[2] Against this uninspiring background, Oscar Wilde entered his life. Their first intersection was in 1883, five years before their first meeting at W.E. Henley's house when Wilde invited Yeats for Christmas dinner:

> On November 20, 1883, Oscar Wilde was scheduled to appear in Dublin to speak on poetry, and Willie, even though he wasn't feeling well, wanted to hear him . . . despite his illness, [he] caught the return train to Dublin and attended the lecture.[3]

Although Wilde's lecture was either "Impressions of America" or "The House Beautiful", Yeats was interested in Wilde, perhaps the man more than his text.[4]

Yeats's connections with the Wildes were strengthened by Oscar's mother, Lady Jane Wilde, the "Speranza" of 1848, patriotic poet, folklorist, and enthusiastic patron of young Irish artists; Sir William Wilde, too, had long been a friend of the Yeatses. Both parents were known to Yeats as fellow-folklorists: Lady Wilde, for her influential *Ancient Legends, Mystic Charms and Superstitions of Ireland*, and Sir William, for his *Irish Popular Superstitions*, from which Yeats extracted material for his own anthology. Yeats's letters from 1888 to 1895 show Lady Wilde constantly encouraging, praising, and publicizing the poet Katharine Tynan and himself, and, from 25 July, 1888, he was

4

regularly at her at-homes, greeted as "My Irish Poet"![5]

When Yeats met Wilde in December, he was dazzled by Wilde's brilliant, spontaneous wit, and his social grace. Imposing and strikingly dressed, Wilde had an audacious ease. He was an Irish writer enviably at home in London society, unlike Yeats, a self-confessed Sligo provincial, and he vividly displayed what Yeats would later call ". . . personality . . . our delight in the whole man – blood, imagination, intellect running together".[6] Yeats dined with Wilde a few days later; the invitation was a charming artifice – although Yeats had attended Lady Wilde's gatherings with his father and sisters, Wilde "affected to believe that he was a lonely young man without family and invited him to Christmas dinner at his Chelsea house".[7] The dinner was not entirely successful, for both men showed some disappointment in each other. Yeats's lack of poise made Wilde uneasy, and Yeats later wrote that he was "abashed before [Wilde] as wit and man of the world alone".[8] Perhaps sensing Yeats's disapproval of his art, Wilde responded with a memorable compromise: "We Irish are too poetical to be poets; we are a nation of brilliant failures, but we are the greatest talkers since the Greeks."[9] These virtues were the basis of the mythic Wilde Yeats was to envision: "too poetical" for poetry, he lived the ideal which his imperfect art did not reflect. "Brilliant failure" also outweighed unimaginative success, as the battle's nobility was more important than its outcome. Wilde's virtues were also characteristically Irish, to Yeats, as was his praise of talk. The product of a vividly imaginative oral culture, the Irishman created poetry in speech, and, as Wilde's prose became less like his speech, it pleased Yeats less.

Notwithstanding their mutual reservations, a friendship began, for Wilde treated Yeats kindly and flattered him, comparing his story-telling art to Homer's. Yeats also envied Wilde's fame, polish, and verbal brilliance, although he might not have wanted to be Wilde, write, or think as he did. His admiration had a practical foundation, for he was eager to be successful, to be recognized as more than a rural poet from a practically savage country. For all the limitations of Wilde's art, he made money from writing. Something of Wilde's immense effect upon the Yeats of this period can be seen in a 1916 letter from AE to George Moore, an unsympathetic yet accurate portrait:

Yeats . . . began . . . to do two things consciously, one to create a "style" in literature, the second to create or rather re-create W.B. Yeats in a style which would harmonise with the literary style.

People call this posing. It is really putting on a mask, like his actors, Greek or Japanese, a mask over life . . . W.B.Y. began twenty years ago vigourously defending Wilde against the charge of being a poseur. He said it was merely living artistically, and it was the duty of everybody to have a conception of themselves, and he intended to conceive of himself. The present W.B.Y. is the result.[10]

Yeats did not write of the Christmas dinner for many years, even to mention its intellectual value – for, after dinner, Wilde had read him the proofs of "The Decay of Lying" – but it was central to his mythic portrait. After it, however, Yeats began to refer to Wilde and his work in letters and essays, perhaps enjoying the friendship's reflected glory. The two men did not meet often, owing to Yeats's movements from England to Ireland, and reasons Coulson Kernahan has suggested in his memories of Wilde:

> We were friends, we corresponded, I dined with him and Mrs. Wilde at 16 Tite Street, and he with me, and we forgathered now and then at clubs, theatrical first nights, and literary at homes; but the occasions on which we met were not very many, all told; nor did I desire more closely to cultivate him . . . the expensive rate at which he lived made him impossible as other than a very occasional companion . . .[11]

Although Wilde's social life was beyond Yeats's means, Yeats thought, talked, and wrote about him, as in a letter to Katharine Tynan, four weeks after the Christmas dinner, "Fairy book is reviewed in February *Woman's World* by Oscar Wilde, who promises to try and get reviewing of poems for *Pall Mall*." One week later, he reminded her of the "long and friendly notice" of his *Fairy and Folk Tales of the Irish Peasantry*.[12]

Yeats did not exaggerate; Wilde quoted at length from his introduction, where Yeats's talents as a writer were most evident, and praised him unstintingly as an anthologist:

> Mr. Yeats has certainly done his work very well. He has shown great critical capacity in his selection of the stories, and his little introductions are charmingly written. It is delightful to come across a collection of purely imaginative work, and Mr. Yeats has a very quick instinct for finding out the best and most beautiful things in Irish folk-lore.[13]

However, Wilde also repeated Yeats's estimate of Lady Wilde's *Ancient Legends* as ". . . the best book since Croker," revealing "the innermost heart of the Celt . . ."[14] Perhaps Lady Wilde had encouraged her son to review Yeats, and Oscar displayed the compliment to his mother as evidence of Yeats's acuity. In July 1889, Wilde kept his promise and reviewed *The Wanderings of Oisin* for the *Pall Mall Gazette*, with qualified praise. Yeats was given to "strange crudities and irritating conceits", in "one or two places the music is faulty, the construction is sometimes too involved", and he occasionally selected an "infelicitous" word. Yet Wilde predicted a "fine future"; although much was "unequal and uneven", and Yeats was "naive and very primitive", Wilde credited his "nobility of treatment", and "richness of imaginative resource", as well as "something of that largeness of vision that belongs to the epical temper".[15] The review was thus Wilde's generous gesture to a younger artist, gifted although inexperienced.

Yeats's mention of Wilde in an essay for the Boston *Pilot*, several months later, was as Lady Wilde's favoured son, the epitome of Irish talk, the product of expressive parents: "When one listens to her and remembers that Sir William Wilde was in his day a famous *raconteur*, one finds it in no way wonderful that Oscar Wilde should be the most finished talker of our time."[16] In another *Pilot* essay, Yeats depicted an Irish heroism which Wilde came to represent in 1891:

> . . . the same source as the Hell Fire Club and all the reckless braggadocio of the eighteenth century in Ireland; one of that class who, feeling the uncertainty of their tenures . . . lived the most devil-may-care existence.[17]

Yeats came to view Wilde as a modern embodiment of that gallant recklessness, a modern eighteenth-century rake.

Three brief references to Wilde, from early 1890 to April 1891, typify the developing relationship. To Katharine Tynan, Yeats wrote of "Oscar's last good thing", retelling a witticism directed at the poet and mystic William Sharp; reviewing William Watson's poetry, he represented Wilde as a man so famous that to name him was unnecessary, "a certain famous hedonist" who had praised Watson's volume on scented note paper; finally, he revived Wilde's *bon mot* about "brilliant failures", calling its source "the wittiest Irishman of our day".[18] In June, Yeats wrote again to Katharine Tynan, acting, as Wilde had done for him, as guide and mentor:

Take Oscar Wilde for another of your subjects. He is *actual* now because of his just published *Intentions* (a wonderful book) and his enlarged edition of *Dorian Gray*. Describe the serious literary side of his life – his fairy tale book *The Happy Prince* and these last books and mention his poems slightly but not slightingly.[19]

She did not take his advice, but the comment suggests that Yeats had read *Intentions* eagerly and was familiar with much of Wilde's writing.

In an article for the Parnellite *United Ireland*, ''A Reckless Century. Irish Rakes and Duellists'', Yeats repeated his admiring portrait of the eighteenth-century men who ''tried to really live, and not merely exist'':

> . . . the devil came often, the story is, and feasted among these eighteenth-century worshippers of his, leaving on one notable night his hoof-mark on the hearthstone; here a number of the gentry of Ireland were wont to drink to the toast ''May we all be damned'', and to go through the ceremony of the Mass with obscene accompaniments; and here, to show their contempt for that eternal flame thought to be their lot, did they set fire to the building in a drunken spree, and sit on mocking the flames until they were driven out half stifled.[20]

Two weeks later, Yeats reviewed *Lord Arthur Savile's Crime and Other Stories* for *United Ireland*. Although mildly disappointed by it, he celebrated Wilde's gallant mockery of tradition and English expectations, and saw him as a descendent of that rakish Irish past:

> We have the irresponsible Irishman in life, and would gladly get rid of him. We have him now in literature and in the things of the mind, and are compelled perforce to see that there is a good deal to be said for him. The men I described to you the other day under the heading ''A Reckless Century'' thought they might drink, dice, and shoot each other to their hearts' content, if they did but do it gaily and gallantly, and here now is Mr. Oscar Wilde, who does not care what strange opinions he defends or what time-honoured virtue he makes laughter of, provided he does it cleverly. Many were injured by the escapades of the rakes and the duellists, but no man is likely to be the worse for Mr. Wilde's shower of paradox.

Yeats made Wilde acceptable to Irish conservatism by portraying his mockery as harmless; however, he also saw Wilde as an Irish warrior, attacking English dullness:

> . . . a part of the Nemesis that has fallen upon her is a complete inability to understand anything he says. *We* should not find him so unintelligible – for much about him is Irish of the Irish. I see in his life and works an extravagant Celtic crusade against Anglo-Saxon stupidity. "I labour under a perpetual fear of not being misunderstood", he wrote, a short time since, and from behind this barrier of misunderstanding he peppers John Bull with his pea-shooter of wit, content to know there are some few who laugh with him. There is scarcely an eminent man in London who has not one of those little peas sticking somewhere about him.

Amidst his enthusiasm for Wilde's heroic iconoclasm, Yeats expressed doubts about Wilde's most recent work; although his judgment was often colored by his friendship with the author (as in his selections for the *Oxford Book of Modern Verse*), he preferred Wilde to his art:

> "Dorian Grey" [sic] with all its faults of method, is a wonderful book. "The Happy Prince" is a volume of as pretty fairy tales as our generation has seen; and "Intentions" hides within its immense paradox some of the most subtle literary criticism we are likely to see for many a long day. To this list has now been added "Lord Arthur Savile's Crime and Other Stories". . . . It disappoints me a little, I must confess. The story it takes its name from is amusing enough in all conscience. "The Sphinx without a Secret" has a quaint if rather meagre charm, but "The Canterville Ghost" with its supernatural horseplay, and "The Model Millionaire," with its conventional motive, are quite unworthy of more than a passing interest.[21]

After this essay, and another reprinting of the "brilliant failures" anecdote, Yeats wrote little about Wilde in a period of Wilde's greatest dramatic productivity. The period ended with his trials and imprisonment, which would have made Yeats less eager to champion Wilde in print, but it was also the time in which *Salomé* was published, and *A Woman of No Importance, An Ideal Husband,* and

The Importance of Being Earnest were performed. For whatever reasons, only two letters from October 1892 to March 1895 are public evidence of Wilde's place in Yeats's thought, the first, from John Butler Yeats to Lily Yeats in June 1894:

> Arthur Lynch is going in for Galway as a Parnellite candidate. It must gall Willie that A Lynch should be on the same side of politics as himself, but more amusing still, Lynch has retired from the Literary Society founded here in London by Willie and Rolleston because he Lynch disapproves so much of Oscar Wilde.
> Willie and Lionel Johnson have condemned A. Lynch – he does not come up to their high standards. And *now* Lynch won't associate ever so remotely with Willie's great Friend.[22]

Yeats defended Parnell and Wilde as aristocratic outcasts against the conservative world, morally revolted by his "great Friend". The second letter is the only known from Wilde to Yeats, written between August and September 1894. Yeats had asked permission to include "Requiescat" in his *A Book of Irish Verse*, and Wilde graciously suggested that other poetry was more typical of his work. Although unremarkable, the letter was cordial; without suggesting an intimate friendship, it eliminates the conventional notion that the two men ceased their friendship after 1889.[23]

In March 1895 (when *A Book of Irish Verse* was published), Yeats reviewed *A Woman of No Importance*; his title, "An Excellent Talker", showed that he preferred Wilde's conversational wit:

> All of 'The Woman of No Importance' [sic] which might have been spoken by its author, the famous paradoxes, the rapid sketches of men and women of society, the mockery of most things under heaven, are delightful; while, on the other hand, the things which are too elaborate in their development, or too vehement and elaborate for a talker's inspiration, such as the plot, and the more tragic and emotional characters, do not rise above the general level of the stage . . . many another epigram, too well known to quote, rings out like the voice of Lear's fool over a mad age. And yet one puts the book down with disappointment. Despite its qualities, it is not a work of art, it has no central fire, it is not dramatic in any ancient sense of the word . . . whenever Mr. Wilde gets beyond those inspirations of an excellent talker which served him so well in 'The Decay of Lying'

and in the best parts of 'Dorian Grey' [sic], he falls back upon the popular conventions, the spectres and shadows of the stage.[24]

This review, praising the witty courtier more than his conventional art, marked a change in the relations between the two men, although not because of its severity. Because of Wilde's notoriety and downfall, beginning in February and continuing until after his death, Yeats wrote nothing for publication about him while Wilde was alive – perhaps he did not wish to endanger his career, and essays on Wilde would not have been accepted. He did go to Wilde's house with Irish letters of support and sympathy, although he did not sign the petition for the reduction of Wilde's sentence. Maud Gonne recalled that Yeats wanted to help Wilde escape from prison "in a boat with painted oars", but the tale was more mythic elaboration than an accurate picture of Yeats's response.[25] For these reasons, and the inevitable changes in Yeats's literary ideology and purpose, the second half of the decade – a time of persecution and exile for Wilde and one of greater mastery for Yeats – did not mirror their closeness of the first half.

Wilde was imprisoned until May 1897, so contact between the two men was almost nonexistent. Wilde asked Robert Ross to send him a copy of Yeats's *The Secret Rose* in prison; perhaps its first tale, "The Crucifixion of the Outcast", seemed appropriate.[26] John Butler Yeats wrote his son in September 1898, sympathetically commenting on York Powell's view of Wilde, the "poor wretch", exiled, in debt, and unable to work, but Yeats did not attempt to re-establish contact with Wilde, who died on 30 November, 1900.[27] Yeats's tribute came almost one year later, when he commemorated him among other heroic and doomed artists who had been cast out by the uncomprehending world: "... I have known two or three men of philosophic intellect like Wilde or Beardsley who spent their lives in a fantastic protest against a society they could not remake".[28] Here, Yeats remembered Wilde symbolically, the heroic victim of "bankers, schoolmasters, clergymen", not the flawed artist; he had become a mythic warrior in the sacred conflict with those who would destroy beauty because of their inability to appreciate it.[29]

Yeats's next evocation of Wilde was similarly elegiac; in his 1904 inscription in John Quinn's copy of *The Land of Heart's Desire*, he recalled his final meeting with Wilde in 1894:

Wylde [Wilde] came late to the theatre & so missed the play, & to make amends he came up and was full of extravagant enthusiasm over a story of mine later 'The Crucifixion of the Outcast'. This was the last time I had any conversation with him, though I saw him for a moment in the same theatre a few weeks later. He was an unfinished sketch of a great man and showed great courage and manhood amid the collapse of his fortunes.[30]

In the 1905 *Samhain*, Yeats critically considered Wilde as an Irish writer, revealing that Yeats's process of Celtic absorption was now complete, for Wilde had all of the race's hereditary artistic flaws:

All fine literature is the disinterested contemplation or expression of life, but hardly any Irish writer can liberate his mind sufficiently from questions of practical reform for this contemplation. Art for art's sake, as he understands it . . . seems to him a neglect of public duty . . . We all write, if we follow the habit of the country, not for our own delight but for the improvement of our neighbours, and this is not only true of such obviously propagandist work as *The Spirit of the Nation* or a Gaelic League play, but of the work of writers who seemed to have escaped from every National influence like Mr. Bernard Shaw, Mr. George Moore, or even Mr. Oscar Wilde. They never keep their heads for very long out of the flow of opinion . . . Mr. Wilde could hardly finish an act of a play without denouncing the British public . . . .[31]

Wilde was no longer the courageous antithesis of the effete dandy; his rakish mockery was a distraction from artistic truth – hardly typical of Yeats, but an expression of his anger at the Irish emphasis on practical politics, not art.

In May, Yeats had his first encounter with *Salomé*, which did not improve his view of Wilde's drama; he wrote to John Quinn, "The audience was curiously reverential, and as I came away I said to somebody, 'Nothing kept us quiet but the pious memory of the sainted author'."[32] Appropriately, when Yeats replied to T. Sturge Moore, one year later, commenting on the Literary Society's plans to produce *Salomé*, he was vehemently negative:

I am sorry you have chosen *Salomé*. . . . I think the Wilde audience is limited to a few hundred who have already been; but

my real objection is that *Salomé* is thoroughly bad. The general
construction is all right, is even powerful, but the dialogue is
empty, sluggish and pretentious. It has nothing of drama of any
kind, never working to any climax but always ending as it begun.
A good play goes like this [Here Yeats drew an ascending wavy
line with its peaks marked "climax".] but *Salomé* is as level as a
table. Wilde was not a poet but a wit and critic and could not
endure his limitations. He thought he was writing beautifully
when he had collected beautiful things and thrown them together
in a heap. He never made anything organic while he was trying to
be a poet. You will never create an audience with a liking for
anything by playing his poetic works.[33]

This admonition judged Moore's lack of foresight and Wilde's play
with equal severity. As in his review of *A Woman of No Importance*,
Yeats denied that Wilde's drama was art, even reverting to diagrams
in his intensity. Yeats could discuss Wilde's limitations charitably
until he thought of Wilde as a degenerative influence on an audience
he was trying to enlighten so that they would appreciate his own
work. However, *Salomé* did remain in Yeats's mind, for all his
vehemence, when he wrote *A Full Moon in March* and other later
plays.

Writing to his father in 1909, Yeats considered Wilde more
calmly as a forerunner: "Wilde wrote in his last book, 'I have made
drama as personal as a lyric', and I think, whether he has done so or
not, that it is the only possible task now".[34] Although he would not
praise Wilde's dramas, he acknowledged him (on the basis of his
reading of *De Profundis*), as a worthy theoretician. In Yeats's journal
of the time, Wilde, as a historical figure, was not immediately
relevant, but his life was philosophically profound:

There is a relation between discipline and the theatrical sense. If
we cannot imagine ourselves as different from what we are and
try to assume that second self, we cannot impose a discipline upon
ourselves, though we may accept one from others. Active virtue
as distinguished from the passive acceptance of a current code, is
therefore theatrical, consciously dramatic, the wearing of a mask.
It is the condition of arduous full life. One constantly notes in very
active natures a tendency to pose, or a preoccupation with the
effect they are producing if the pose has become a second self.
One notices this in Plutarch's heroes, and every now and then in

some modern who has tried to live by classical ideals, in Oscar Wilde, for instance . . .[35]

Its basis was Wilde's "What people call insincerity is simply a method by which we can multiply our personalities."[36] Wilde's pose was heroic creativity, which required intense self-discipline, a continual artistic re-creation of the self. In writing "Style, personality – deliberately adopted and therefore a mask – is the only escape from the hot-faced bargainers and the money-changers",[37] Yeats showed that Wilde's self-dramatization was not only a means to social grace, but a way to the greatest self-realization.

In 1910, Yeats spoke twice of Wilde as a dramatist whose virtues and flaws were again peculiarly Irish; first, he placed Wilde in the great tradition of Irish fantasy, remembering the duellists, alongside Synge, Lady Gregory, and Shaw, and asserting that "the greatest English dramatists for two hundred years have nearly all been Irishmen, or have had Irish blood in their veins".[38] Part of Yeats's joy in Wilde was always his pride in Irish work, and his delight at reclaiming Wilde from the English. In an essay on Synge, Yeats reverted to his plaint of the "alien trick of zeal" that limited Shaw and Wilde, but praised them both for energy and extravagance that had made them "the most celebrated makers of comedy in our time", although Wilde's gifts had "sounded plainer" in his conversation.[39]

In the next years, Yeats spoke of Wilde and "our generation" at length in interviews; in 1912, he placed Wilde among other notable Irish individualists:

> During Shaw's childhood, the Ireland created by English politics reached its climax, and its products were men like Shaw, Wilde, and George Moore. . . . They had no home in Ireland, and England was always a foreign country. The effect of this on Wilde and Moore was to make them personally irresponsible. Deprived of a resting-place, they became spiritual adventurers. And England drew them with the attraction of strangeness. That explains to me what some people call Wilde's snobbishness. It was not snobbishness; it was the wonder of a traveller. The English aristocrats were as marvelous to Wilde as nobles of Baghdad.[40]

Although some aspects of this portrait were puzzling, it was generally favourable as he attempted to explain Wilde to an audience that remembered him only as the destroyer of souls. A few months later, he spoke as one who had known Wilde well, remembering the Christmas dinner:

> He was incomparably the best talker of his epoch. It was, perhaps, because I admired his conversation so much that I never fully appreciate his books. They remind me of something else, incomparably more spontaneous . . . there was a story (fabulous, perhaps) that he filled notebooks with the casual inspirations of his own conversations and made the plays out of these notebooks.[41]

Presenting Wilde to a British audience as a brilliant and spontaneous artist whose life was incompletely realized, and by not aggressively defending him, Yeats made it possible for readers to approach the subject without violent prejudice.

Speaking with Charles Ricketts in May 1914, Yeats "spoke with great intelligence of the British public during its quite senseless bursts of revengeful hypocrisy and morality such as it displayed in the Parnell case, the Wilde case . . .":

> He explains the unanimity of the mob by the fact that it has become hypnotized by a word, by a notion, and shows the senseless behaviour of a man under the effect of hypnotic suggestion. The rage against Wilde was also complicated by the Britisher's jealousy of art and the artist, which is generally dormant but called into activity when the artist has got outside his field into publicity of an undesirable kind; this hatred is not due to any action of the artist or eminent man, it is merely the expression of an individual hatred and envy, become collective because circumstances have allowed it to become so.[42]

Wilde's downfall resembled Parnell's in the ignorant malice which had destroyed them; both outcasts were crucified by the "senseless" mob.

During this time, Yeats composed the first draft of his autobiography. Since it was "for my own eye alone",[43] it was free from certain restraints and was occasionally more vivid than later, more polished versions. His portrait of Wilde was more expansively elaborate, as Yeats remembered him as a mythic hero as well as a departed friend. After beginning with a standard description of the

Christmas dinner, Yeats remembered Wilde's "self-possession" and "easy courtesy", as opposed to his youthful "shapelessness".[44] Although his reservations about Wilde's art had not vanished, Yeats developed the image of a heroic duellist: ". . . it was the man I admired, who was to show so much courage and was so loyal to the intellect . . . 'he would be a good leader in a cavalry charge' ".[45] Yeats saw him as a man of action – an idea that Wilde himself had little patience for, as Vincent O'Sullivan remembered:

> W.B. Yeats said to me that he thought Wilde was meant for a man of action. I told Wilde this at Naples. He thought it over and observed: "It is interesting to hear Yeats's opinion about one", and then gave a disparaging picture of English political life. Balfour, whom he placed very high in his esteem, had told him that he was often depressed at a political meeting by the thought that he could always bring down the house by simply exclaiming: "After all, gentlemen, you know – Rule, Britannia!"[46]

Wilde had misinterpreted Yeats's heroic vision, seeing in it the political manipulator, but Yeats remembered Wilde's courage with pride, as in his memory of a visit to Wilde's house in May 1895, after the first trial:

> . . . I was soon to discover that my world, where historical knowledge had taken away the horror or disgust at his form of vice prevalent elsewhere in England, had many stories of his courage and self-possession. I myself on hearing the first rumours at Sligo had said . . . 'He will prove himself a man.' I had always felt the man in him and that the wit was, as [it] were, but the sword of the swashbuckler.[47]

Although Yeats's sexual liberalism might have been that of a more mature man superimposing his feelings on the more naive man of 1895, his loyalty to Wilde's memory was exceptional, for "the condemnation of Wilde had brought ruin upon a whole movement in art and letters".[48]

This portrait of Wilde Yeats had set down in his first draft – generally admiring but fragmented – was artfully shaped in the next years. C.M. Bowra wrote of a 1917 luncheon in which Yeats, speaking at length "in praise and gratitude" concerning Wilde, was "shaping" his memories in preparation for *The Trembling of the Veil*.

Bowra shrewdly perceived Yeats reshaping memory and history into artistically recreated myth. A less sympathetic listener, St. John Ervine, heard similar stories in 1920 and saw Yeats only as hopelessly trapped in the past; from Yeats's memories of Wilde, Beardsley, and others, Ervine could only conclude that "one imagines he has not had a friend since 1890".[49] The result of Yeats's artistic rearrangement of his memories was his portrait of Wilde in *The Trembling of the Veil*, completed in May 1922. Although it began conventionally, with Wilde at Henley's, it quickly became art, not history: ". . . I constantly see people, as a portrait painter, posing them in the mind's eye before such and such a background":

> My first meeting with Oscar Wilde was an astonishment. I had never heard a man talking with perfect sentences, as if he had written them all overnight with labour and yet all spontaneous. There was present that night at Henley's, by right of propinquity or of accident, a man full of the secret spite of dullness, who interrupted from time to time, and always to check or disorder thought; and I noticed with what mastery he was foiled and thrown . . . he could pass without incongruity from some unforeseen, swift stroke of wit to elaborate reverie.

Against a familiar background, Yeats recreated Wilde as an Irish swashbuckler, gracefully and gallantly foiling dullness. He was a hero too bold for modern London: ". . . he seemed to us . . . a triumphant figure, and to some of us a figure from another age, an audacious Italian fifteenth-century figure".[50] As a heroic anachronism, Italian or Irish duellist, Wilde embodied Yeats's Mask: ". . . every passionate man . . . is, as it were, linked with another age, historical or imaginary, where alone he finds images that rouse his energy".[51]

Yet Yeats was happiest when establishing countertruths to apparently unshakable truths. Having portrayed Wilde as graceful, gallant, and spontaneous, he wrote of him as R.A.M. Stevenson's inferior, displaying an "unpardonable insolence": "His charm was acquired and systematised, a mask he wore only when it pleased him, while the charm of Stevenson belonged to him like the colour of his hair." Having spoken kindly of Wilde's Christmas dinner, he turned his youthful enthusiasm into colder scrutiny: "It was perhaps too perfect in its unity . . . and I remember thinking that the perfect harmony of his life there . . . suggested some deliberate artistic

composition.'' The pleasure taken in art for its artifice had been
Yeats's delight in Wilde's thought, but, as Yeats saw earlier
enthusiasms as fancies, his criticisms became more severe. The
perspective of 1922, not 1889, was most evident in Yeats's
judgments on Wilde's art. No longer the youthful provincial, he
spoke as an experienced artist:

> . . . the vague impressiveness . . . spoilt his writing for me. Only
> when he spoke, or when his writing was the mirror of his speech
> . . . had he words exact enough to hold a subtle ear.

> I was abashed before him as wit and man of the world alone.

> . . . the dinner table was Wilde's event and made him the greatest
> talker of his time, and his plays and dialogues have what merit
> they possess from being now an imitation, now a record, of his
> talk.

Although Wilde's art had diminished, the memory of his grace had
remained; Yeats could still call to mind ''wearing shoes a little too
yellow'' and attempting to tell Wilde's young son a terrifying fairy
tale, embarrassments that remained vivid.[52]
 To explain the enigma he had presented, Yeats always returned
to Wilde as the gallant hero. Paradoxically, that heroism limited his
art, as Yeats saw him as too active for creative toil – yet that
heroism was his essence, even when completed and realized in
defeat. Even ''cultivated London'', that had ''mocked his pose and
his affected style'', was now ''full of his advocates . . . artists and
writers who praised his wit and eloquence in the witness-box . . .''.
That heroism expressed itself in martyrdom, which helped Wilde,
ironically, to realize himself. Prison, suffering, and tragedy were
essential:

> Before his release, two years later, his brother and mother were
> dead, and a little later his wife, struck by paralysis during his
> imprisonment, I think, was dead, too; and he himself, his
> constitution ruined by prison life, followed quickly; but I have
> never doubted, even for an instant, that he made the right
> decision, and that he owes to that decision half his reknown.[53]

Wilde's heroism was self-destructive, but it was the only act possible when in combat with the mob; those who hounded him defined him as a courageous man – only those who the Gods love do they destroy. In *The Trembling of the Veil,* the more mature Yeats of 1922 considered many facets of Wilde as well as considering himself; in judging Wilde, he reflected upon the changes he had undergone. In understanding Wilde as artist and as heroic martyr, he had to make his own past and Wilde's part in it comprehensible to himself as myth superimposed upon history.

Although this was Yeats's most comprehensive portrait, and might have seemed his final word, Wilde appeared also as an exemplar in *A Vision.* It is difficult to fix *A Vision* precisely in time, because its lineage spanned 1918 to 1937, but it was the supernatural countertruth to Yeats's autobiographical rearrangement of history. A passage from *The Trembling of the Veil,* however, dealt with Wilde as part of Yeats's "System":

> . . . men who belong by nature to the nights near to the full are still born, a tragic minority, and how shall they do their work when too ambitious for a private solution, except as Wilde of the nineteenth Phase, as my symbolism has it, did his work? He understood his weakness, true personality was impossible, for that is born in solitude, and at his moon one is not solitary; he must project himself before the eyes of others, and, having great ambition, before some great crowd of eyes; but there is no longer any great crowd that cares for his true thought. He must humour and cajole and pose, take worn-out stage situations, for he knows that he may be as romantic as he please, so long as he does not believe in his romance, and all that he may get their ears for a few strokes of contemptuous wit in which he does not believe.[54]

Even in this context, Yeats balanced Wilde's image between the details of his life and the larger confines of *A Vision's* philosophical cycles. In the "Table of Four Faculties", Yeats characterized Wilde's phase:

Will: The assertive man
True Mask: Excess
False Mask: Limitation
True Creative Mind: Moral iconoclasm
False Creative Mind: Self-assertion
Body of Fate: Persecution[55]

Loosely interpreted – for there were few absolutes in the
"System", – Yeats saw Wilde as assertive, fulfilling himself in
excess (not a negation, remembering Blake's praise of it). Such
assertiveness could be heroic self-definition or "unpardonable
insolence". "Excess" was also appropriate, not only as financial
extravagance, but as the wildness of his art's satiric energies.
"Limitation" referred to that art's inadequacies, and "Moral
iconoclasm" may have been apparent in Wilde's decision to
prosecute the Marquess of Queensberry on principle, in a case a
more reasonable man would have known was lost. "Self-assertion"
reflected Wilde's Will: when True, it asserted an intellectual creation
outside the self; when False, it asserted only the self, and was thus
closer to an obsessive domination. "Persecution", finally, was
familiar as the fate towards which he moved inexorably.

In a more thorough delineation of Phase 19, Yeats altered these
characteristics slightly: True Mask became "Conviction"; True
Creative Mind, "Emotional Intellect"; False Creative Mind, "The
Unfaithful". These were less specifically applicable to Wilde,
because the phase now included other exemplars: "Gabriele
d'Annunzio (perhaps) . . . Byron, a certain actress". Body of Fate
was, however, now "Enforced failure of action", perhaps reflecting
Wilde's inability to escape persecution.[56] Yeats's connection of
Wilde and Byron was revealing, for Yeats had celebrated both as
men and moral rebels rather than as artists. Byron was "one of the
great problems, the great mysteries – a first-rate man, who was
somehow not first-rate when he wrote . . . yet the very fascination of
him grows from the same root as his faults. One feels that he is a
man of action made writer by accident . . .". To H.V. Nevinson,
Yeats called Byron "the last *man* who made poetry", thus Wilde's
equal as an audacious hero.[57]

Although the details of Wilde's personal history were often
abstracted to more general conceptions, Phase 19 was firmly based
on him:

> This phase is the beginning of the artificial, the abstract, the
> fragmentary, and the dramatic. Unity of Being is no longer
> possible, for the being is compelled to live in a fragment of itself
> and to dramatise that fragment . . . direct knowledge of self in
> relation to action is ceasing to be possible.

Wilde was visible in "artificial" and "dramatic", and his

fragmentation and the impossibility of Unity of Being were echoes of Yeats's earlier conception of him as an "unfinished sketch". The discontinuity between self and action suggested another sort of fragmentation, perhaps also the pose, but it was a result of the social convention that forced Wilde to lead separated lives, thus limiting the possibility of his unity. The intellect of the man of Phase 19, as well, reflected Wilde's:

> His aim is so to use an intellect which turns easily to declamation, emotional emphasis, that it serves conviction in a life where effort, just in so far as its object is passionately desired, comes to nothing. He desires to be strong and stable, but . . . he passes from emphasis to emphasis . . . His thought is immensely effective and dramatic, arising always from some immediate situation, a situation found or created by himself, and may have great permanent value as the expression of an exciting personality. This thought is always an open attack; or a sudden emphasis, an extravagance, or an impassioned declamation of some general idea, which is a more veiled attack.

However effective and dramatic, Wilde's artistic efforts were overshadowed by his personality, extravagant, even belligerent. In this new context, Yeats also remembered Wilde's "unpardonable insolence" in a life "lived out of phase":

> . . . there is a hatred or contempt of others, and instead of seeking conviction for its own sake, the man takes up opinions that he may impose himself upon others. He is tyrannical and capricious . . .[58]

Wilde's failure was thus most comprehensible in terms of his personality, and Yeats developed this by examining the relationships characteristic of the phase, perhaps with Lord Alfred Douglas's treacheries in mind:

> Here one finds men and women who love those who rob them or beat them, as though the soul were intoxicated by its discovery of human nature, or found even a secret delight in the shattering of the image of its delight. It is as though it cried, "I would be possessed by" or "I would possess that which is Human. What do I care if it is good or bad?" There is no "disillusionment", for

they have found that which they have sought, but that which they
have sought and found is a fragment.

When Yeats noted Wilde as a specific illustration of the phase, his
estimate was severe, contrary to his elegiac visions, and only
understandable as Yeats's reservations about his art:

> I find in Wilde, too, something pretty, feminine, and insincere,
> derived from his admiration for writers of the 17th and earlier
> phases, and much that is violent, arbitrary and insolent, derived
> from his desire to escape.[59]

The condemnation of Wilde as "insincere" was unusual, for
Yeats had known it as the way to multiply one's personalities. Yet
it was the nature of *A Vision* to blame as well as praise, for it
chronicled a passage through the phases, not celebrating one
phase above all, for that would negate the "System" as cycle and
attempt a static perfection. However, Yeats's summation of
Phase 19 was more generous: in it, "we create through the
externalised Mask an imaginary world, in whose real existence
we believe, while remaining separate from it . . .".[60] Such self-
dramatization made personal and artistic unity possible, and
Yeats had also described the artist's task and goals. For all its
reservations, *A Vision* still celebrated Wilde's potential for
creation through self-dramatization, whether personal or public.
Although fragmented, the man of that phase was capable of great
intellectual power.[61]

Yeats returned to his characteristic vacillation between gentler
praise and blame of Wilde, as in his introduction to *The Happy Prince
and Other Fairy Tales* (one volume of a 1923 collected edition), which
contained much familiar material, altered subtly through Yeats's
changing perspective. He began with praise of Wilde that perhaps
only he could suggest seriously – Wilde had been internationally
adopted by non-Western cultures as their writer, for Yeats "had
already heard that 'The Soul of Man Under Socialism' was much
read in the Young China party". From this, Yeats fantasized about
his earliest meetings with Wilde:

> My mind went back to the late eighties when I was but just
> arrived in London with the manuscript of my first book of poems,
> and when nothing of Wilde's had been published except his

poems and "The Happy Prince". I remember the reviews were generally very hostile to his work, for Wilde's aesthetic movement was a recent event and London journalists were still in a rage with his knee breeches, his pose – and it may be with his bitter speeches about themselves; while men of letters saw nothing in his prose but imitations of Walter Pater or in his verse but imitations of Swinburne and Rossetti. Never did any man seem to write more deliberately for the smallest possible audience or in a style more artificial. . . . then in the midst of my meditation it was as though I heard him saying with that slow precise, rhythmical elocution of his, "I have a vast public in Samarkand". Perhaps they do not speak Arabian in Samarkand, but whatever name he had chosen he would have chosen it for its sound and its suggestion of romance. His vogue in China would have touched him even more nearly, and I can almost hear his voice speaking of jade and powdered lacquer.

In the way that Swift would haunt Yeats, Wilde's voice and presence were still tangibly available to him. Yeats also placed him in the greatest tradition of Irish talk and wit, here transformed by a joyous mind without practical aims into pure art:

> . . . when I remember him with pleasure it is always the talker I remember, either as I have heard him at W.E. Henley's or in his own house or in some passage of a play, where there is some stroke of wit which had first come to him in conversation or might so have come. . . . He talked as good Irish talkers always do – though with a manner and music that he had learnt from Pater or Flaubert – and as no good English talker has ever talked. He had no practical interest, no cause to defend, no information to give, nor was he the gay jester whose very practical purpose is our pleasure. Behind his words was the whole power of his intellect, but that intellect had given itself to pure contemplation.

As a result, only that art which captured his talk was memorable; as Wilde abandoned his improvisatory "method of speech", he became less "original", less "accomplished". Yeats could only enjoy a fairy tale if he could "hear his words once more, and listen once more to that incomparable talker".

"The Doer of Good" again epitomized Wilde's tragic life, the paradox of success and ruin:

It has definiteness, the simplicity of great sculpture, it adds
something new to the imagination of the world, it suddenly
confronts the mind – as does all great art – with the
fundamental and the insoluble. It puts into almost as few as
possible words a melancholy that comes upon a man at the
moment of triumph, the only moment when a man without
dreading some secret bias, envy, disappointment, jealousy, can
ask himself what is the value of life. Wilde, when I knew him first,
was almost a poor man . . . now he had three plays running at
once, had earned it was said ten thousand pounds in a year:
"Lord, I was dead and you raised me into life, what else can I do
but weep?"

Commending Wilde to the discredit of his natural opposite, Shaw,
who had "never cast off completely the accidental and the soluble",
Yeats concluded with unusually determined praise of Wilde's art,
although its potential was incompletely realized:

When his downfall came he had discovered his natural style in
"The Importance of Being Earnest", constrained to that
discovery by the rigourous technique of the stage, and was about
to give the English theatre comedies which would have been to
our own age what the comedies of Goldsmith and Sheridan were
to theirs.[62]

In 1924, Wilde emerged in various contexts as a point of reference
for Yeats. "Wilde told me that he had read this somewhere" was
sufficient documentation in a revision of a 1900 essay on Shelley,
and Yeats repeated treasured anecdotes and epigrams to Lady
Gregory as she wrote her autobiography, the accuracy of his
memory ample testimony to the value he placed on these
memories.[63] In "Compulsory Gaelic", a mock-dialogue fashioned
after "The Decay of Lying", Yeats created three characters who
discussed the enforcement of Gaelic in Ireland and commented on
Wilde, an Irish writer, forced to express himself in English. "Paul"
encouraged the literary and cultural unity Gaelic would bring, if the
Irish spoke only one language "well enough for intimacy": "Would
not Ireland have gained if Mr. Bernard Shaw and Oscar Wilde . . .
thought they were strangers everywhere but in Ireland."[64] Wilde
was lost to Ireland because it could not give him a proper intellectual
home; had British internationalism not attracted him he might have

fostered an Irish Unity of Culture.

During the latter half of the decade, Yeats retold stories of Wilde to new listeners, proudly displaying himself as that tragic generation's survivor. Gabriel Fallon remembered a January 1926 meeting when Yeats "fittingly tempered his tales of Wilde" for mixed company, and Micheal MacLiammoir remembered a similar luncheon when Yeats spoke of Wilde, Beardsley, Dowson, and Lionel Johnson.[65] Even if the art that Yeats's friends had made had faded, their richly shaped lives were still vivid. In 1929, Yeats read Lord Alfred Douglas's autobiography, and wrote scathingly of its author to Olivia Shakespear; thirty years later, Wilde's life and times still fascinated him, and he remained loyal to Wilde's heroic memory. Other letters of the next few years, to Olivia Shakespear and Mrs. Yeats, brought Wilde into disparate contexts: Balzac, Catholicism. No matter what the subject, Yeats often considered Wilde's attachment to it, haunted by Wilde's image and memory.[66]

In his commentary to "A Parnellite at Parnell's Funeral", Yeats remembered Wilde as one of a singular trio shaping the Irish intellectual and political mind before Parnell's death: ". . . three men too conscious of intellectual power to belong to party, George Bernard Shaw, Oscar Wilde, George Moore, the most complete individualists in the history of literature, abstract, isolated minds, without a memory or a landscape".[67] Yeats had abandoned his criticism of Wilde as an artist ruined by political zeal; here, he was a pure thinker whose joy was in imaginative art without external purpose. In the political context Yeats remembered – the madness of Irish party politics surrounding Parnell's fall – it was the highest praise to portray Wilde as contemplative, not fervently political.

In 1934, Yeats wrote and saw produced *The King of the Great Clock Tower* and *A Full Moon in March*, both indebted to images Wilde had evoked in *Salomé*: her dance, and the severed head (notable in Celtic myth, as in the *Táin Bó Cualinge*). However, calling his work "more original than I thought it", he disavowed any connections between it and Wilde's:

> . . . when I looked up *Salomé* I found that Wilde's dancer never danced with the head in her hands – her dance came before the decapitation of the saint and is a mere uncovering of nakedness. My dance is a long expression of horror and fascination.[68]

In his preface to the play, he acknowledged Wilde's potential influence, yet defended the idea's originality by constructing an elaborate genesis:

> The dance with the severed head, suggests the central idea of Wilde's *Salomé*. Wilde took it from Heine who has somewhere described Salomé in Hell throwing into the air the head of John the Baptist. Heine may have found it in some Jewish religious legend for it is part of the old ritual of the year: the mother goddess and the slain god. In the first edition of *The Secret Rose* there is a story based on some old Gaelic legend. A certain man swears to sing the praise of a certain woman, his head is cut off and the head sings. A poem of mine called 'He Gives His Beloved Certain Rhymes' was the song of the head. In attempting to put the story into a dance play I found that I had gone close to Salomé's dance in Wilde's play. But in his play the dance is before the head is cut off.[69]

Whether Yeats was amending, rejecting, or forgetting Wilde's images, his attempts to disavow Wilde's influence showed its power.

At this time, Yeats was editing and writing an introduction to *The Oxford Book of Modern Verse*. His drastic revision of *The Ballad of Reading Gaol* showed how his taste had changed from his 1895 request to include "Requiescat" in an anthology; only by recreating Wilde's work in his own image could Yeats consider it poetic. In his introduction, he also judged Wilde from the double perspective of "a young man" of the eighties and as a mature poet:

> Nor would that young man have felt anything but contempt for the poetry of Oscar Wilde, considering it an exaggeration of every Victorian fault, nor, except in the case of one poem not yet written, has time corrected the verdict. Wilde, a man of action, a born dramatist, finding himself overshadowed by old famous men he could not attack, for he was of their time and shared its admirations, tricked and clowned to draw attention to himself. Even when disaster struck him down it could not wholly clear his soul. Now that I have plucked from *The Ballad of Reading Gaol* its foreign feathers it shows a stark realism akin to that of Thomas Hardy, the contrary to all its author deliberately sought. I plucked out even famous lines because, effective in themselves, put into the Ballad they become artificial, trivial, arbitrary . . . I have stood in judgement upon Wilde, bringing into the light a great, or

almost great poem, as he himself had done had he lived; my work gave me that privilege.[70]

In April 1938, Yeats's final reference in print to Wilde appeared – Yeats's sole reference to him in his poetry, which had often celebrated friends and historical figures by name. "The Statesman's Holiday" mocked and renounced a degenerate modernity: "I lived among great houses, / Riches drove out rank, / Base drove out the better blood, / And mind and body shrank. / No Oscar ruled the table."[71] With men such as Wilde, "the better blood", gone, the only choice was to renounce the world and sing "an old foul tune". Although that song was joyous and his renunciation the only possible act, Yeats's backward glance was a regretful one at a vanished era, its culture, his lost friend.

To understand Wilde's complexity – hero and martyr, admired friend and artistic failure – we must view Yeats's modification of his myth through fifty-five years. His first admiration was for the older, successful artist, the epitome of social grace. In his example, Yeats saw an Irishman with power over himself and England granted through his art, not politics. As Yeats matured, however, he cast off his earlier artistic models; as he wrote later, "We are never satisfied with the maturity of those whom we have admired in boyhood . . . we remain to the end their harshest critics."[72] Had Wilde not fallen from grace, he might have been a minor figure in Yeats's history, but that fall revealed his aristocratic courage when faced by the traditional enemies of the Irish artist: England and moral stupidity. Thus, he became a heroic ideal, one of those "personages" Yeats revered instead of orthodox religious icons, a man whose heroic grace neither poor art nor insolence could erase.

In considering the effects of Wilde's art upon Yeats, we face the paradox of his early admiration and later scorn. To understand this, we will examine those works Yeats read, his reactions, and their effects on his art and thought. We begin with Wilde's poetry, as did Yeats, to reconcile the contraries of hero and limited artist that Yeats celebrated so extensively.

3   Yeats and Wilde's Art

Had Wilde truly "lived his poems", as he asserted, Yeats would have found his life unworthy of celebration.[1] His verse was, first, highly derivative; his *Poems* (1881) abounded with echoes which made their context seem insubstantial. More disturbing, however, was his traditionalism, in content, approach, and method. As Yeats attempted to revitalize Ireland through myth and saga, Wilde glorified British imperialism. "Ave Imperatrix" praised an England "girt and crowned with sword and fire" that "Climbs the steep road of wide empire".[2] Such art was politically disloyal, and, as propaganda, poor art as well. As Yeats sought new possibilities in mysticism, Wilde worshipped an orthodox Christianity without his later irreverences. In "E Tenebris", he found traditional solace traditionally satisfying, and in "Santa Decca", he returned to themes familiar to Milton, the death of pagan deities and their replacement by Christ: "Great Pan is dead, and Mary's Son is King".[3]

Had his manner been artful, Yeats could have overlooked the traditionalism, but Wilde clung to exhausted forms, diction, and conventions. For Yeats, in "The Song of the Happy Shepherd", Arcady was dead; in Wilde's "The Garden of Eros", it was real and possible.[4] Wilde also enjoyed much that was purely decorative – catalogues of flowers and semi-precious stones – and rhetorical amplification often became numbing repetition. Emotion was expressed in suitably sentimental, timeworn images: "For the crimson flower of our life is eaten by the canker-worm of truth, / And no hand can gather up the fallen withered petals of the rose of youth."[5] At his most florid, his diction alternated between anachronism and cliche: "nathless", "wight", "insapphrine", "white as milk", "heart of stone".[6]

Thus, Yeats's evaluation of Wilde's poetry as an inorganic collection of Victorian error was amply supported by such evidence. Three poems, however, deserve specific note. Although Yeats admired "Requiescat", it was illogical, a collection of "ritual utterances" in a traditional formula.[7] Wilde's paen to Lily Langtry, "The New Helen", might seem a possible antecedent to Yeats's use of Helen, as in "No Second Troy", but Wilde's Helen was only another "decorative image", a quick way to praise Langtry's beauty.[8] Yeats's Helen was not simply praise of Maud Gonne: the image had danger as well as beauty, historical and political resonances. *The Ballad of Reading Gaol* was Wilde's only poem that Yeats would even consider including in the *Oxford Book of Modern Verse,* but to find the "stark realism" in it, contrary to Wilde's intentions, Yeats excised more than two-thirds of the poem, keeping only those stanzas in which Wilde was direct, free from ostentation, moralizing, or melodrama – perhaps his most severe judgment of Wilde's poetry.

Any attempt to claim Wilde as one of Yeats's poetic ancestors must ignore Yeats's self-education in his craft, for the effect of Wilde's poetry was "only in antithesis", its lessons purely negative.[9] A letter from Yeats to Katharine Tynan in 1888 shows why he did not follow Wilde. Yeats had written the poetry "of longing and complaint – the cry of the heart against necessity", and wished "some day to alter that and to write poetry of insight and knowledge", a type of art he could not find in Wilde's verses.[10]

In his September 1891 review of *Lord Arthur Savile's Crime and Other Stories,* Yeats remembered *The Picture of Dorian Gray* as the artistic summit from which Wilde had fallen. For "all its faults of method", it was "a wonderful book".[11] The faults – its melodrama of tone and phrase and its extravagant catalogues – were evident. However, its contrived plot, which might have been its gravest fault, became an asset to Yeats, as the relationship between Dorian's life and portrait was appropriate to *A Vision,* where the dance of two simultaneous antinomies was a philosophical foundation. One can hardly read *A Vision* without being reminded of Wilde's conception, as in Yeats's frequent quotation from Heraclitus, "Dying each other's life, living each other's death", and ". . . a being racing into the future passes a being racing into the past, or two footprints perpetually obliterating each other, toe to heel, heel to toe", or in his reference to Flaubert's "La Spirale": "It would have described a man whose dreams during sleep grew in magnificence as his life grew more and more unlucky, the wreck of some love affair coinciding with his marriage to a dream princess".[12] Although Yeats never acknowledged such a philosophical or structural debt, we need not discount it as an inspiration, for in his 1928 introduction to *A Vision,* answering whether he actually believed in his "System", he provided the terms by which we may understand his use of the novel, as providing yet another "stylistic arrangement of experience".[13] As such, Wilde's explorations of the contraries influenced Yeats's:

> The portrait would be to him the most magical of mirrors. As it had revealed to him his own body, so it would reveal to him his own soul. And when winter came upon it, he would still be standing where spring trembles on the verge of summer. When the blood crept from its face, and left behind a pallid mask of chalk with leaden eyes, he would keep the glamour of boyhood.
>
> The very sharpness of the contrast used to quicken his sense of pleasure. He grew more and more enamoured of his own beauty, more and more interested in the corruption of his own soul.[14]

The novel also enabled Wilde to boldly present ideas in monologue and dialogue; it reproduced his witty voice, although it now belonged to "Sir Henry Wotton": "It is perfectly monstrous . . . the way people go about nowadays saying things against one behind one's back that are absolutely and entirely true."[15] More than charming paradox, its artful shape influenced the way Yeats formed ideas. As the paradox of the plot influenced *A Vision,* Wotton's mode of expression became the best way to present paradoxical heart-truths. His lament, "The tragedy of old age is not that one is old, but that one is young", reappeared in Yeats's understandable preoccupation with the rigours of old age, but it had retained its singular shape in Yeats's comment to Sir William Rothenstein: "When I was young my mind was a grub, my body a butterfly; now, in my old age, my body is a grub, my mind a butterfly."[16] When Yeats first read the novel, old age was not yet oppressive, but paradoxes remained valuable artistic forms. In the words of "Mr. Erskine", ". . . the way of paradoxes is the way of truth. To test Reality we must see it on the tight-rope. When the Verities become acrobats we can judge them."[17]

The novel's ideas were not entirely subordinated to their shape: Wilde's musings on the conduct of one's life, the purpose of art, and the Mask, were, when filtered through Yeats's sensibility, influential in themselves. Since much of the novel was didactic – Lord Henry education Dorian, and Dorian educating others – Wilde had many opportunities to instruct, as in Lord Henry's secular gospel:

> The aim of life is self-development. To realize one's nature perfectly – that is what each of us is here for. People are afraid of themselves, nowadays. They have forgotten the highest of duties, the duty that one owes to one's self.

> To be good is to be in harmony with one's self. . . . Discord is to be forced to be in harmony with others.[18]

"Perfection of the self", like Unity of Being, could be attained through inner harmony and self-discipline, and that perfected self was the highest artistic good. In his struggle to free Irish art from the demands of nationalism, another idea was valuable support for the necessity of art for its own sake: "Art has no influence upon action. It annihilates the desire to act." Yeats repeated this in 1897, defending an art stripped of political or social responsibilities:

> Art should be used only for its own sake. In literature the art that aims at moral ends in the copybook and the headlines – in Ireland many have the idea that literary art should be used for political ends, and this would lead us to Spirit of the Nation after Spirit of the Nation to the end of time. Art should be for its own sake only – Art is the reflection of the heavenly vision, and its end should be, for peace.[19]

Dorian Gray also dramatized Wilde's ideas on the Mask's use and abuse, as it portrayed a man, given the opportunity to attain Self and Anti-Self, who ruined himself and many others by submerging himself wholly in one. It was thus a cautionary tale on the necessity of the contraries, pose, and Mask: "Being natural is simply a pose, and the most irritating pose I know." Contemplating the divided self brought enlightened harmony: "Perhaps one never seems so much at one's ease as when one has to play a part." By treating one's life as raw material to be re-formed artistically, one could "multiply our personalities" and "escape the suffering of life".[20]

These ideas also shaped Yeats's poetry. A Wotton epigram came to fruition in "A Dialogue of Self and Soul", "To get back one's youth, one has merely to repeat one's follies", was recreating by an aging Yeats who declared himself willing to repeat the process for the peace it would bring, willing to "Endure that toil of growing up", for he was "content to live it all again/And yet again . . .".[21] The more famous paradox of "Easter 1916" was born in Wootton's commentary on the artistic limitations of Sybil Vane's tragedy: ". . . the real tragedies of life occur in such an inartistic manner that they hurt us by their crude violence, their absolute incoherence, their absurd want of meaning, their entire lack of style". This was to be revealed in the process Yeats went through in transforming the deaths of the Easter Rising into art: how to make the tragic yet inartistic into emotionally potent art. If we wonder at the generality of the connection, for Easter 1916 was not the only inartistic tragedy of Yeats's life, we have only to read Dorian's characterization of his part in Sybil's suicide: "It has all the terrible beauty of a Greek tragedy, a tragedy in which I took a great part, but by which I have not been wounded."[22] Certainly that phrase and the artist's stance, contemplating tragedy but being removed from it, were echoed in "Easter 1916". Although Yeats was far less responsible for the Irish tragedy than Dorian had been for Sybil's, he was wounded by it and blamed himself: "Did that play of mine send out / Certain men the English shot?"[23]

If only as the source of that "terrible beauty", *The Picture of Dorian Gray* would have been influential, but it also transmitted many of Wilde's ideas to him – although it did not give him a unified aesthetic or philosophical statement.

Although Yeats remembered Wilde's fairy tales with pleasure, his enjoyment did not affect his work. Having collected his own stories about the people of Faery, Yeats would have been ambivalent about Wilde's mixtures of Jesus and selfish giants, talking rockets and a water-rat who sounded much like a hostile London critic. Wilde's tales were essentially for children; he had not intended to rebuild a national consciousness through myth. The tales also ended more happily; unlike the protagonists of Yeats's tales, who were often scarred or "taken" to the other world (appropriately, Yeats had frightened Wilde's son with his fairy tale), Wilde's characters were usually saved through more orthodox moral or Christian means. Even when both writers shared a motif, their treatments were antithetical, as a comparison of "The Fisherman and his Soul" and "The Mermaid" shows. Similarly, Yeats was hardly affected by *Lord Arthur Savile's Crime and Other Stories*; as in *The Picture of Dorian Gray,* he appreciated Wilde's profound wit, but found the plots and contrivances of the short stories tiresome and predictable.

"The Soul of Man Under Socialism" was another matter. Although Yeats's political thought had not crystallized at the time of its publication, February 1891, he responded to its aesthetic view of political reality, with political and economic salvation possible only through complete self-realization and self-fulfillment – the goal was to be "perfectly and absolutely" oneself.[24] He also proposed an ideal relationship between the artist and the public: ". . . *Art should never try to be popular. The public should try to make itself artistic. . . . The work of art is to dominate the spectator, the spectator is not to dominate the work of art.*"[25] The receptive audience was free from ignorance and narrowness, as well as the traditional critical criteria common to the educated. Wilde also criticized the public's condemnation of art they did not understand as "immoral", which anticipated Yeats's conflicts with the mob, church, and state, as forces limiting artistic freedom. The public's violent antipathy to Wilde's art intensified during his lifetime, and his grim depiction applied to English and Irish audiences alike:

A fresh mode of Beauty is absolutely distasteful to them, and whenever it appears they get so angry and bewildered that they always use two stupid expressions. . . . When they say a work of art is grossly unintelligible, they mean that the artist has said or made a beautiful thing that is new; when they describe a work as grossly immoral, they mean that the artist has said or made a beautiful thing that is true. . . . *There is not a single real poet or prose-writer of this century, for instance, on whom the British public have not solely conferred diplomas of immorality . . .*

These attacks were badges of artistic honour: ". . . an artist in England gains something by being attacked. His individuality is intensified. He becomes more completely himself". Wilde's view of the public's moral backwardness was also reassuring: ". . . *the popular novel that the public call healthy is always a thoroughly unhealthy production . . .*".[26] The influence of this upon Yeats was most evident in his 1903 "Moral and Immoral Plays":

A writer . . . has said that I told my audience after the performance of *The Hour-Glass* that I did not care whether a play was moral or immoral. . . . I did not say that I did not care whether a play was moral or immoral. . . . My objection was to the rough-and-ready conscience of the newspaper and the pulpit in a matter so delicate and so difficult as literature. Every generation of men of letters has been called immoral by the pulpit or the newspaper, and it has been precisely when that generation has been illuminating some obscure corner of the conscience that the cry against it has been more confident.[27]

In his 1928 essay, "The Censorship and St. Thomas Aquinas", Yeats again paid Wilde homage by recreating the idea: "There is such a thing as immoral painting and immoral literature, and a criticism growing always more profound establishes that they are bad paintings and bad literature . . .".[28]

A secondary focus of the essay (aside from its secular re-creation of Christ) was its discussion of Parnell. Although Wilde never named his subject, his references were clear, especially in the prevailing political climate. Yeats might not have agreed precisely with Wilde's political view, but he would have shared Wilde's estimate of modern journalism: "In the old days men had the rack. Now they have the Press. That is an improvement certainly." He also deplored journalism's destructive intrusions into the private lives of public leaders:

> . . . harm is done by the serious, thoughtful, earnest journalists, who, solemnly, as they are doing at present, will drag before the eyes of the public some incident in the private life of a great statesman, of a man who is a leader in political thought as he is a creator of political force, and invite the public to discuss the incident, to exercise authority in the matter, to give their views, and not merely to give their views, but to carry them into action, to dictate to the man upon all other points, to dictate to his party, to dictate to his country; in fact, to make themselves ridiculous, offensive, and harmful. The private lives of men and women should not be told to the public. The public have nothing to do with them at all. In France they manage these things better. They do not allow the details of the trials that take place in the divorce courts to be published for the amusement or criticism of the public . . . they limit the journalist, and allow the artist almost perfect freedom.[29]

When Yeats read *De Profundis*, Wilde's letter to Lord Alfred Douglas from Reading Gaol, Robert Ross had expurgated Wilde's personal recriminations; thus, Yeats read it as a record of

Wilde's intellectual development in prison and as the self-portrait of a man "who stood in symbolic relations to the art and culture" of his age. In it, Wilde's courage was impressive, and self-realization, leading to Unity of Being, was still the hero's work:

> When first I was put into prison some people advised me to try and forget who I was. It was ruinous advice. It is only by realizing what I am that I have found comfort of any kind. Now I am advised by others to try on my release to forget that I have ever been in a prison at all. I know that would be equally fatal.[30]

In "The Soul of Man Under Socialism", Christ had realized himself perfectly; this, combined with His ability to transform sorrow into beauty, made him the ultimate artist in *De Profundis*: the connection between the true life of Christ and that of the artist was "intimate and immediate", and "nothing that either Plato or Christ had said . . . could not be transferred immediately into the sphere of Art and there find its complete fulfillment". This did not encourage Yeats to embrace Roman Catholicism, but he saw the possibilities of Wilde's reinterpretation of Christian mythology. Christ's art was not only externalized; His "place indeed is with the poets", but He was the self-creating artist of his own life: ". . . of his own imagination entirely did Jesus of Nazareth create himself". As a result, He was also the supreme Romantic, embodying all "the accidentals, the wilfulnesses even, of the romantic temperament also. He was the first person who ever said to people that they should live 'flower-like lives' ".[31] As beauty's epitome, Christ was also misunderstood and criticized by the Philistines, in "the war every child of light has to wage":

> In their heavy inaccessibility to ideas, their dull respectability, their tedious orthodoxy, their worship of vulgar success, their entire preoccupation with the gross materialistic side of life, and their ridiculous estimate of themselves and their importance, the Jew of Jerusalem in Christ's day was the exact counterpart of the British Philistine of our own.[32]

This idealized portrait was not entirely without Wilde's characteristic irony of tone, however:

> His justice is all poetical justice, exactly what justice should be.

The beggar goes to heaven because he had been unhappy. I can't conceive a better reason for his being sent there. The people who work for an hour in the vineyard in the cool of the evening receive just as much reward as those who had toiled there all day long in the hot sun. Why shouldn't they? Probably no one deserved anything.[33]

This was crucial to Yeats's secular recreation, showing that a sacred subject did not demand unrelieved seriousness. This mildly heretical vision impressed Yeats more than did Wilde's worship of Christ as heroic fellow-artist and fellow-victim, for such exaltation resembled orthodoxy. At His most fascinating, Christ was a mythic figure full of human frailty: "It is the feet of clay that make the gold of the image precious."[34]

In "Poems in Prose", published in July 1894, Wilde recreated Christ as secular myth in six tales, which, although "ruined" for Yeats by Wilde's transformation from speech to prose, revealed the myth's possibilities. "The Disciple" commented ironically on mutual love and discipleship – at best, symbiotic, and, at worst, parasitic. Although Wilde used classical myth as his foundation, it also described the relations between Christ and all men. Not only did each man kill the thing he pretended to love, but he loved only the reflection of his own image. Thus, betrayal by one's disciples was inevitable, and even Christ only loved men narcissistically (which Yeats remembered in *Calvary*). In "The Master", Wilde undermined Christ's uniqueness by telling of a young man whose feats duplicated His, but who despairingly envied Christ His crucifixion. Salvation through good deeds was thus futile, and it was useless for anyone to imitate Christ. "The finest short story in the world",[35] "The Doer of Good", also developed these themes, as the saviour brought all mankind, especially a reluctant Lazarus, greater pain through His best intentions. As in "The House of Judgment", life was Hell; Christ was well-meaning but His system had failed. No longer unique, His inferior miracles were thwarted by their recipients and the mortal world. "What else can I do?" showed salvation as impossible and Christ as impotent, and from these tales, especially from Lazarus's cry, Yeats developed *The Resurrection* and *Calvary*, his visions of sacred myth re-examined.

Testing the dramatic possibilities of theology, Wilde told Yeats another "Christian heresy":

. . . a detailed story, in the style of some early father, of how Christ recovered after the Crucifixion, and escaping from the tomb, lived on for many years, the one man upon the earth who knew the falsehood of Christianity. Once St. Paul visited his town and he alone in the carpenters' quarter did not go to hear him preach. Henceforth the other carpenters noticed that, for some unknown reason, he kept his hands covered.[36]

Here, Christ hid from the basic fraudulence of orthodoxy. Wilde's delight in such heretical re-creation is most vivid in the tale he told André Gide in late 1891:

"Would you like me to tell you a secret? . . . but promise me not to tell it to anyone. . . . Do you know why Christ did not love his mother? It's because she was a virgin! . . ."[37]

Although its purpose may have been only to amuse or to scandalize, Wilde was still remaking orthodoxy into art. The range between the supreme artist of *De Profundis* and these heresies appealed to Yeats, and it led him to a freer use of Christ as a dramatic character. In 1918, he wrote the first of two heresies, here contained in an idea for a play:

. . . where a Sinn Feiner will have a conversation with Judas in the streets of Dublin. Judas is looking for somebody to whom he may betray Christ in order that Christ may proclaim himself King of the Jews. The Sinn Feiner has just been persuading a young sculptor to leave his studio and shoulder a rifle.

Judas is a ghost, perhaps he is mistaken for the ghost of an old rag-picker by the neighborhood.[38]

In 1935, Yeats also mentioned an old plan for a short story on the Second Coming, in which the Last Supper would be held at the Ritz.[39] This echoed Wilde's comic ingenuity in the incongruous juxtaposition of the sacred and mundane, as the previous heresy had juxtaposed the historical and the spiritual. Although Yeats's purpose was not comic, he benefited from Wilde's imaginative reworkings of Christ and Christian myth.

In prose, Yeats's most notable example was his 1897 "The Crucifixion of the Outcast",[40] with Christ as a travelling gleeman. Christ as poet reflected Wilde explicitly, but Yeats's tale was also bitter commentary on the fate of the creative in an unappreciative society. Whether creating theology, politics, or poetry, all artists were hated, feared, and destroyed by the unimaginative. Had Christ returned, He would have been crucified again for disrupting the established order. It was appropriate that Wilde had praised the tale, for it reflected his myth and depicted his fate.

Yeats's versions of Christian myth in his poetry varied in scope. Often, he adapted Christian elements into his own myth, or established pagan, physical, or astrological countertruths to them the contraries inherent in Christ also intrigued him, the violence and love of the Annunciation, the divinity and human pain of the Crucifixion, for he was always concerned with divine intrusion into the mortal world, especially when it combined sexual love and terrifying force. In "The Magi", the magi themselves believed in Yeats's philosophy and were unfulfilled by Christianity, "by Calvary's turbulence unsatisfied". "The Dolls", its companion poem, showed the incompatibility of human, supernatural, and subnatural in a parable, whose closing lines echoed "The Magi", as the dollmaker's wife murmured, after uncontrollable turbulence, "My dear, my dear, O dear,/It was an accident." This was the strife between the natural and divine, and also Yeats's recreation of the difficulties of Mary and Joseph. Art disdained Nature, as in "The Decay of Lying", yet the child was aesthetically disturbing, the dolls morally offensive. Both Christ and the dolls were incongruous in the mortal world; both were unfulfilling and made their human counterparts uneasy.[41] Yeats's most famous merging of Christ and his cycles, "The Second Coming", echoed "The Magi" in evoking destructive potential, although the violence would come from Christ's antithesis, that "rough beast", which "Slouches toward Bethlehem to be born".[42] "A Prayer for My Son" portrayed Christ as simultaneously human and divine; although omnipotent, He had known "All of that worst ignomy / Of flesh and bone", an inexpressible human suffering beyond divine comfort. However, Christ was rescued from Herod's men by "human love"; salvation from pain was possible.[43] In "Two Songs From A Play", from *The Resurrection*, Yeats linked Dionysisiac and Christian, as the Muses sang of Magnus Annus, "As though God's death were but a play". Whether the ritual was historical, pagan, or Christian, the death and rebirth of the slain god were inevitable. The second song returned to the contraries within Christ, of "Galilean turbulence" and the "Odour of blood when Christ was slain"; the mystery was uncontrollable because a divine phantom had suffered a human death.[44] Like "The Dolls", "Oil and Blood" suggested that divinity might be terrible as well as sacred; all experience outside the human was essentially mysterious and unpredictable, whether benevolent or ghoulish. Typically, Yeats began with an apparent orthodoxy, but quickly moved to a real or profane countertruth to the sacred vision: vampire and saint were equally plausible.[45] "Veronica's Napkin" established human and astrological contraries to Christ's Passion, as the Cross balanced between "Tent-pole of Eden" and "a different pole, and where it stood / A pattern on a napkin dipped in blood".[46] Although the centre of Christian cosmology and a divine symbol, the Cross was also a wooden structure, a part of human history. In "The Mother of God", Yeats explored the human response to the divine, as in "Leda and the Swan"; the Annunciation contained the "terror of love" as well as divine majesty.[47] Christian dove and Ledaen swan brought fear as well as exaltation, and Mary's frightened confusion was essential to Yeats's recreation of myth, for he saw her as human, not only the honoured vessel for the sacred infant. His concern was not an orthodox acceptance of the myth, but an imaginative exploration of its human significance: what did Mary feel? Having considered this, Yeats investigated St. Joseph's feelings in "A Stick of Incense", where his curiosity about the sexual relations between Mary and Joseph after Christ's birth grew from Wilde's cheerfully blasphemous yoking of the exalted and the erotic. The intellectual background to Yeats's irreverence was in "Private Thoughts", from *On the Boiler*: ". . . we must hold on to what we have that the next civilization may be born, not from a virgin's womb, not a tomb without a body, not from a void, but of our own rich experience". Conception without sexual reward denied that "rich experience" and was unthinkable to Yeats, especially when its product was the prime symbolic figure of Western religion. Thus, the poem's "fury" was orgasmic, and its final couplet, "Saint Joseph thought the world would melt / But liked the way his finger smelt,"[48] showed that the pure joy of mortal sexual play was its own divinity, and that love must, as Crazy Jane knew, "Take the whole / Body and soul."[49] In his final poetic recreation of this myth, "A Nativity", Yeats returned to the Annunciation and "The Mother of God": considering paintings of the Nativity, he balanced "terror" and "mercy", wondering at the effects of this transfiguration on human life, and the powers of the divine to interrupt and disturb human experience.[50]

Yeats's dramatic versions of Christian myth, *Calvary* and *The Resurrection,* showed the same creative freedom. In the 1920 *Calvary,* Yeats returned to Christ as the unwelcome saviour of "The Doer of Good", who confronted an aggressively dissatisfied Lazarus, who no longer wept. Having desired death, he was angered by Christ's burdensome gift of life, which had "dragged" him back to the light. Christ's announcement that He had "conquered death, / And all the dead shall be raised up again" was the ultimate affront to Lazarus, bitterly unhappy with life on earth; Christ would "disturb that corner / Where I had thought I might lie safe for ever". Faced by such unexpected defiance, Christ turned to His higher authority, only to be rebuked by Lazarus for evading the issue: Christ was thus only an ineffective subordinate, following His Father's orders, not fulfilling himself or mankind. Yeats had strengthened Wilde's original confrontation; now, Lazarus was eloquently rebellious, defeating Christ's feeble arguments. Where Wilde had shown human despair, expressed in helpless weeping, beyond divine salvation, Yeats showed the limitations of divine power. Judas again tested Christ and proved Him inadequate; as Lazarus was made unhappy by Christ's good intentions, Judas, trapped by Christ's power, found it unbearable. Only in betrayal could he proclaim his freedom; to defy Christ's love made him the only free man – for even Christ was shackled by His Father's will – and only in revolt against repressive divinity was individual self-realisation possible: ". . . I did it, / I, Judas, and no other man, and now / You cannot even save me".[51] In refusal and rejection, Lazarus and Judas became completely and absolutely themselves – Christ's perfection in "The Soul of Man Under Socialism". When Yeats wrote of Judas in *A Vision,* he saw him as an artist rebelling against a stifling orthodoxy: ". . . Judas, who betrays, not for thirty pieces of silver, but that he may call himself creator".[52]

In *The Resurrection* (1927), characters attempted, as had Wilde and Yeats, to interpret Christ's mystery. The Hebrew, Syrian, and Egyptian served as Hic and Ille, or Cyril and Vivian, voices in dialogue, exploring differing perspectives, attempting to understand in terms of human predilections and experiences. To the Hebrew, Christ was self-deluded; "brooding always" on human unhappiness, He "became unhinged and called himself 'God's Only Son' ". Made mad through intense love and pity, Christ's divinity was only the deception of a God who "had turned juggler". The more orthodox Egyptian cherished Christ as "an image of God's own incorruptible essence'', who had only seemed to die. When the Syrian brought news of Christ's empty tomb, the debate continued: had Christ been deluded, a phantom, or the Master of all men? At the play's climax, when the phantom of Christ appeared, and the Egyptian found that its heart beat, he saw it as the entity outside human experience that would utterly transform it: "Rome, Greece, Egypt – it has come, the miracle, that which must destroy you, irrational force."[53] Using secular dialogue, full of human doubts, Yeats reached a relatively orthodox conclusion, proclaiming Christ as divine mystery – neither wholly divine nor human – an unpredictable and powerful force beyond human comprehension. However, this apparent orthodoxy was part of Yeats's "System", as miracle signified the beginning of the historical cycle's second phase, transfiguration with violent potential, as in "The Second Coming".

Purgatory (1938), Yeats's last exploration of Christian heresy in drama, recreated a Christian Purgatory as part of the "System", drawing on ideas Yeats had advanced in *The Words upon the Window-Pane*:

> Some spirits are earth-bound – they think they are still living and go over and over some action of their past lives, just as we go over and over some painful thought, except where they are thought is reality. For instance, when a spirit which has died a violent death comes to a medium for the first time, it relives all the pains of death. . . . Sometimes a spirit re-lives not the pain of death but some passionate or tragic moment of life . . . the murderer repeats his murder, the robber his robbery, the lover his serenade, the soldier hears the trumpet once again. If I were a Catholic I would say that such spirits were in Purgatory. In vain do we write *requiescat in pace* upon the tomb, for they must suffer, and we in our turn must suffer until God gives peace.[54]

No true purgation was possible, no expiation of sins or passions; souls were committed to repeat their crimes without hope of change, escape, or purification. Yeats had removed the hope inherent in Christian myth, for there was no way to "Appease / the mystery of the living and the remorse of the dead."[55] Stirred by Wilde's example, Yeats had entirely recreated Christian truths in his art, transfiguring doctrine into myth.

In *A Full Moon in March*, Yeats again freely recreated Biblical mythology, drawing on Wilde's original heresy, *Salomé*. Because the story of Salomé, as told by Matthew and Mark, was spare and undramatic, Wilde had swelled it with exotic dialogue and luxuriant images, attempting to create a foreign atmosphere, which Yeats amended. Before he had written *A Full Moon in March* or its predecessor, *The King of the Great Clock Tower,* Yeats had written of Salomé in *A Vision*:

> When I think of the moment before revelation I think of Salome
> – she, too, delicately tinted or maybe mahogany dark – dancing
> before Herod and receiving the Prophet's head in her indifferent
> hands, and wonder if what seems to us decadence was not in
> reality the exaltation of the muscular flesh and of civilisation
> perfectly achieved. Seeking images, I see her anoint her bare
> limbs . . . and remember that the same impulse will create the
> Galilean revelation and deify Roman emperors whose sculptured
> heads will be surrounded by the solar disk. Upon the throne and
> upon the cross alike the myth becomes a biography.[56]

She epitomized physical, sensual beauty, as Christ stood for spiritual knowledge and Caesar political power. Christ and Caesar, antithetical masks, were also linked in March, the month Christ rose and Caesar died, the month "of victims and saviours".[57] In his notes to the play, Yeats added another mythic element: the dance came from Celtic legend and pagan ritual, "the mother goddess and the slain god".[58] Thus, the play grew from myths and themes familiar to Yeats – the combinations of spiritual, erotic, and political exaltations, of divine knowledge and physical power. However, as Marilyn Rose has noted, this mythic background was secondary to the more elemental experience of human relations. Heart-truths were its basis, especially the merging of opposites for sexual fulfillment.[59]

Unlike Yeats's Christian heresies, Wilde's *Salomé* was frankly erotic. Although symbolically enacted, the determined lusts of various characters dominated the play. When Yeats recreated the myth, there was no longer a puddle of blood on the stage, but an emblematic pattern of red on the Queen's dress, and red gloves and masks for both Queen and Swineherd. Her dance of erotic adoration before the severed head, the violation of her self, her orgasm, were all represented in quickening shivers; lust was expressed in stylized worship, not elaborate prose. Here Yeats asked Freud's question, What do women want?" and dramatized his answer, "Their desecration and the lover's night,'' in the relations between Queen and Swineherd.[60] Hers was the unrealized destructive power of women, as in "No Second Troy", and a fierce virgin cruelty because she was unfulfilled. Once her aloneness had been shattered, she could succumb to her bodiless lover, alluring and refusing in a dance of consummation. Completeness came only through violence and bodily desecration: "For nothing can be sole or whole / That has not been rent", and opposites merged, Self realizing itself in Anti-Self.[61] Courtship was represented in antithesis, the Swineherd's defiance and death, the Queen's surrender and fulfillment in being torn. In *Salomé*, consummation was possible only through destruction of the lover's body; only by being beheaded could the Swineherd complete himself and his task. The play expanded Yeats's 1931 statement, ". . . the tragedy of sexual intercourse is the perpetual virginity of the souls".[62] Isolated, haughty, and pure, the Queen could complete herself only in the earth's physicality the Swineherd's drop of blood represented, and her spirit could only be reborn from her violation and his death, in the ritual of the mother-goddess who must slay the male god for the world's rebirth into spring.

Some fundamental impulses for this came from Wilde, although Yeats had found much to dislike in *Salomé*, and Yeats's simpler spareness showed a conscious rejection of Wilde's excess. The dance's dramatic potential was so immense that it is difficult to accept Yeats's disclaimer entirely; indeed, the vigour of his disavowal suggests that he knew how close the dance's origins were to Wilde's. Even if Yeats had wanted the idea as purely his own (with the severed head appearing also in *The Green Helmet,* from Celtic myth), Wilde's theatrics were memorable. Yeats had absorbed the idea as another development of his many dance-images in poetry, and would revise it in *The Death of Cuchulain.* To suggest that Wilde's influence on *A Full Moon in March* was only in the dance would severely limit *Salomé*'s importance as a powerful myth. Although Yeats had established his own dramatic tradition, and would not consciously have relied upon Wilde's dramatic example, nuances of *Salomé* remained, in its merging of holy and erotic opposites, and in the sexual consummation attained only through violence and desecration.

The gulf between Yeats's drama and Wilde's four domestic plays – *Lady Windermere's Fan, A Woman of No Importance, An Ideal Husband*, and *The Importance of Being Earnest* – was vast. Generally,

Wilde's melodrama was contrived, relying on hints of scandal, blackmail, and illicit affairs for dramatic momentum. His plays were also inescapably realistic, set in the London present, and populated with almost-real varieties of English nobility. Yeats's aversion to drawing-room drama was exceeded only by his hatred of realism, which was "created for the common people . . . the delight to-day of all those whose minds, educated alone by schoolmasters and newspapers, are without the memory of beauty and emotional subtlety".[63] Wilde's realism was comprehensive, in plot, language, setting, and scenery: in 1883, he had proudly designed the scenery and costumes for *Vera*, wishing to have "as much fact as will convey the impression of reality", even boasting that "A crown used in one of the acts is a reproduction of the crown used at the recent coronation of Alexander III."[64] Yeats's theory was antithetical: ". . . poetic or legendary drama . . . should have no realistic, or elaborate, but only a symbolic and decorative setting . . . an accompaniment not a reflection of the text".[65] Yeats's rejection of Wilde's drama was also because it had nothing to do with an Irish national spirit, or his vision of a national theatre which would present drama reflecting Irish experience. Wilde's drama expressed alien ideas in alien speech: "if you would ennoble the man of the roads you must write about the roads, or about the people of romance or about great historical people".[66] Thus, Yeats wrote of Cuchulain and beggars, not of an English aristocracy, of an epic past, not the London present.

However, some aspects of Wilde's work transcended these limitations, and Yeats again delighted in Wilde's wit and paradox. As in *Dorian Gray*, he took them as patterns for his thought; as expressed in *A Woman of No Importance*, the paradox of unaging intellect and bodily decrepitude was pertinent:

Lord Illingworth
    I never intend to grow old. The soul
is born old but grows young. That is the
comedy of life.
Mrs. Allonby
    And the body is born young and grows
old. That is life's tragedy.
Lord Illingworth
    Its comedy also, sometimes . . .[67]

In *An Ideal Husband,* Wilde described the dandy as a man "who plays with life", a portrait of the artistically-shaped life, as in Mrs Cheveley's comment on the "only really Fine Art we have produced in modern times", which fathers could learn from their sons, "The art of living".[68] Yeats remembered little from Wilde's comic masterpiece, *The Importance of Being Earnest,* for it was unified, without melodromatic inconsistencies. Individual epigrams were not set off by banalities, but the play advanced ideas which Yeats knew well from Wilde's conversation and criticism, such as the superiority of art over fact, a "perfectly phrased" epigram being better than a true one: "In matters of grave importance, style, not sincerity is the vital thing."[69] It also reflected "The Decay of Lying", which impressed Yeats greatly: Life was influenced by Art, not the reverse. Ugly realism ruined human beauty – which Yeats treated seriously in *The King's Threshold* – here, the doctrine was applied comically as Cecily Cardew noted the destructive effects of an inartistic language on her beauty: ". . . German . . . isn't at all a becoming language. . . . I look quite plain after my German lesson".[70] Yeats was no less affected by the comic treatment of a serious idea, and in the same way that he absorbed influential fragments from Wilde's apparently frivolous work, he was affected by Wilde's popular theatre, although he disdained it in his conception of a dramatic ideal.

Wilde's criticism impressed Yeats early: at the 1888 Christmas dinner, Wilde had read him the proofs of "The Decay of Lying", and Yeats praised *Intentions* enthusiastically. In it, Wilde's thought was freed from the restrictions of tale, poem, or play, and his audacious and idosyncratic style was fully expressed. To Yeats, forming critical approaches, this modern iconoclasm was more satisfying than the orthodoxies of Dowden or Arnold.

In "The Decay of Lying", Wilde lamented the abandonment of imaginative lying in art and its replacement by realism. As practiced by Zola and others, scientific realism was "tedious" and the artistic pursuit of truth was "morbid and unhealthy". A "degraded race", we had "sold our birthright for a mess of facts", which were "usurping the domain of Fancy, and have invaded the kindgom of Romance".[71] Changing "Fancy" to "Faery" gives us a statement of Yeats's Celtic Twilight position, as in Yeats's letter of December 1893, "The Silenced Sister", where he applied Wilde to contemporary politics:

Do not our newspapers with their daily tide of written oratory,
make us cry out, "O God, if this be sincerity, give us a little
insincerity, a little of the self-possession, of the self-mastery that
go to a conscious lie."[72]

Realism in drama was also futile; to Wilde, the characters in modern
English drama were "taken directly from life and reproduce its
vulgarity down to the smallest detail",[73] which Yeats agreed with in
theory and practice; heroic sagas needed no contemporary
verisimilitude, as Emer could not have spoken or dressed as a
modern Dubliner. Drama should also not attempt to reproduce the
modern world: "the two things that every artist should avoid are
modernity of form and modernity of subject matter".[74] Thus,
through creativity unfettered by fact and realism, art could regain
lost "distinction, charm, beauty, and imaginative power", rather
than being "an account of the doings of the lower orders".[75] This
was liberating for Yeats, another inspiration to celebrate the heroic,
not the socially or economically wretched; in 1938, he wrote, "I still
think that artists of all kinds should once again praise or represent
great or happy people".[76] The essay supported his repudiation of
the grim modern world for the happier one of Faery, or the heroic
Irish past.

For Wilde, art's truth was in its integrity, and truth was "entirely
and absolutely a matter of style". Imagination was all, for "the
object of Art is not simple truth but complex beauty. . . . Art itself is
really a form of exaggeration . . .".[77] Yeats usually saw
"exaggeration" as "extravagance", and used it as praise; defending
The Playboy of the Western World, he attributed a characteristically
Wildean statement to "a French writer": "Art . . . is exaggeration
apropos. . . . All great literatures . . . dealt with exaggerated types,
and all tragedy and tragi-comedy with types of sin and folly. A
dramatist is not a historian."[78] In "Poetry and Tradition", it was
the mark of joyous artistic style: ". . . that leaves one, not in the
circling necessity, but caught up into the freedom of self-delight
. . .".[79]

As Wilde undermined realism, he also attempted to free art from its
traditional debt to Nature as its primary inspiration. It was no longer
Nature's mirror, for Art improved on Nature, and Nature had
attempted and failed to imitate Art. A "glorious sky" was "simply a
very second-rate Turner, a Turner of a bad period, with all the
painter's worst faults exaggerated and overemphasized".[80] Art's

ideals also influenced human behaviour and beauty, reflecting Yeats's Mask: an artistic stance of heroic pose could produce an artistic or heroic life. Yeats remembered Wilde's "Think of what we owe to the imitation of Christ, of what we owe to the imitation of Caesar", and repeated in in several contexts. Properly chosen images of the imitation of certain heroes could inspire the artist or shape a culture:

> . . . I began to believe that our culture, with its doctrine of sincerity and self-realisation, made us gentle and passive, and that the Middle Ages and the Renaissance were right to found theirs upon the imitation of Christ or of some classic hero. Saint Francis and Caesar Borgia made themselves overmastering, creative persons by turning from the mirror to meditation on a mask.[81]

Art, which was Art "because it is not Nature",[82] created and shaped human beauty:

> A great artist invents a type, and Life tries to copy it, to reproduce it in a popular form, like an enterprising publisher. Neither Holbein nor Vandyck found in England what they have given us. They brought their types with them, and Life with her keen imitative faculty set herself to supply the master with models. The Greeks, with their quick artistic instinct, understood this, and set in the bride's chamber the statue of Hermes or of Apollo, that she might bear children as lovely as the works of art that she looked at in her rapture or her pain.[83]

Yeats used this in *The King's Threshold* – first, as the poet Seanchan's lesson on why poetry was honoured:

> . . . the poets hung
> Images of the life that was in Eden
> About the child-bed of the world, that it,
> Looking upon these images, might bear
> Triumphant children.

Poets provided the ideals and inspirations for all beauty; if realism triumphed, all would perish:

> The world that lacked them would be like a woman
> That, looking on the cloven lips of a hare,

Brings forth a hare-lipped child.[84]

Wilde's views also provided a foundation for the play; because art shaped beauty and behaviour, the poet was thus essential to the state, and when the government was inartistic, it and society collapsed.

Yeats's poetry also reflected the idea; in "The Statues", statues and images created individual and racial personality, as art reshaped life: "Phidias / Gave women dreams and dreams their looking-glass."[85] In "The Gyres", philosophers affected the world as did artists: "Empedocles has thrown all things about".[86] "The Dolls" explored the relationship between supreme art and imperfect life, as the dolls "bawl" and "out-scream" each other, proclaiming the nastiness of human creation. It was, however, ironic – art condemned life for the faults it displayed itself in its denunciation: as the baby was "a noisy and a filthy thing", the dolls became noisy and filthy in their outrage.[87] "Under Ben Bulben" reaffirmed the artist's power to form the race; if young Irish poets learned their trade, their heroic visions would continue "the indomitable Irishry":

> Poet and sculptor, do the work,
> Nor let the modish painter shirk
> What his great forefathers did,
> Bring the soul of man to God,
> Make him fill the cradles right.[88]

Although the artist was supreme in his power to make images for men to use as patterns for their life, Wilde had removed responsibilities from the artist's shoulders. He was not responsible for social reform, for his reformation of the world was in making it able to appreciate beauty:

> We try to improve the conditions of the race by means of good air, free sunlight, wholesome water, and hideous bare buildings for the better housing of the lower orders. But these things merely produce health, they do not produce beauty. For this, Art is required . . . .[89]

This emphasis on art, not social activism, as the artist's rightful task, helped Yeats to justify it in a hostile environment, as in the 1902 "The Irish Drmatic Movement":

In Ireland, where we have so much to prove and to disprove, we are ready to forget that the creation of an emotion of beauty is the only kind of literature that justifies itself. Books of literary propaganda and literary history are merely preparations for the creation or understanding of such an emotion.[90]

Finally, Wilde reiterated art's fundamental independence:

Art never expresses anything but itself. It has an independent life, just as Thought has, and develops purely on its own lines. It is not necessarily realistic in an age of realism, nor spiritual in an age of faith. So far from being the creation of its time, it is usually in direct opposition to it, and the only history it preserves for us is the history of its own progress. Sometimes it returns upon its footsteps, and revives some antique form . . . other times it entirely anticipates its age, and produces in one century work that it takes another century to understand, to appreciate, and to enjoy. In no case does it reproduce its age.[91]

This defended all Yeats held sacred: art's pure independence from modernity, realism, and the spirit of the times. As the creator's mind was free and powerful, so was his art; thus supported, Yeats could revive an ancient Irish heroism, rather than being forced to glorify "this filthy modern tide".[92]

In its style, "The Decay of Lying" proved the importance of manner to matter; its form, the dialogue, also attracted Yeats as an expression of the Mask's double nature. Fittingly, when Wilde first read the proofs to Yeats, the scene itself combined dialogue within dialogue, mask upon mask, as Wilde read to Yeats what Vivian read to Cyril. Here and in "The Critic as Artist" Wilde showed, by example and commentary, the form's potential. Dialogue was natural to Wilde, as a brilliant conversational artist; it was "that wonderful literary form which . . . can never lose for the thinker its attraction as a mode of expression":

By its means he can both reveal and conceal himself, and give form to every fancy, and reality to every mood. By its means he can exhibit the object from each point of view, and show it to us in the round, as a sculptor shows us things, gaining in this manner all the richness and reality of the effect that comes from those side issues that are suddenly suggested by the central idea in its progress, and really illumine the idea more completely, or from those felicitous after-thoughts that give a fuller completeness to the central scheme, and yet convey something of the delicate charm of chance

It enabled the artist to "invent some imaginary antagonist, and convert him when he chooses by some absurdly sophistical argument", thus dramatically enacting the interplay between Self and Anti-Self, objective and subjective. He could thus "multiply his personalities", thus dramatizing the contraries.[93] It embodied Wilde's dictum: "in art there is no such thing as a universal truth. A Truth in art is that whose contradictory is also true".[94]

Yeats had used the form before he read *Intentions*, but Wilde's extravagant developments of it showed new possibilities: it became pastoral elegy in "Shepherd and Goatherd", or, in "Ego Dominus Tuus", it showed Self and Anti-Self, represented by Hic and Ille. Like Cyril and Vivian, they represented inner tensions as well as being asker and answerer: Cyril defended simplicity, sincerity, tradition as Vivian insisted on imaginative insincerity. Hic would have held the poet to that which could be realized – why seek unorthodoxy in the intricacies of the gyres? – and Ille defended fancy, the limitless opposite to tangible, established truths. In both cases, the subjective visionary, imaginative liar vanquished the objective realist; an expansive mysticism was worth venturing beyond the known for "an image, not a book".[95] As well as presenting internalized contraries, whether Hic and Ille or Robartes and Aherne in "The Phases of the Moon", Yeats also used dialogue as externalized drama, in discussions with another individual or voice – Maud Gonne's sister Kathleen Pilcher, in "Adam's Curse", Iseult Gonne, in "Michael Robartes and the Dancer", and his wife, in "Solomon and Sheba". But, as in "A Dialogue of Self and Soul" and "Vacillation", it was most rewarding as internal questioning, balancing Heart and Soul, Self and Soul. In his last dialogue, "The Man and the Echo", he had not finished with such questioning, for the form had brought no resolution, only an implacable Echo and the inevitable vacillation between joy and pain. Fifty years of variations on Wilde's structure took their shape from his criticism, but were charged with the energies of Yeats's emotions.

The opening lines of "Pen Pencil and Poison", Wilde's study of the artist and poisoner, Wainewright, defended the artist's apparent narrowness of vision, for his responsibility was to his art alone. The "concentration of vision and intensity of purpose" were intentional modes of "limitation". "To those who are pre-occupied with the beauty of form nothing else seems of much importance." Wilde also commended the artistically-realized man, who concentrated his energy on the possibilities of an internal beauty of form, rather than the "Philistine", relying on "the vulgar test of production".

> The young dandy sought to be somebody, rather than do something. He recognised that Life itself is an art, and has its modes of style no less than the arts that seek to express it.

Referring to the "fanciful pseudonyms" Wainewright adopted, Wilde casually celebrated the mask: "A mask tells us more than a face. These disguises intensified his personality."[96] In his sketch of the artist as poisoner – itself a comment on the artist's relation to his society – Wilde continued ideas influential to Yeats, which reached from his earliest work to *De Profundis*.

The idea of the Mask was also developed in "The Truth of Masks", for costume exposed character, rather than concealing it; appearance, as Yeats saw in "The Mask", was the more attractive reality.[97] Wilde's commentary on dramatic practice might also have remained with Yeats in his Abbey experience – on the proper way to speak dialogue and to gesture, and the necessity of artistic harmony; both men were frustrated by the inability of the finest actors to grasp the simplicity essential to acting, as in "The Fascination of What's Difficult" and in Yeats's essays on theatre. Wilde also suggested that Shakespeare's goal had been similar to Yeats's:

> . . . to create . . . a national historical drama, which would deal with incidents with which the public was well acquainted, and with heroes that lived in the memory of a people.

The essay's conclusion was as striking as Wilde's dialogue: not simply a scholarly examination of historical costuming, which Yeats would have respected as erudite, it was in itself a mask, embodying the concept it celebrated:

> Not that I agree with everything that I have said in this essay. There is much with which I entirely disagree. The essay simply represents an artistic standpoint, and in aesthetic criticism

attitude is everything. For in art there is no such thing as a universal truth. A Truth in art is that whose contradictory is also true. And just as it is only in art-criticism, and through it, that we can apprehend the Platonic theory of ideas, so it is only in art-criticism, and through it, that we can realize Hegel's system of contraries. The truths of metaphysics are the truths of masks.[98]

Intentions's longest essay, "The Critic as Artist", repeated familiar ideas – Wilde's praise of art, of criticism as an art form, and of art as a criticism of life. Much of the essay, however, was his rejection of the man of action as futile (which Yeats re-interpreted, envisioning Cuchulain fighting the waves, not successful politicians): "When a man acts he is a puppet. When he describes he is a poet." Action itself was accidental, aimless:

> . . . a blind thing dependent on external influences, and moved by an impulse of whose nature it is unconscious. It is a thing incomplete in its essence, because limited by accident, and ignorant of its direction, being always at variance with its aim. Its basis is the lack of imagination.[99]

Echoing "The Decay of Lying", Wilde saw action as "a base concession to fact"; as Yeats would do in "Adam's Curse", he denied the traditional definition of heroism, for "the world is made by the singer for the dreamer".[100] He also returned to the source of Yeats's "terrible beauty", from *Dorian Gray*, in his view of Life as an artistic failure, "terribly deficient in form":

> Its catastrophes happen in the wrong way and to the wrong people. There is a grotesque horror about its comedies, and its tragedies seem to culminate in farce. One is always wounded when one approaches it.[101]

The Mask, as a tool to expand human and artistic possibilities, was characteristically seen: "Man is least himself when he talks in his own person. Give him a mask, and he will tell you the truth." "To arrive at what one really believes, one must speak through lips different from one's own."[102] Appropriately, the essay had begun with an eloquent defence of dialogue, the form suited to the Mask.

Wilde's summary of his arguments also summed up the revolutionary nature of *Intentions*:

You have told me that it is more difficult to talk about a thing than to do it, and that to do nothing at all is the most difficult thing in the world; you have told me that all Art is immoral, and all thought dangerous; that criticism is more creative than creation, and that the highest criticism is that which reveals in the work of Art what the artist had not put there; that it is exactly because a man cannot do a thing that he is the proper judge of it; and that the true critic is unfair, insincere, not rational.[103]

This was the Gospel of Paradox – which justified Yeats's editing of *The Ballad of Reading Gaol*, for he found in it "what the artist had not put there". This, as well as its companion essays, gave Yeats a reassuring sense that others were fighting the battle for art's sake against Philistines. Although he did not agree with all of Wilde's ideas and disregarded others, he recognized a fellow-warrior, eloquently and wittily undermining the bourgeois world, attempting to make the love of beauty essential in a society devoted to the ugly.

Wilde's effect and influence on Yeats, as artist and hero, is not difficult to measure. Although he usually offered only glittering fragments, the ideas Yeats absorbed were impressive: the necessity and uses of the Mask and dialogue, the supreme duty of self-realisation, and the freedom and example to reinterpret Christian myth. Yeats rearranged, recreated, and revised what he found, often not caring to acknowledge Wilde's inspiration, but the result was as significant as Wilde's example of heroic martyrdom. Wilde's philosophy of art for its own sake had almost conquered the British, as he won money, fame, and respect from the enemy, in a way that Irish political activism had not. For however short a time, he had made himself another Irish uncrowned King of London, of which Yeats was admiringly aware.

Wilde represented another path for Yeats to follow, often at odds with nationalistic duty, but one of uncompromising devotion to one's art, no matter how derisive or seductive the world might be. His example showed that it was possible and gratifying to follow that revolutionary path of personal expression and idiosyncratic creation, and that one could display one's vision to the uncomprehending crowd, if one did it with transcendent style. That style, reflected in his heroic pose and in his best work, made Wilde one of the "unpractical people who see beyond the moment, and think beyond the day".[104] Yeats would not imitate Wilde, but he never forgot him as an image of the most desirable artistic life.

4   Parnell: "A proud man's a lovely man"

Charles Stewart Parnell appeared to be Wilde's countertruth: aloof, solitary, uninterested in literature, and, as John Morley noted, "No public man of his time was more free of the evil arts of Pose, nobody more disdainful of playing to the gallery . . .".[1] Yet these two men shared a heroic style greater than the distance between aesthetics and agrarian reform. Both were aristocratic Protestants, attacked by the mob, the Church, and the state for violating moral and sexual codes. Although Yeats had vacillating, even abivalent feelings about Parnell, he mythologized him as he had done with Wilde. In superimposing his heroic creation over the historical Parnell, Yeats had to reconcile Parnell as the force that had submerged Ireland in mad political rancour and Parnell as a martyr to that violent nation.

Five figures helped to shape Yeats's political thought and background before Parnell's fall: his father, John O'Leary, Maud Gonne, Katharine Tynan, and George Pollexfen. The elder Yeats disliked Parnell and saw him as inferior to the man he had deposed, Isaac Butt, a family friend and a "lovable" man, full of "the charm of personality". Parnell was "a cold logician and politician" who appealed to Irish "spite", and whose only qualifications for the task were "an intense, unrelenting, inexorable hatred . . .".[2] John O'Leary, "the old Fenian", disliked Parnell less, yet there was a palpable distance between Parnell's constitutional nationalism and his own Republican separatism. To O'Leary, Parnell's tactics were distractions, and he waited for "Parnellism" to "play itself out".[3] However, he respected Parnell as an individual, admired his courage under attack, and disliked other alternatives – Michael Davitt's land nationalization and the terrorism of the "Dynamitards" – even more. Yeats may have rebelled against his father's disdain for Parnell, but he adapted O'Leary's view of Parnellism as obstruction to his purposes, as he lamented the energies it diverted from culture and literature. Like O'Leary, Maud Gonne felt that Parnellism would have a limited effect, for parliamentary politics was insufficiently dramatic and revolutionary. However, she had met both Parnell and his wife shortly before his death, and spoke eloquently of him after his death, even though she felt that his last triumph had come only through an alliance with "the hillside men".[4]

Katharine Tynan was a profoundly Parnellite contrary, admiring, idealizing, even adoring him, and she made him mythic before Yeats, creating images of heroic passion controlled by fierce self-restraint. Also, Tynan, a published poet, had met Parnell and had been greeted warmly. "I remember you perfectly", he had said. "I have been reading your poems".[5] This recognition and encouragement signified that "the Chief" supported the literary and cultural enthusiasm Yeats and Tynan shared, and might have been receptive to Yeats's work. The least known influence upon Yeats was his maternal uncle, George Pollexfen. Although not a Parnellite, he was a familial link to him, as Yeats remembered in *The Trembling of the Veil*:

> When Parnell was contesting an election at Sligo a little before his death, other Unionist magistrates refused or made difficulties when asked for some assistance, what I do not remember, made necessary under election law; and so my uncle gave that assistance. He walked up and down some Town Hall assembly-room or some courtroom with Parnell, but would tell me nothing of that conversation, except that Parnell spoke of Gladstone with extravagant hatred. He would not repeat words spoken by a great man in his bitterness, yet Parnell at the moment was too angry to care who listened.[6]

Although this contact was brief and cryptic, it was the basis of myth, which Yeats remembered proudly as his family's connection to Parnell.

Even considering the influences of Tynan and Pollexfen, Yeats's early indifference to politics was not surprising, as he was too young to have been politically active before Parnell's rise and many hotly-debated issues did not affect him or his family. The Yeatses were neither tenant farmers nor landlords, although John Butler Yeats had once owned land in Ireland, and they were more concerned with economic survival than the "No Rent" manifesto. Political issues soon became relevant to him; however, they were often intrusive distractions from his art.

We do know that Yeats and his father discussed politics with Douglas Hyde, Davitt, John F. Taylor, O'Leary, and other men they met at the Contemporary Club between 1885 and 1887, but we have no record of the discussions or of Yeats's views of the time. In 1889, at one of William Morris's Sunday evening Socialist gatherings of "educated workmen", Yeats showed his preference for Parnell:

> I was told by one of them, on a night when I had done perhaps more than my share of the talking, that I had talked more nonsense in one evening than he had heard in the whole course of his past life. I had merely preferred Parnell, then at the height of his career, to Michael Davitt, who had wrecked his Irish influence by international politics.[7]

Yeats's comments on the forger Richard Pigott, in letters to Katharine Tynan, show a developing interest. Although his references to "poor Pigott" and his "pathetic" end were not orthodox Parnellism, even though Mrs Parnell later wrote that "It was a painful affair, and Parnell was sorry for the poor creature",[8] they mark the beginning of an exuberant fascination with political excitement.

His first reference to Parnell in print was in an October 1889 article on William Carleton, published at the peak of Parnell's popularity, after his victory over the Pigott forgeries and a few weeks before his meeting with Gladstone at Hawarden:

> . . . a now famous agitator called on an old Fenian (since dead) and asked him, Would the people take up a land cry? 'I am only afraid', was the answer, 'they would go to the gates of hell for it', . . .[9]

Yeats agreed with O'Leary, who had told the story of Parnell's meeting with Kickham, and disapproved of the land war's results. Yeats's epithet for Parnell was revealing; he was not the "archpolitician" John Butler Yeats detested, but Yeats had noted his ability to stir the masses, disrupt the British, and create tumultuous drama.

In 1890, Yeats mentioned Parnell's name only twice in print, particularly neutral contexts, as if he wished to dissociate Parnell and himself from the furor that had arisen when Captain O'Shea filed for divorce, citing Parnell as co-respondent. He noted that Parnell had ''just added his name'' to the list of subscribers for O'Leary's memoirs, information he had seen ''by the evening papers''. Here, his emphasis was on O'Leary, and Yeats distanced himself from Parnell by obtaining his information through the public press. Also, in a review of the 1890 Arts and Crafts Exhibition, he noted Parnell's contribution of the ''over-glaring'' Irish banner.[10] Finally, in his introduction to a volume of selections from Irish novelitsts, *Representative Irish Tales,* published after the divorce petition but before Parnell's fall. Yeats acknowledged that Ireland's overwhelming passion was politics, and hoped for more literary activity: ''We are preparing likely enough for a new Irish cultural movement – like that of '48 – that will show itself at the first lull in this storm of politics.''[11] An intellectual movement was more necessary than Home Rule, more desirable than the current political hatreds, for politics had become only a noisy distraction from the proper work of the Irish mind.

Two events of November 1890 – the divorce trial and Gladstone's withdrawal of support – marked the beginning of Parnell's fall. Because Parnell and Katharine O'Shea had lived as husband and wife for almost a decade, and because Parnell did not oppose the divorce, Captain O'Shea was not cross-examined at the trial, and acted the role of an innocent and deceived husband. Thus, Parnell appeared immoral, for he could not offer evidence that O'Shea had connived at his wife's adultery for political and financial gain without incriminating both himself and the woman he wished to marry. (In 1936, Yeats would learn what had happened from Henry Harrison, but no such vindication was possible in 1890.) As a result of the public outcry against the Protestant adulterer, Parnell and ''Kitty O'Shea'', ''the were-wolf woman of Irish politics'', were denounced by the clergy and the press.[12] Faced with this explosion of public morality, Gladstone reconsidered his advocacy. Although he felt he had no right to ask Parnell to resign, he wrote a letter stating that if Parnell remained the head of the Irish Party, Gladstone's political effectiveness as leader of the Liberals would become ''almost a nullity''.[13] Yeats's comment, in a letter to O'Leary, showed him receptive to the intense drama:

This Parnell business is most exciting. Hope he will hold on, as it is he has driven up into dust & vacuum no end of insincerities. The whole matter of Irish politics will be the better of it.[14]

He was optimistic: Parnell would purge Irish politics, and, in that new atmosphere, perhaps the new literary movement would flourish. Although he wearied of it quickly, public battle between Irish political forces and between England and Ireland was initially stimulating. A letter of January 1891 to O'Leary indicated a continuing optimistic interest:

> It seems as though Parnell's chances had greatly improved these latter weeks. His last two speeches were wonderfully good. I wish I was over in Ireland to see and hear how things are going. The Hartlepool victory should help him by showing that his action has not injured the cause over here as much as people say. My father is bitterly opposed to Parnell on the ground chiefly, now, of his attacks on his followers. To me, if all other reasons were absent, it would seem plain that a combination of priests with the 'Sullivan gang' is not likely to have on its side in political matters divine justice. The whole business will do this good anyway. The Liberals will have now to pass a good measure if any measure at all – at least so I read the matter.[15]

This was unusually political for Yeats, but he had moral reasons to support Parnell against the common enemy, that combination of mob and Church which repressed individualism in art and politics.

In an early October article for *United Ireland,* Parnell's newspaper, published three days before his sudden death, Yeats announced that the local Young Ireland Societies had banded together to form a literary society, the Young Ireland League. Commenting on the inability of Irish and English newspapers to understand the League's intentions, Yeats depicted the Irish press as "the old hurdy-gurdy" that could play "but one tune – the wickedness of Mr. Parnell". Here, his aim was singularly apolitical:

> . . . to . . . train up a nation of worthy men and women who shall be able to work for public good, whether we are about to win an Irish Parliament or whether the old war against English domination is still to go on. The general election, or the coming of Home Rule itself, will not do away with the need for our work, for our enemies are ignorance and bigotry and fanaticism, the

eternal foes of the human race which may not be abolished in any way by Acts of Parliament . . . we welcome Parnellite and M'Carthyite equally . . . perhaps, in ours alone of national organizations may they find the peace that comes from working for distant purposes. We desire to make the fanatic, on which side soever he may be found, less fanatical. . . . In no other sense have we to do with parties.[16]

Loyal readers would have seen this as an attack on those who persecuted Parnell, but Yeats disdained all political solutions, for none would purify the Irish heart of hatred. An essay that began as an orthodox statement of Parnellite gospel rejected politics as destructive fanaticism.

On Tuesday, 6 October, 1891, Parnell died, and Yeats's response was a memorial poem for *United Ireland,* "Mourn – And Then Onward!" which was traditional, even anachronistic, in style. However, Yeats had not altered his view of the situation for the elegiac demands of the occasion. The way had been "bitter", and Parnell had been lonely, "derided, hated". Rather than entirely lamenting Ireland's loss or commemmorating Parnell's achievements, Yeats reproached all parties for fanaticism, and ended with the sharp directness of "there is no returning".[17] Mourning should properly give way to activity; "onward" was equivalent to "outward", finding new solutions and "peace", as in the Young Ireland League, beyond political strife. The day after the poem's publication on 10 October, Parnell's body was brought back to Ireland, and Yeats met the boat, because Maud Gonne was a passenger. Yeats did not attend the funeral, although he wrote of it in later accounts, but he saw the procession and wrote of it to Lily Yeats:

I send you a copy of *United Ireland* with a poem of mine on Parnell written the day he died to be in time for the press that evening. It has been a success.

The Funeral is just over. The people are breathing fire and slaughter. The wreaths have such inscriptions as 'Murdered by the Priests' and a number of Wexford men were heard by [a] man I know promising to remove a Bishop and seven priests before next Sunday. Tomorrow will bring them cooler heads I doubt not.[18]

The poem's "success" was only a momentary exultation; he excluded it from the *Collected Poems*, refused to rewrite it, and reacted strongly when it was reprinted in another context many years later. However, he had moved "onward" quickly and expected others would also – although his prediction that all would be peaceful on Monday underestimated the anger and tenacity of Irish political energy.

Late in 1892, Yeats was involved in a fierce dispute over control of the League's publications, battling Sir Charles Gavan Duffy, a man characterized by "a domineering obstinacy and an entire lack of any culture I could recognize". The dispute took on a familiar intensity, as the older men, who believed in the patriotic poetry of Thomas Davis, opposed Yeats and his younger colleagues, who favoured more contemporary art. Writing to T. Fisher Unwin, Yeats viewed it in political terms:

> . . . I am afraid that . . . our movement may split up on lines which the press will soon turn into a dispute of Parnellite Dublin and the Parnellite young men in the country parts, against what they will call 'West British' and 'Whiggish' Duffy and Rolleston. All the most ardent of the young men are Parnellites and would be only too ready to raise such a cry against Duffy . . .[19]

Although Yeats feared a recasting of an artistic dispute in these terms, he was willing to play Parnell's role in this split, assuming the heroic mantle as the leader of defiant youth battling orthodoxy. His attempt failed because Duffy insisted on an unreadable volume by Thomas Davis, but the drama had played itself out along Parnellite lines, with Yeats as the rebellious leader, crushed by the unimaginative.

At the end of 1893, Yeats defended Richard Ashe King, who had lectured on the destructive effects of political partisanship; in the second of two articles in *United Ireland,* he attacked political oratory, but also condemned the inconsistencies that had ruined Parnell: ". . . have we not seen a number of our politicians affirm with every mark of passionate sincerity that Mr. Parnell was the only possible leader and then a few hours later, with equal passion that he was the one leader quite impossible"?[20] As before, whad had seemed to favour Parnell quickly became an even-handed rejection of all political sides. We have noted John Butler Yeats's letter of June 1894, connecting his son, Wilde, and Parnell: it, too, was evidence of Parnellite leanings, but he would have shunned the issue if possible.

As a spokesman for an emerging literary movement, Yeats wrote on "Contemporary Prose Writers" for the August 1895 *Bookman*. Writing of Standish O'Grady's *The Story of Ireland*, Yeats praised him as the one "historian who is anything of an artist", because he had recorded "with careful vividness some moment of abrupt passion, some fragment of legendary beauty, and for no better reason that because it did interest him profoundly", but showed that his feelings about Parnell were not equal to O'Grady's mythic adoration:

> . . . Ireland is hardly ready for . . . a whimsical impressionism which respects no traditional hatred or reverence, which exalts Cromwell and denounces the saints, and is almost persuaded that when Parnell was buried, as when Columba died, "the sky was alight with strange lights and flames".[21]

Some of Yeats's reaction mocked Irish provincialism, but "almost persuaded" sounded a note of gentle scepticism – although he would later adopt O'Grady's tale of cosmic portents.

In 1897, the year Yeats later characterized as his beginning of "an active Irish life",[22] he took steps as a political organizer that reflected Parnell's influence; his attempts to unify political opposites for a Wolfe Tone monument recalled Parnell's methods:

> . . . I formed a grandiose plan without considering the men I had to work with, exactly as if [I] were writing something in a story. The Dublin committee . . . was a large body – two or three hundred perhaps . . . Why could we not turn this council into something like an Irish Parliament? There were then four parties in Ireland. . . . Why not, after the laying of the stone, invite all these parties to make a statement before us? . . . our council should sit permanently, and the representatives of the various Irish parties should agree to sit in Westminster only as a deputation from us, and only when we had decided that a vital Irish issue had arisen. They would be less expense to the nation and, as English parties would polarize in a new way, the occasional attendances, never to be foreseen, would produce great disturbance.[23]

As autocratic organizer and intellectual stimulus, Yeats would rule, reining in dissident parties, as had Parnell. His scheme directly reflected Parnell's party pledge, where members were pledged to vote according to the party line, not to disagree or abstain. Also, the potential of Yeats's party to "produce great disturbance" by selectively attending Parliament modernized the obstruction of Parnell and Joseph Biggar had perfected. Both the details of the plan and Yeats's self-conceived role were greatly indebted to Parnell's inspiration and model. Although the plan failed because of Yeats's political inexperience, it was an unspoken homage to Parnell as a masterful ruler.

Although his emulation was unsuccessful, Yeats continued his public praise of Parnell's virtues, claiming them as characteristically Irish. At a dinner party at Lady Gregory's in February 1897, Yeats "let off fireworks all evening" in response to the "dogmatic ultra-English mind" of a "Miss X": "Yes, Parnell was a representative Irishman, he lived for an idea; Englishmen will only live for an institution." When he dined there a month later, with Horace Plunkett and Barry O'Brien, the conversation returned to Parnell:

> Mr. Plunkett thinks he was quite unlike an Irishman, but Yeats says it is quite Celtic to have that strong will. The Englishman, he says, is reserved, because of his want of sensibility. Parnell was reserved in spite of it. When he was taunted by Foster in the House he answered with no change from his usual cold manner, but afterwards it was seen blood streaming from his hands, wounded by the clutch which had driven in the nails. The Irish are a feminine nation with masculine ideals; the English, a masculine nation with feminine ideals. . . . England would never like a masculine nature, Napoleon or Parnell, as Ireland would do. He said also, "In Ireland we care too much for action, to succeed in literature. We are not satisfied to sit down and meditate, we all want to be doing something. I myself had a faint feeling of satisfaction the other day when a man in the street said, 'How are you *Mr. Redmond*?'."[24]

Yeats shaped a mythic anecdote he was to repeat several times – Parnell's fierce control of his passions when taunted by William E. Forster, who had linked him to the Phoenix Park murders, and the resulting spectacle, which approached self-crucifixion. Yeats had also changed his theory of Irish failure: dining with Wilde, he had agreed that Irish writing was slight because talk was the natural Irish art. Among more political men, he saw failure caused by Irish restlessness; every poetic exterior hid an eager man of action. In his casual mention of being mistaken for John Redmond was a political impulse, incompletely subordinated to art. Although he had failed as a powerful politician, he was undaunted; that "faint feeling of satisfaction" may have motivated his acceptance of a Senate seat.

In February 1898, Yeats reviewed Lionel Johnson's *Ireland, with Other Poems*, for the *Bookman*, making special mention of Johnson's "Parnell" as a poem which ". . . will become part of the ritual of that revolt of Celtic Ireland . . . the Celt's futile revolt against the despotism of fact or his necessary revolt against a political and moral materialism". The poem, however, was an uninspired reflection of "Mourn – And then Onward!" Johnson's images were traditional: Parnell was a fallen morning light and morning star, and Ireland was a bereaved mother; to remove "Night from our mother's heart", the Irish were to carry on his mission. When Yeats edited a selection from Johnson's poetry for a Cuala edition in 1904, he excluded "Parnell", although he included a patriotic poem along similar lines, "Ireland's Dead". "Parnell", although he reviewed it graciously, represented an outmoded approach.[25]

When Yeats addressed a Wolfe Tone banquet in April, after a giant procession had marched and a cornerstone had been laid, he reflected on the immediate past and future of Irish politics:

> This year will do much, not only for union, but much to reawaken our country after a great disillusionment. The political movement which has just passed away did some things which had to be done, but it left Ireland rent in pieces and full of an immense scepticism. It was utilitarian, and the Celt, never having been meant for utilitarianism, has made a poor business of it . . .[26]

His disillusionment was not with Parnell but with those who had deserted; the "intense scepticism" was characteristic of his own feelings about all political solutions. In rejecting "utilitarianism", he returned to the need for intellectual and cultural solutions to the acrimony of the split, for the answer was again "onward". Late in the year, Lionel Johnson again brought Parnell to Yeats's attention, with more fortunate effect, by reviewing Barry O'Brien's *The Life of Charles Stewart Parnell* and comparing Parnell and Daniel O'Connell in a way that Yeats remembered: O'Connell was gregarious and "loved the very physical contact with crowds, whom his voice

swayed irresistibly''. Parnell, his undemocratic opposite, ''was alone
and aloof, doing his duty and hating it''.[27] This was the foundation
of Yeats's later portraits of the two men as comedian and tragedian,
in his speech on divorce and in ''Parnell's Funeral''. In March
1899, Yeats again met O'Brien at Lady Gregory's dinner party;
now an authority on Parnell, O'Brien told an anecdote of Parnell
bowing ''meek and mild'' to Katharine's will during the divorce
case.[28] Yeats's reaction was unrecorded, but the antithetical portrait
of Parnell, aloof aristocrat in public and devoted husband in private,
remained in mind for ''Come Gather Round Me, Parnellites''.

We may assume that Yeats read O'Brien's biography; although he
never referred to it directly, it was the most comprehensive and reliable
source available, and his interest in Parnell would have extended to it.
Whether he had read it and forgotten it, or had heard similar tales at
the dinner party and other occasions, aspects of it influenced his later
portrait of Parnell. Conor Cruise O'Brien and F.S.L. Lyons, modern
biographers of Parnell, have noted its unavoidable defects. Because so
many participants were alive in 1898, it was extremely cautious of
O'Shea matters and O'Brien relied greatly on anonymous sources in
other areas.[29] Yeats might have regretted O'Brien's reticence, but it
was a welcome change from the lurid emphasis placed on Parnell's
private life, and he might have found O'Brien's mysterious sources
dramatic – as valuable to myth as they were useless as historical
evidence. As ''Parnell's Boswell'', O'Brien had given the book an
unequalled intimacy.

Yeats might have remembered his younger self in the sketch of
Parnell in 1876, an undistinguished orator:

'He was a bad speaker then – had a bad, halting delivery. In fact, it
was painful to listen to him. You would think he would break down
every moment. He seemed to be constantly stuck for want of a
word. It was horribly awkward for the people listening to him, but,
oddly enough, it never seemed awkward to him. I remember a
number of us who were on the platform near him would now and
then suggest a word to him in the pauses. But he never once took a
word from any one of us. There he would stand, with clenched fists,
which he shook nervously until the word he wanted came. And
what struck us all, and what we talked of afterwards, was that
Parnell's word was always the right word, and expressed exactly the
idea in his head; our word was simply makeshift, for which he did
not even thank us.'[30]

Here was passion vehemently controlled, and a stubborn independence in his aristocratic refusal to be indebted to anyone, even in public distress. Sir Frederic Harrison's memory of Parnell's self-control reflected similar mythic characteristics, although Parnell's hands had changed slightly:

> He had one hand behind his back, which he kept opening and closing spasmodically all the time. It was curious to watch the signs of nervous excitement and tension which one saw looking from the back, while in front he stood like a soldier on duty, frigid, impassive, resolute – not a trace of nervousness or emotion. He did not seem to care about putting himself in touch with his audience. He came to say something, and said it with apparent indifference to his surroundings.[31]

Finally, Yeats would have found inspiration in an unlikely place, O'Brien's conversation with Gladstone. Responding to O'Brien's "May I ask if you considered that Parnell should have retired from public life altogether, or only from the leadership of the Irish party?" Gladstone said, "From public life altogether. There ought to have been a death, but there would have been a resurrection," which recalled the Christ-image in Parnell, as well as that of the king slain and reborn, which Yeats would use in "Parnell's Funeral". O'Brien also ended the interview with a memory of Parnell in his last days, when he "suffered intense pain . . . though he tried to conceal it", to which Gladstone replied, "Poor fellow! Poor fellow! I suppose he did; dear, dear, what a tragedy! I cannot tell you how much I think about him, and what an interest I take in everything concerning him. A marvellous man, a terrible fall."[32] The last six words characterized Yeats's feelings – Parnell's magnificence was matched by the immensity of his downfall.

Although Yeats was intrigued by Parnell, he was, by 1899, eager to set aside the angers of the split; a typical example of his irritation was in a March article defending Douglas Hyde, who had been attacked by a Trinity College professor, Robert Atkinson, who had called the folklore Hyde wished to encourage "at bottom abominable".

> . . . Dr. Atkinson, like most people on both sides in politics of the generation which had to endure the bitterness of the agrarian revolution, is still in a fume of political excitement and cannot

consider any Irish matter without this excitement. . . . Ireland will
have no dispassionate opinion on any literary or political matter
till that generation has died or fallen into discredit . . . men often
of great natural power . . . cannot talk, whether in public or
private, of any Irish matter in which any living affection or
enthusiasm has a part without becoming bitter with the passion of
old controversies in which nobody is any longer interested.[33]

Although Yeats did not refer to Parnell, the passions he had
provoked were destructive, and Ireland's future was only in
abandoning the acrimonious past and moving to cultural self-
realization. This perspective continued in a May essay, "The
Literary Movement in Ireland", which Yeats revised for Lady
Gregory's 1901 collection, *Ideals in Ireland*. In it, Yeats put historical
distance between himself and the split, a historical landmark, not an
emotional issue. Parnell's fall now marked the literary movement's
birth and a new cultural awareness, the results of the energies which
Yeats had hoped to divert. The Irish mind prior to 1891 was now
seen as simplistic; its imagination "uttered itself, with a somewhat
broken energy" in simple stories and ballads of Irish martyrs; its
writers were bourgeois, devoted to "civic virtues" and "unbounded
patriotism". Parnell's fall, "the wreck of his party and of the
organisations that supported it", symbolized, if not caused, a new
energy and a "new utterance" for Ireland.[34] Parnell had vanished,
and was notable only for the vacuum his fall had created, which
Yeats filled with the literary movement. However, one aspect of the
essay was not concerned with the announcement of the new
movement's birth and history, and Yeats's leadership – his
distinction between English and Irish heroic ideals:

> Contemporary English literature takes delight in praising
> England and her Empire, the master-work and dream of the
> middle class . . . it must long continue to utter the ideals of the
> strong and wealthy. Irish intellect has always been preoccupied
> with the weak and the poor . . .

> Ireland has no great wealth, no preoccupation with successful
> persons to turn her writers' eyes to any lesser destiny. Even the
> poetry which had its form and much of its matter from alien
> thought dwelt . . . on ideas living in the perfection of hope, on
> visions of unfulfilled desire, and not on the sordid compromise of

success. The popular poetry of England celebrates her victories, but the popular poetry of Ireland remembers only defeats and defeated persons.[35]

Historically justifiable, this was most evident in Yeats's heroic portraits of Wilde, Parnell, Casement – men who had failed by English standards. Yeats celebrated their defeats as part of their heroism. In this year, he wrote, ". . . the arts are at their best when they are busy with battles that can never be won"; in 1917, "The desire that is satisfied is not a great desire, nor has the shoulder used all its might that an unbreakable gate has never strained"; in 1929, "The one heroic sanction is that of the last battle of the Norse Gods, of a gay struggle without hope",[36] and it reached its fullest expression in "Lapis Lazuli", which celebrated gaiety in the face of apocalypse. Heroism was always measured by the attempt's nobility, even by the magnificence of one's defeat.

Although February 1900 marked the formal truce between the warring parties of the split, when John Redmond was elected head of the unified Parliamentary party, this political unification was of limited importance to Yeats, for he had made a split of his own – not between Parnellite and anti-Parnellite, but between literature and politics. He had seceded, leaving the politicians to battle among themselves on concerns he had come to see as obsolete and irrelevant to himself and the nation. Yet his irritated abandonment of politics for pure literary agitation was never absolute or permanent.

Parnell had become history, a stimulus for the "old controversies" Yeats gladly would have forgotten. Ironically, however, his January 1900 letter to the *United Irishman* concerned itself with Parnell, albeit indirectly, as Yeats delivered a cultural lecture on the choice of the best sculptor for a statue of Parnell.[37] Two years later, Yeats was interviewed by *The Echo* on Irish politics, and he agreed that the split was responsible for the aloofness of the young from contemporary politics:

Ten years of discord . . . took away the air of romance that had gathered round Parliamentary politics. The fading of romance from Parliamentary life has had this good effect; it has liberated all the other pent-up forces of the nation – all the forces, in fact, which were absorbed by revolutionary politics of past time. . . . It is better, perhaps, that our politics should be done in a more humdrum spirit . . .[38]

This was characteristically ambivalent – with Parnell gone, the dramatic excitement Yeats had enjoyed was gone, but his loss made it possible to re-direct Irish energies.

In October 1903, Yeats wrote in defence of Synge's *Shadow of the Glen*, defending singular art against an "opinion-ridden" community, for the demands of patriotism were art's ruin.[39] Synge and Parnell were closely connected in Yeats's mind because the attack on Synge was led by *The Irish Independent* – once a Parnellite paper but now controlled by the Catholic businessman William Martin Murphy, who had acted as Archbishop Walsh's intermediary in 1890, attempting to undermine Parnell's leadership. Murphy had denounced Parnell; in his current attack on Synge and Yeats's theatre, he represented many villainies, and his outrages against Parnell grew in importance to Yeats until they were equal to his present offenses. Yeats's most direct reply to Murphy's demand for a "true, pure and National" dramatic art was "The Irish National Theatre and Three Sorts of Ignorance", where Murphy's violence against Parnell and Synge sprang from the same hatred of thought:

> I have listened of late to a kind of thought . . . among some who fought hard enough for intellectual freedom when we were all a few years younger. Extreme politics in Ireland were once the politics of intellectual freedom also, but now, under the influence of a violent contemporary paper, and other influences more difficult to follow, even extreme politics seem about to unite themselves to hatred of ideas.

This proud ignorance, resenting cultural enlightenment as anti-clerical and un-Irish, was so widespread that it had three sources: the Gaelic propagandist, the priest, and the politician.[40] Yeats's position greatly resembled Parnell's defiance of the controlling forces in Irish life; defending artistic freedom, Yeats was attacked by the same regressive nationalism, rigid religion, and expedient politics that had oppressed Parnell.

In his February 1904 speech in New York to the Clan-na-Gael, commemorating the 126th anniversary of Robert Emmet's birth, Yeats depicted more traditional Irish enemies: first, the English "slander" an Irish young man might suffer, ". . . some charge such as that Parnell had to meet when the *Times* newspaper accused him of recommending assassination". The "young man" gradually became more specific, as Yeats recast all Irish heroism in Parnell's image. Yet his heroic evocation was brief, for he remembered the past obsession with "the politics of the hour . . . the pursuit of some great political measure":

When I was a young lad all Ireland was organized under Parnell. Ireland then had great political power; she seemed on the verge of attaining great amelioration, and yet when we regret the breaking up of that power – and we may well regret it – we must remember that we paid for that power a very great price. The intellect of Ireland died under its shadow. Every other interest had to be put aside to obtain it. I remember . . . an article which contrasted the Parnell movement with the movement that had gone before it by saying: "The last movement was poetry plus cabbage garden" (meaning poetry and the failure of Smith O'Brien) "but this movement is going to be prose plus success". When that was written Ireland was ceasing to read her own poetry. . . . That great Parnellite movement tried now to bully England by loud words, and now to wheedle England by soft words, and Ireland herself, her civilization and her ideals, were forgotten in the midst of it all. . . . Idealists and poets had once been of importance to her, but I can remember some verses . . . addressed to the poet . . . saying "Take a business tour through Munster; Shoot a landlord; be of use." We poets were expected to be of use. The day had come when Ireland was to be content with prose plus success; but then it turned out to be not prose plus success but prose plus Committee Room 15.[41]

Parnell had been heroic, but Yeats still found the political emphasis of the time infuriating in its dismissal of art, and was still angered bitterly by its utilitarian nature. His tone, however, became more cheerful when he could talk of the movement Parnell's fall had made possible, an idealist's revenge on the useful:

Then suddenly Parnell fell. The new school of practical and ecclesiastical politicians sold him to the enemy for nothing. Let us mourn his tragic fall, but let us remember that it brought, besides much evil, a new life into Ireland . . . it was the transformation of the whole country.[42]

For the first time since "Mourn – And Then Onward!" Yeats

asked his audience to mourn Parnell's tragic fall, although the movement, replacing "mere ignoble quarrelling", was more important. That movement had "unconquerable energy" and it was continuously active, not intermittently vital: "We have had a period of intense life – Fenianism, Parnellism, whatever it may be – and then it dies down again."[43] Ultimately, Yeats wished most to publicize the movement outside Ireland; although Parnell was heroic and his fall tragic, politics was still an unworthy distraction of Irish energies.

In his introduction to Lady Gregory's *Gods and Fighting Men*, written that year, Yeats considered heroic self-dramatization in terms that linked Wilde and Parnell to Cuchulain: "When we read of the Fianna, or of Cuchulain, or of some great hero, we remember that the fine life is always a part played finely before fine spectators."[44] In *Samhain,* he reflected on the singular nature of Irish heroism:

> I do not think it a national prejudice that makes me believe we are harder, a more masterful race than the comfortable English of our time, and that this comes from an essential nearness to reality of those few scattered people who have the right to call themselves the Irish race. It is only in the exceptions, in the few minds where the flame has burnt, as it were, pure, that one can see the permanent character of a race. If one remembers the men who have dominated Ireland for the last hundred and fifty years, one understands that it is strength of personality, the individualising quality in a man, that stirs Irish imagination most deeply in the end. There is scarcely a man who has led the Irish people, at any time, who may not give some day to a great writer precisely that symbol he may require for the expression of himself.[45]

The heroic figures of Parnell and Swift, especially, signified Irish glory and the heights of human potential; playing a heroic part, one could become symbolic in art, and that image would help others to attain that heroism, whether by emulating Parnell or Cuchulain.

In April 1905, Yeats had a brief conversation with the tireless theatregoer and diarist, Joseph holloway, where Yeats said "he had Charles Stewart Parnell in his mind when he wrote *On Baile's Strand:* 'People who do aught for Ireland,' he said, 'ever and always have to fight with the waves in the end.' "[46] Both Parnell and Cuchulain had been Irish warriors, lonely and doomed, fighting the "ungovernable sea" with gallant intensity. Their heroic independence was unendurable to the common, and their aristocratic individualism had to be sacrificed to the collective will. Neither hero could be made "as biddable as a house-dog" by the orthodoxy, Catholicism or Conchubar; that singularity had to be destroyed.[47] In the play, Yeats had done more than give Parnell a mythic context, recreating him as a hero of saga – he had given him a tragic hero's majesty, in his battle with a powerful society unable to accept his noble majesty.

1907 began for Yeats with the opening of Synge's *The Playboy of the Western World* on January 26, and the riots its "immorality" and the word "shifts" caused. When interviewed, Yeats called up Parnell's name as the lone figure against the mob:

> When I was a lad, Ireland obeyed a few leaders; but during the last years a change has taken place. For leaders we have now societies, clubs, and leagues. Organised opinion of societies and coteries has been put in place of these leaders, one of two of whom were men of genius. Instead of a Parnell, a Stephens, or a Butt, we must obey the demands of commonplace and ignorant people . . . [48]

Ironically, Yeats had been cheered by remembering that Parnell's fall had freed the national imagination to turn to literature. When confronted by a monstrous democracy, which opposed art, he regretted Parnell's loss and wished to return to a single man's masterful autocracy. In the August "Poetry and Tradition", Yeats returned to the problem; since John O'Leary was dead, his noble example gone, the mob seemed even more bleakly oppressive:

> . . . a new class, which had begun to rise into power under the shadow of Parnell, would change the nature of the Irish movement, which, needing no longer great sacrifices, nor bringing any great risk to individuals, could do without exceptional men, and those activities of the mind that are founded on the exceptional moment.[49]

Parnell's fall had brought a new mediocrity, not the imaginative freedom Yeats had hoped for; when the nation turned from his heroism to the Abbey mobs, Yeats valued what had been discarded: "I sing of what was lost and dread what was won."[50]

Yeats was also involved in a minor controversy over the play *The*

Piper, by "Norreys Conell" (Conal O'Riordan), which depicted Irish politics as bitter squabbling. The Abbey audience rejected it as an unflattering portrait, and they were also incensed because a character, "Black Mike", shouted "God damn Father Hanningan!" In February 1908, he spoke at the Abbey, averting mass violence. First, however, he spoke to Joseph Holloway, who did not understand him: "Yeats told me the author meant *The Piper* for a satire about Parnell. How or why I could not tell." Satire might seem antithetical to heroic myth, but it was directed at the split:

> The play meant to me a satire on those dreadful years of the Parnellite split – those years of endless talk, of endless rhetoric, and drivelling folly – years which were taken out of the history of this nation and made nothing of, because of the folly of this nation. . . . In Mr. Connell's play I see the generous impulses, the underlying heroism, which is in the midst of all that folly. I see the ceaseless heroic aspirations of the Irish people imaged in the character of the Piper. I see a figure which had deeply impressed my boyhood in the character of Black Mike. I see in that character Charles Stewart Parnell. I see that angry, heroic man once again as I saw him in my boyhood face to face with Irish futility.[51]

Again, Parnell was separated from the split – a hero in valiant battle, but a historical figure from the past of Yeats's "boyhood". No longer was the split the impetus for new movements, but the worst example of Irish frustration of its heroes. Once a distraction from the rightful work of the Irish mind, Parnell had become Yeats's dominant heroic image.

The journal Yeats began also concerned itself with Parnell; in February 1909, writing of Synge, he mentioned Goethe's characterization of the Irish, ". . . always like a pack of hounds dragging down some noble stag", which would stand for Parnell as well. When he wrote of his desire for an aristocracy to oppose democratic excesses, he praised Protestant "directness and simplicity of mind", not Catholic "slackness and vagueness":

> The lack of the moral element in Irish public life today comes largely from the badness of Catholic education, and the small number of Catholic families with traditions. The sense of form, whether that of Parnell or Grattan or Davis, of form in active life, has always been Protestant in Ireland. O'Connell, the one great

Catholic figure, was formless. The power of self-conquest, of elevation has been Protestant, and more or less a thing of class. All the tragedians were Protestant – O'Connell was a comedian. He had the gifts of the market place, of the clown at the fair.

The Protestant virtues, "form" and "the power of self-conquest", both reflected Unity of Being, the artistically-conceived man, and the ability to master oneself by realizing one's opposite, qualities related to the heroic images of Wilde and Parnell. Much of this came from Yeats's pride at being one of this aristocracy of artistic independence and moral heroism, defining itself against O'Connell and the Catholic mind.[52]

In a September 1910 letter to his father, Yeats mentioned Lady Gregory's new "symbolical" play, "ostensibly about Moses really about Parnell". She described *The Deliverer* as "a crystallising of the story, as the people tell it, of Parnell's betrayal", and of an incident that had happened ten years earlier at a festival at Spiddal:

> In the evening there were people waiting round the door to hear the songs and the pipes again. An old man among them was speaking with many gestures, his voice rising, and a crowd gathering about him. 'Tha se beo, tha se beo' – 'he is living, he is living,' I heard him say over and over again. I asked what he was saying and was told: 'He says that Parnell is alive yet.' I was pushed away from him by the crowd to where a policeman was looking on. 'He says that Parnell is alive still', I said. 'There are many say that', he answered. 'And after all no one ever saw the body that was buried.'

The play, produced in January 1912, showed Parnell as symbolically powerful as Moses or Christ. Betrayed, he could rise again to lead the Irish to freedom; although supposed dead, he could be summoned back, as in "To a Shade". However, Lady Gregory concentrated more on the collective impulse to betray than on the sacrificed hero; although Parnell was to return to "get satisfaction" from those who had rejected, betrayed, and devoured him, she emphasized the treachery more than his Messianistic potential.[53]

Yeats was interviewed in that month, because of the tumultuous American response to *The Playboy*; here, Parnell pointed up a lost Irish courage:

'WE IRISH ARE ALWAYS AFRAID OF THINGS',
said a celebrated theatrical manager to me, added Mr. Yeats, and
there is some truth in the remark. Ireland used to be a nation of
soldiers; to-day it trembles before a play or a newspaper article or
the report of a divorce case. Our nationality and our purity seem
such fragile things when they can perish at a shadow. It is only a
passing fit of panic. Ireland will recover its courage and
remember its past.[54]

Synge and Parnell were again connected because they had been
betrayed by a particularly Catholic cowardice, although Yeats
optimistically saw the fear as temporary. In 1912, Yeats also wrote
an introduction to *Selections from the Writings of Lord Dunsany*, in which
he compared the books and ideals of the old "Library of Ireland" to
the Cuala Press, O'Connell to Parnell:

> . . . some analogy of the old with O'Connell's hearty eloquence,
> his winged dart shot always into the midst of the people, his mood
> of comedy; and of the new, with that lonely and haughty person
> below whose tragic shadow we of modern Ireland began to
> write.[55]

O'Connell was still the democratic comedian, although portrayed
with less disdain; here, Parnell's mythic image was that of the
future, as Yeats hoped for a return of aristocratic heroism and the
literature that would make it possible.

1913 was a year of great political passion for Yeats, as he again
battled William Martin Murphy, "Mr. Healy's financial supporter
in his attack upon Parnell." The artistic issue was complicated by
money: Hugh Lane, Lady Gregory's nephew, had a valuable
collection of modern French art, which he was willing to donate to
Dublin if a suitable gallery, to be designed by Sir Edward Lutyens,
would be built. In *The Irish Independent*, Murphy argued that the
paintings were immoral and useless, and, in *Poems Written in
Discouragement*, Yeats defended Lane and the art he represented
against the "blind and ignorant town", suspicious of all culture.[56]
Although the scene had changed, the quarrel had not, and Yeats
responded with anger intensified cumulatively through past conflict
with the same enemies. He was not only defending individual artistic
expression, but his alliances had been formed by Murphy's personal
attacks, as well as Murphy's involvement in the Dublin lock-out

of August 1913, where he opposed the workers and Jim Larkin's Irish Transport and General Workers' Union. Larkin and his men were hardly predictable allies, considering Yeats's aristocratic feelings, but Larkin was a powerful force against Murphy.

In September, Yeats voiced his feelings in two poems. The refrain of ''September 1913'' reflected his despair at new Irish commonness: ''Romantic Ireland's dead and gone, / It's with O'Leary in the grave.''[57] As in ''To a Wealthy Man'', he lamented vanished wisdom and courtesy, replaced by mercantilism. Hugh Lane became the newest incarnation of the Parnell principle: to be noble in Ireland was to be scorned and betrayed by the unworthy. Although its subject was Murphy's attacks on Lane, Parnell's image dominated ''To a Shade''. Depicting Dublin crassness, Yeats showed Parnell as its noble opposite without open praise. He began with ''If '': suggesting Parnell's shade might have come back to visit Dublin, but allowing for uncertainty: ''If you have revisited this town, thin Shade, / Whether to look upon your monument / (I wonder if the builder has been paid).'' The third line, a deflation characteristic of Swift and later Yeats, was an ironic counter-voice, depicting the fraudulent world of unpaid debt, opposed by the honest generosity of Lane and Parnell. Parnell's possible haunts continued the contrast, as they strikingly opposed the urban scene. At the stanza's end, Yeats had possibly called up a ghost who might or might not come, and abruptly sent that ghost from Dublin with a warning: ''Let these content you and be gone again; / For they are at their old tricks yet.'' By ''yet'', not ''again'', Yeats recalled more than twenty continuous years of ignobility, and he equated Lane and Parnell – not as precise evocations of the same image – as men of a ''passionate serving kind'', similarly attacked by the ungrateful. Along with Synge (and the shadow of Wilde), all were heroes ''driven from the place'' by their tormentors, Goethe's savage beasts: ''. . . insult heaped upon him for his pains, / And for his openhandedness, disgrace; / Your enemy, an old foul mouth, had set / The pack upon him''. The society, personified by Murphy, attacked the virtues it lacked: Lane's generosity and culture, Parnell's political and moral honesty, and Synge's artistic truth. The poem's second stanza moved from ''old tricks'' to a vivid description of Lane's offer and Murphy's response, with Parnell's ghost as a corollary. The third stanza intensified Yeats's necessary dismissal of Parnell's shade, with ''Go, unquiet wanderer'', gesture transformed into admonition. Finally, concerned for Parnell's safety, Yeats ended with an indictment of Dublin: "You had enough of sorrow before death – / Away, away! You are safer in the tomb."[58] By his example, Parnell condemned modern Ireland as dangerously unworthy, heroic generosity's enemy.

The poem was Yeats's angry revision of *The Deliverer*: Parnell would have saved the Irish, but they would only have crucified him again. Revolted by what he saw, Yeats directed the ghost from the sordid scene, wishing to avoid another tragedy. To Lady Gregory, the Irish were worth the trouble of saving; Yeats, disagreeing, protected Parnell's shade from their evil. In the treachery against Lane, Yeats rediscovered their treachery against Parnell – the pattern that would result from his reading of *Parnell Vindicated* and *The Forged Casement Diaries* in the 1930's; in 1913 and later, Yeats condemned baseness and celebrated Parnell anew, as a moral standard from which the Irish had fallen.

In his 1914 notes to his poems on Hugh Lane, he explicitly linked Parnell with Lane and Synge, in "three public controversies" that had "stirred his imagination":

> The first was the Parnell controversy. There were reasons to justify a man's joining either party, but there were none to justify, on one side or the other, lying accusations forgetful of past service, a frenzy of detraction. And another was the dispute over *The Playboy*. . . . The third prepared for the Corporation's refusal of a building for Sir Hugh Lane's famous collection of pictures. . . . These controversies, political, literary, and artistic, have showed that neither religion nor politics can of itself create minds with enough receptivity to become wise, or just and generous enough to make a nation . . .[59]

Fourteen years after its official end, the split was the most vivid example of ill-breeding and vindictiveness. Perhaps because his unhappy memory of the period was still so strong, Yeats's first draft of his autobiography contained little reference to Parnell, who appeared parenthetically, indicating the political climate or how it had changed since his fall. He was almost insubstantial, existing almost exclusively as a shadow of other personalities: Maud Gonne, W.E. Henley, C.H. Oldham.[60]

In the spring of 1914, Mrs Parnell's two-volume biography, *Charles Stewart Parnell: His Love Story and Political Life*, was published; Yeats, his father, and Lady Gregory read it.[61] Written under the supervision of her son, Gerald H.W. O'Shea, who was "jealous for his father's honour", it inaccurately suggested that Captain O'Shea had been deceived by his wife and Parnell. Yeats, however, did not read the book as a historical document, and valued it as the intimate corollary to O'Brien's public and political biography, for it was personal testimony by the only remaining authority on the private Parnell, devoted to his "own little Wifie." As Yeats had done with O'Brien's book, he took evidence from it which supported and enlarged his mythic portrait. Parnell's amorous life, Mrs Parnell's view of the public outcry, and the contrast between Parnell's honour and the charges of dishonour against him were new, as was her assertion that her marital life with the Captain was, by 1881, "accepted as a formal separation of a friendly sort", because "Years of neglect, varied by quarrels, had killed my love for him long before I met Parnell, and since the February of 1882 I could not bear to be near him."[62] Thus, Parnell had not ruined a happy marriage; he had been moral, wishing only to marry her as soon as possible – and, if that were impossible, to live with her in the most traditional way:

> . . . as regards the marriage bond his honest conviction was that there is none where . . . love . . . does not exist, *or where it ceases to exist.* To Parnell's heart and conscience I was no more the wife of Captain O'Shea when he (Parnell) first met me than I was after Captain O'Shea had divorced me, ten years later. He took nothing from Captain O'Shea that the law of the land could give, or could dispossess him of, therefore he did him no wrong.[63]

Her view of public reaction to their transgression also coincided with Yeats's, especially in her condemnation of Gladstone, who had known of their relations and used her as his intermediary, but, when forced to acknowledge this, had become orthodox and denounced them. He had obeyed the hypocritical morality that had destroyed Wilde, ". . . the eleventh commandment of social life: 'Thou shalt not be found out' (publicly) . . ."[64]

Certain fragments particularly impressed Yeats: Mrs Parnell remembered watching Parnell from the Ladies' Gallery "in moments of passion against his own and his country's foes", clenching his hands "until the 'Orders of the Day' which he held were crushed into pulp, and only that prevented his nails piercing his hand". This passion was matched by his aristocracy, as when she wanted him to apologize for missing a meeting:

. . . this he would never do, saying, "You do not learn the ethics of kingship, Queenie. Never explain, never apologize"; adding, with his rare laugh: "I could never keep my rabble together if I were not above the human weakness of apology."[65]

One anecdote epitomized the passionate man, lover, and husband, usually hidden beneath the impassive exterior, and Yeats referred to it in *The Trembling of the Veil* and *A Vision*: the Parnells at Brighton pier on "one rough, stormy day":

. . . we had been much worried and were wondering whether the time of waiting we had imposed upon ourselves . . . till the way could be opened to our complete union before the world, was not too long for our endurance. It was a wild storm, and Parnell had to hold me as we slowly beat our way to the pier-head. The chains were up to prevent anyone going on to the lower deck, but Parnell lifted me over . . . we stood looking at the great waves – so near, and shaking the whole pier-head in their surge. Parnell remarked that the old place could not last long, and as I turned to get a fresh hold on him, for I could not stand against the wind, and the motion of the sea sickened me, the blazing fires in his eyes leapt to mine, and, crushing me roughly to himself, he picked me up and held me clear over the sea, saying, "Oh, my wife, my wife, I believe I'll jump in with you, and we shall be free for ever."

Had I shown any fear I think he would have done it, but I only held him tight and said, "As you will, my only love, but the children?" He turned then, and carried me to the upper deck, hiding my eyes from the horrible roll and sucking of the sea beneath our feet.[66]

This heroism, verging on a mad disdain for personal safety, was Parnell's inner self; emotionally reminiscent of the cult of love-suicides from Yeats's Romantic past, it depicted Parnell as an amorous Cuchulain, fighting the Brighton waves. Although Yeats did not acknowledge Mrs Parnell's book extensively, material such as this emerged in later portraits – especially the evidence that showed Parnell's private passion, corollary to impassive public heroism.

When the occasion demanded, Yeats returned to Parnell and O'Connell as contrary symbols, as in his November 1914 speech at the Thomas Davis Centenary. Referring to the ballad "The Lament for Owen Roe", Yeats stated that "to read it is to remember Parnell and Wolfe Tone, to mourn for every leader who has died among the ruins of the cause he had all but established . . .". Here, no denigrating references to the split marred his vision of lost leaders. O'Connell, however, was the enemy, whose "personal influence had been almost entirely evil":

> His violent nature, his invective, his unscrupulousness, are the chief cause of our social and political divisions. . . . When at the Clare election, he conquered the patriots of a previous generation by a slanderous rhetoric, he prepared for Committee Room No. 15 and all that followed. In his very genius itself, there was demoralisation, the appeal – as of a tumbler at a fair – to the commonest ear, a grin through a horse-collar.[67]

Yeats had found a source for the split's virulence, as well as Parnell's destruction – as opposed to Parnell's aristocratic grace, almost lost in democratic frenzy and rage.

When John, Viscount Morley's *Recollections* were published in 1917, Yeats and his father read them, and Yeats used them as one source for his portrait of Parnell in *A Vision*:

> . . . in our protracted dealings for some four or five years, I found him uniformly considerate, unaffectedly courteous, not ungenial, compliant rather than otherwise. In ordinary conversation he was pleasant, without much play of mind; temperament made him the least discursive of the human race.[68]

At the year's end, Parnell emerged in a dramatic context, in Lennox Robinson's play, *The Lost Leader,* which Yeats characterized to Lady Gregory as "a very fine play – the supposed return of Parnell – your old subject – nearly a great play but not quite."[69] The play added psychoanalysis to the myth of Parnell's empty coffin. Set in contemporary Ireland, unlike *On Baile's Strand* or *The Deliverer,* its protagonist was the elderly Lucius Lenahan, who, under hypnotic trance, revealed that he was Parnell – hidden, not dead, and reappearing during the Troubles. Appropriately, Lenahan, heroic and scornful, was killed by a blind beggar, Houlihan – like Cathleen, symbolizing Ireland – ironically, Lenahan's most fervent supporter. Robinson, like Yeats, saw the passions of Irish love and betrayal as intertwined and equally violent. Lenahan's death was emotionally in keeping with Yeats's myth of Parnell's crucifixion, but Yeats preferred his dramatic freedom to Robinson's historically-grounded fantasy, and Robinson's extensive discussion of the psychoanalytic nature of Lenahan's malady would have seemed superfluous to Yeats, draining the play's elemental myth of energy.

Yeats turned to a more detailed characterization of Parnell in a November 1920 interview, where Parnell's aristocracy was part of an essential Irish pride:

> Pride is not the antithesis of humility . . . but the antithesis of vanity. The vain man cares for the good opinion of the crowd. The proud man is content with his own good opinion, because he respects himself. The vain man loves rhetoric because it pleases the crowd. The proud man speaks simply. . . . Daniel O'Connell represented normal Ireland, Ireland of the crowd, but Parnell – there was never a man less of the crowd than Parnell. It is recorded of him that the members of Parliament did not salute him first, but awaited his recognition, according him the position of a superior, as of natural right.[70]

On Easter Sunday 1922, Yeats, John Michael Henry (author of the 1920 *Evolution of Sinn Fein*), and John Dillon, who had turned against Parnell in the split, lunched at Lady Gregory's. Two days earlier, Yeats had obviously been thinking of Dillon, as Lady Gregory recorded in her journal: "Y. asked who it was that had no peace because he slew his master, and I told him Zimri, and that I used to apply it to John Dillon after the split with Parnell and he says that is what he is going to do." She also recorded Dillon's view of Parnell's fall:

> Parnell would have got all we wanted but for the woman. Have you read the life? It is a wonderful love story. It would have been all right if it had not been made public. No man is allowed to stay in public life when that is so . . . I always refused to attack him on moral grounds, but only because he had unfitted himself to be leader of the party. If he had lived a little longer he would have had no follower left.[71]

Yeats was unaffected by this view, which resembled Gladstone's hypocrisy, and Dillon's suggestion that Parnell was failing, not betrayed at the height of his powers, did not fit a hero's portrait.

In June, Yeats had finished *The Trembling of the Veil*; in it, Parnell had developed from the first draft's peripheral figure to one of the principal actors, influential in life and death – as one-fifth of the volume was titled "Ireland after Parnell". There was the traditional opposition between "the bragging rhetoric and gregarious humour of O'Connell's generation and school . . . and . . . the solitary and proud Parnell", but the portrait was enlarged by Yeats's delight in the heroic:

> . . . whenever we did not speak of art and letters, we spoke of Parnell. We told each other that he had admitted no man to his counsel; that when some member of his party found himself in the same hotel by chance, that member would think to stay there a presumption, and move to some other lodging; and, above all, we spoke of his pride, that made him hide all emotion while before his enemy. Once when he had seemed callous and indifferent to the House of Commons, Foster had accused him of abetting assassination, but when he came among his followers his hands were full of blood, because he had torn them with his nails. What excitement there would have been, what sense of mystery would have stirred all our hearts, and stirred hearts all through the country . . . had we known the story Mrs Parnell tells of that scene on Brighton Pier. He and the woman that he loved stood there upon a night of storm, when his power was at its greatest height, and still unthreatened. He caught her from the ground and held her at arm's length out over the water and she lay there motionless, knowing that, had she moved, he would have drowned himself and her. Perhaps unmotivated self-immolation, were that possible, or else at mere suggestion of storm and night, were as great evidence as such a man could give of power over self and so of the expression of the self.[72]

Parnell was pre-eminent as the fiercely proud man of the O'Leary mould, and the passionate man, whose passions could have transformed the Irish imagination, in his merging of impassivity and bloodied hands, callousness and self-immolation. In Yeats's last line, Parnell emerged as an image of Unity of Being, as control of the self led to its greatest expression: the anecdotes had coalesced, transformed, into unified heroic myth.

On 12 August, Arthur Griffith, founder of the *United Irishman*, once Yeats's ally but later an enemy in the conflict over Synge, died.

His death affected Yeats little, but Yeats was incensed by the reprinting of "Mourn – And Then Onward!" as a memorial to Griffith. Lady Gregory recorded that he was "very indignant" and could see no "trace of merit" in it, a poem he had "hoped forgotten", and he commented on the incident in her autobiography:

> . . . I remember once seeing a quotation on a wooden shield on the wall of a National League Hall that I thought was from the Bible; and then I found that it was from myself. It was in a poem that I had written on Parnell's death and that I hope has never been reprinted – something about his 'leading us from the tomb.'[73]

His objection was aesthetic – notwithstanding his distaste for Griffith – that his poem should serve as a universal elegy, and it was indicative of his development, as poet and myth-maker, that he should so decisively reject his earlier and more traditional vision of Parnell.

Later that year, he completed the major portions of *A Vision*, which he had written simultaneously with the revision of his memoirs. It contained a portrait of Parnell which both duplicated and opposed that of his autobiography; as he had done with Wilde, he found a place in the "System" for individual examples. In the "Table of the Four Faculties", he placed Parnell at Phase 10. His Will was "The Image-breaker", the political and moral rebel; when true, his Mask was "Self-reliance", and, when false, "Isolation", both reflecting his dependence on no one and his avoidance of everyone except Katharine, to his political disadvantage. When true, his Creative Mind was "Dramatisation of the Mask"; when false, "Self-desecration". The latter may have been linked to his bloodied hands. Finally, his Body of Fate was "Humanity", perhaps Yeats's nod to Mrs Parnell's book or to the suffering of the crucified hero. Notably, the characteristic associated with Phases 8 through 12 was "Rage"; Yeats saw the general character of the Creative Mind of Phase 10 as "Intellectually passionate", and Phase 10's Body of Fate as affected by "Tension". All reflected the heroic political man in opposition to hostile forces, not only the tragic lover. Some characteristics shifted in Yeats's extended description of the phase: the Mask, when true, was now "Organisation"; when false, "Inertia", as Yeats depicted Parnell's actions as reflections of character. Creative Mind, when true, became "Domination through emotional construction"; when false, "Reformation"; the first was characteristic of Parnell's dramatic power, and perhaps Yeats saw him as reforming politics by purging it of hypocrisy. The Body of Fate was now "Enforced emotion", less explicable because of Parnell's repression of emotion in public.[74]

Yeats's application of these qualities to Parnell, as the sole example of Phase 10, was less cryptic. Out of phase, he gave himself up to "rudderless change", perhaps Yeats's vision of Parnell's absences from leadership or the way he was manipulated for his love of Katharine. Even when out of phase, he was powerfully disruptive; he "disturbs his own life, and he disturbs all who come near him . . . ". When true to phase he could "create some code of personal conduct, which implies always 'divine right' ", and he became "proud, masterful and practical". This was the image of an imperial man who led by political intelligence, strong will, and noble example, although his majesty could easily be undermined by forces beyond his control, not O'Connell's "gregarious sympathies", but "some woman's tragic love almost certainly". Parnell's attraction to Katharine, as Yeats saw it, was destructive, founded in "circumstances rather than by any unique beauty of body or of character". Although Yeats never doubted that love's sincerity, he doubted that Katharine was worthy of such all-consuming adoration. The intensity of Parnell's restraint of his passions was expressed in an image reminiscent of the burning pillar of "Mourn – And Then Onward!":

> . . . a kind of burning restraint, a something that suggests a savage statue to which one offers sacrifice. This sacrifice is code, personality no longer perceived as power only. He seeks by its help to free the creative power from mass emotion, but never wholly succeeds, and so the life remains troubled, a conflict between pride and race, and passes from crisis to crisis.[75]

His passion was self-corrosive, expressed only in conflict, as an outraged nation prevented Parnell from expressing his self. The conflict was internal, between passion and restraint, but it was also the struggle between private desires and public restrictions.

Like Wilde, Parnell's life was shaded by his rage to escape, "to destroy all that trammels the being from without", for both men were trapped by the conflict between self and collective law. Parnell was also viewed as a kind of actor, although different from Wilde as self-dramatist; Parnell saw ''all his life as a stage play where there is only one good acting part; yet no one will accuse him of being a stage player, for he will wear always that stony *Mask*. . . ''.[76] Acting brought the power of ''action'' and ''command''; one could fulfill the passions within by acting impassively. Parnell also embodied aspects of godhood, as well as that of the savage statue to which sacrifice was offered. In his autocracy, he had the ''ambition . . . of the solitary lawgiver'', and was simultaneously god and sacrificial victim, ''like that god of Norse mythology who hung from the cliff's side for three days, a sacrifice to himself''.[77] Only in pain could he realize himself; as in the split, he was both the idol and victim of the masses. Although he needed ''the submission of others'' to realize himself heroically, he was vanquished by those who worshipped him.[78]

Finally, Yeats recalled the anecdotal portraits of Morley and Mrs Parnell:

> John Morley says of Parnell, whose life proves him of the phase, that he had the least discursive mind he had ever known, and that is always characteristic of a phase where all practical curiosity has been lost wherever some personal aim is not involved, while philosophical and artistic curiosity are still undiscovered. He made upon his contemporaries an impression of impassivity, and yet a follower has recorded that, after a speech that seemed brutal and callous, his hands were full of blood because he had torn them with his nails. One of his followers was shocked during the impassioned discussion in Committee Room No. 15 that led to his abandonment, by this most reticent man's lack of reticence in allusion to the operations of sex, an indifference as of a mathematician dealing with some arithmetical quality, and yet Mrs Parnell tells how upon a night of storm on Brighton pier, and at the height of his power, he held her out over the waters and she lay still, stretched upon his two hands, knowing that if she moved, he would drown himself and her.[79]

This was generally a familiar portrait of the simultaneous contraries, but one change was notable, aside from Yeats's heightened dramatization of the Parnells at Brighton, in the incident of Parnell's bloodied hands. Yeats had characterized Parnell as having appeared ''callous and indifferent'' to charges of having abetted assassination;

here, the "brutal and callous" speech was Parnell's.[80] It had been self-crucifixion; here, it reflected an internal duality. As Parnell spoke brutally, his bloodied hands were a self-flagellation, an atonement for his words, a reminder of his "Humanity". The change was characteristic of Yeats's myth and his incorporation of Parnell into the "System", for it emphasized simultaneous opposites – although Parnell's strengths, in biography or in philosophy, never diminished.

1922, the year in which these views of Parnell were completed, was eventful for Ireland, in that the conflict with England was ended, but it marked the beginning of civil war. For Yeats, it was the start of his years in the Irish Senate, as "one of three Senators appointed to advise the government on matters concerning education, literature, and the arts".[81] In this role – as public and political man – Yeats was again offered an opportunity to emulate Parnell. Although the seat was more an honorary one than one of autocratic power, Parnell's shade influenced his actions. In the Senate, Yeats involved himself in varied controversies and spoke eloquently on the arts, politics, and Ireland's future, but the February 1925 controversy over divorce legislation brought Parnell vividly back. The Dáil had requested the Committee on Standing Orders to frame an Order which would make it impossible for any person to introduce a bill of divorce *a vinculo matrimonii*.[82] As the chairman of the Senate had ruled this resolution out of order, Yeats published his undelivered speech on divorce in *The Irish Statesman* on 14 March. The memory of the Parnell divorce case coloured his thoughts, as he found himself in a similar position, defending Protestant liberalism against Catholic dogmatism. Divorce in itself was not the issue, but it represented the larger concerns of intellectual and religious freedom, as the Catholics would have made national law identical to religious doctrine. Yeats's view of marriage was unintentionally an echo of the convictions Mrs Parnell ascribed to her husband:

> Marriage is not to us a Sacrament, but, upon the other hand, the love of man and woman, and the inseparable physical desire, are sacred . . . and it seems to us a most sacreligious thing to persuade two people who hate one another because of some unforgettable wrong, to live together, and it is to us no remedy to permit them to part if neither can re-marry.[83]

His view of the Parnell case, and its reverberation in current history, was an echo of Berkeley's "We Irish think otherwise", with

"Protestants" substituted, defending his intellectual heritage.

Before Yeats spoke in the Senate, he expressed related feelings in "The Three Monuments", which took as its subject the statues of O'Connell, Parnell, and Nelson in O'Connell Street, and the private immoralities of the three men, venerated by an orthodox public for their heroic purity. The "three old rascals" mocked modern Irish hypocrisy and the "popular statesmen", who, lacking courage, praised a rigid morality, abandoning the rakish past. What Yeats prized most, proud intellect and heroic dalliance, would have been replaced by the standardized morality of the common man.[84]

Yeats's "undelivered speech" cannot have prepared the Senators to receive his views calmly, as the 11 June debate showed. Although "The Three Monuments" was not published until 1927, Yeats showed he had the three rascals in mind, and his references to them created a furor. With what appeared heretical boldness, he exalted his Protestant legacy, portraying the Catholics as enslaved by dogma, proposing "exceedingly oppressive legislation" that would "open the way for every kind of intolerance and for every kind of religious persecution". He turned to the three monuments, which were "encouraging":

> We never had any trouble about O'Connell. It was said about O'Connell, in his own day, that you could not throw a stick over a workhouse wall without hitting one of his children, but he believed in the indissolubility of marriage, and when he died his heart was very properly preserved in Rome. . . . We had a good deal of trouble about Parnell when he married a woman who became thereby Mrs Parnell.
>
> AN CATHAIORLEACH: Do you not think we might leave the dead alone?
>
> DR. YEATS: I am passing on. I would hate to leave the dead alone. When that happened, I can remember the Irish Catholic Bishops coming out with a declaration that he had thereby doubled his offense. That is, fundamentally, the difference between us. In the opinion of every Irish Protestant gentleman in the country he did what was essential as a man of honour. Now you are going to make that essential act impossible and thereby affront an important minority of your countrymen.

The issue was Protestant gallantry, as opposed to the Catholic majority, represented by Yeats's slighting reference to the "workhouse wall"; Parnell's honourable behaviour was more valuable than dogma. Yeats closed by championing the heroic lineage of that Protestant minority:

> We against whom you have done this thing are no petty people. We are one of the great stocks of Europe. We are the people of Burke; we are the people of Grattan; we are the people of Swift, the people of Emmet, the people of Parnell. We have created the most of the modern literature of this country. We have created the best of its political intelligence.

Parnell's name was the latest on Yeats's list; although Yeats had spoken primarily of his honour, he was an established man of the cultural aristocracy. To Yeats, "divorce" and "Parnell" had become synonymous, as both represented the oppression of Protestant freedom by a rigid conservatism. Although Yeats, defending himself under attack by the Senators, apologized for his mind's "innate immorality", he did not retract his emphatic praise of the Protestant tradition and its freedom. As hero and victim of oppression, and as a gallantly "irregular" man, Parnell was still its newest member.[85]

The Bounty of Sweden, Yeats's "bread and butter letter" to Stockholm for its reception of him on his way to receive the Nobel Prize, published that year, was less inflammatory. His official lecture to the Swedish Royal Academy, "The Irish Dramatic Movement", used Parnell as a familiar historical and cultural landmark:

> The modern literature of Ireland, and indeed all that stir of thought which prepared for the Anglo-Irish war, began when Parnell fell from power in 1891. A disillusioned and embittered Ireland turned from parliamentary politics; an event was conceived; and the race began, as I think, to be troubled by that event's long gestation.[86]

In November 1928, Yeats retired from the Senate because of poor health, a sense of his political inadequacy, and a disillusionment with his fellow Senators and politics in general – but to see this as his farewell to public politics would be to underestimate his resilient love of controversy, as his later poetry on Parnell and Casement reveals. In his introduction to his "Swift play", *The Words upon the Window-Pane*, written late in 1930, Parnell reappeared as the familiar

historical landmark whose fall had freed the Irish imagination from
political obsession. More intriguing was Yeats's reference in his
October 1930 diary:

> . . . serve nothing from the heart that is not its own evidence,
> what Blake called 'naked beauty displayed', recognise that the
> rest is machinery and should [be] used as such. The great men of
> the eighteenth century were of that beauty; Parnell had something
> of it, O'Leary something, but what have O'Connell and all his
> seed, breed, and generation but a roaring machine?[87]

Yeats praised Parnell's metaphysical beauty, reflecting Wilde's
artistically-conceived man, also taking the opportunity to refer slyly
to the legends of O'Connell's profligacy, representing the
mechanistic logic Yeats despised.

Early in 1932, Yeats completed his introduction to *Fighting the
Waves*, which contained eight lines that would be incorporated into
"Parnell's Funeral". In the introduction, he noted Ireland's
changed mood, and the effects of that change stemming from the
split, on his work: "When Parnell was dragged down, his shattered
party gave itself up to nine years' vituperation, and Irish
imagination fled the sordid scene." This was traditional for him,
even in its echoes: "sordid" characterized the split in a letter twenty
years before to Katharine Tynan, and "dragged down" was a
memory of Goethe's picture of Irish bestiality. He turned, however,
from this traditional beginning to view Parnell amidst the belligerent
"spite and bitterness" of those literary realists who had been
repelled by the split:

> An age is the reversal of an age;
> When strangers murdered Emmet, Fitzgerald, Tone,
> We lived like men that watch a painted stage.
> What matter for the scene, the scene once gone!
> It had not touched our lives; but popular rage,
> *Hysterica passio*, dragged this quarry down.
> None shared our guilt; nor did we play a part
> Upon a painted stage when we devoured his heart.[88]

In this stanza, Yeats considered the fall anew as a symbol and cause
of modern Ireland. Initially, the Irish reaction was the emotional
detachment of spectators: "What matter?" Blaming English

"strangers", they were not provoked to action. The contrary to this detachment was not progressive unity, but Parnell's destruction. Although unidentified, his tragedy needed none, for his stature equalled the three patriots of the first age, and "dragged down" made it inescapable. Now, the Irish were entirely responsible, having devoured him in carnivorous madness. Yeats's final image reflected the Dionysiac myth of "Two Songs from a Play":[89] Parnell had been destroyed by his own people, who had killed their god-king for the power they would get by devouring his heart. Savage malice became primitive ritual, as Parnell was now the mythic victim. Godlike in heroism and in crucifixion, whether as Dionysius, Christ, or a Norse god, Parnell transcended his physical death through a resurrection as lasting image.

In September, Yeats gave a Sunday lecture at the Abbey. Although Joseph Holloway was bored by it, he remembered Yeats's new concept of "the four bells or epochs of Irish literature",[90] which reappeared in the 1934 "Commentary on 'A Parnellite at Parnell's Funeral' " – this commentary and the completed "Parnell's Funeral" had developed from "Modern Ireland", Yeats's American lecture, which he had practiced at the Abbey. That tour, Yeats's last, began in October 1932, and he returned home in late January 1933. Although "Modern Ireland" is undated, internal evidence suggests that it was written after mid-August 1932. It began on the same grim note as "The Second Coming": "We have intellect but not conviction nor will", and continued as Yeats explored ". . . for the sake of my own peace of mind, the origin of what seems to me most unique and strange in our Irish excitement". To do this, he spoke of the historical foundation of modern Ireland, but that soon changed to personal recollection: "At the close of the nineteenth century came the third moment. 'I saw it begin almost exactly forty years ago on a stormy autumn morning." That event, recorded by Maud Gonne, a "friend . . . more tireless than I", was Parnell's funeral and "the stars that fell in the broad daylight as the body was lowered into the grave". Standish O'Grady's myth, "witnessed by thousands", was now acceptable; although Yeats had rejected it as "whimsical impressionism" in 1895, he accepted Parnell as sacred mystery, beyond recorded history. He quickly summarized the past, from Parnell as the guilty adulterer to his death, and the split:

All over Ireland the old Fenians and the young men discussed

Parnell, praised his pride, his loneliness, and denounced not only
the party that deposed him, but the country that slandered and
betrayed. Families were broken up, father and son, brother and
sister, brother and brother were divided by furious hatred. No
one has a better [right] than I to speak of that controversy that
affected national character so powerfully, for I took an active part
in the political and literary societies of the young men.
Everywhere I saw the change take place, young men turning
away from politics altogether, taking to Gaelic, taking to
literature, or remaining in politics that they might substitute for
violent speech more violent action. Ten years later when St.
Gaudens designed the memorial that stands now in O'Connell
Street, he set round its base the ox heads and wreaths that
commemorate the sacrificial victims of classical Rome. From that
national humiliation, from the resolution to destroy all that made
the humiliation possible, from that sacrificial victim I derive
almost all that is living in the imagination of Ireland today.[91]

By 1932, Yeats saw the violence of 1916 and beyond as having
grown from Parnell's tragedy; although it had been a "national
humiliation", he noted, almost proudly, all that come from it – the
strongest forces shaping modern Ireland. He continued, discussing
and summarizing the Christmas dinner scene of Joyce's *A Portrait of
the Artist as a Young Man* as a literary mirror of pervasive conflict, and
retold the incident of *The Piper* to establish the climate of ruin:
"Ireland was humiliated, Ireland was degraded, political method
had been an insincere oratory, an artificial enthusiasm, and it had
proved useless in a moral crisis." The split had encouraged "violent
clericalism and anti-clericalism, and . . . personal jealousies and
rivalries . . . ill-temper . . . casual malice", but it also produced
Joyce, "the most famous of a movement of imagination that
was . . . a direct expression of the national self-contempt that
followed the death of Parnell". Equal and opposite was Parnell's
effect on Irish political self-definition, as in his influence on the
Rising: "Three or four years after the betrayal of Parnell two little
boys, sons of a Dublin stone mason, knelt down beside their beds
and prayed that they might sacrifice their lives for Ireland." They
had been inspired by his example; however, with characteristic
ambivalence, Yeats viewed post-1916 politics as obsessed with self-
sacrifice for its own sake:

Something new and terrible had come in Ireland, the mood of the mystic victim. For a generation speeches, commemorations led before men's minds the martyrs for the national cause, all the more popular national songs were in their praise; not one of them, not Lord Edward, not Wolfe Tone, was the victim. They had served their cause and met their deaths, but they had not deliberately sought suffering. . . . Parnell had been the victim, the nation the priest, but now men were both priest and victim – they offered the nation a terrible way out [of] humiliation and self-detraction. Since then the substitution of the hunger strike for [the] silence of the imprisoned Fenians has helped to make deliberate suffering a chief instrument in our public life . . . it is not wholesome for a people to think much of exceptional acts of faith and sacrifice, least of all to make them the sole test of [a] man's worth.[92]

The dignity and purpose of earlier suffering had changed; Terence MacSwiney seemed masochistic when compared to O'Leary and Parnell. Yeats had praised his power at Brighton to consider self-destruction; now, it had turned to a neurotic fascination without ennobling purpose. In their deliberate search for pain, Yeats found only a perverse desire to be punished, rather than to triumph, as if atonement for past ignobility could come only from self-destruction.

Yeats had proposed to investigate the cause and nature of current Irish excitement, and Parnell was its centre, connecting and transfiguring all: the lecture's proper title was "Ireland after Parnell", for his was the dominant force, and Yeats showed that its magnitude in his imagination had only intensified. "Parnell's Funeral", his completed poetic meditation on the subject, combined the practical history of the lecture with the mythic and ritual conceptions of the untitled stanza.[93] When first published in October 1934, its first section was titled "A Parnellite at Parnell's Funeral"; its second, "Forty Years Later". Although omitted in later publications, these subtitles indicated the areas of Yeats's contemplation: past history and its effects on the present. The first two stanzas drew upon myth: although the scene, Glasnevin cemetery, O'Connell's tomb, suggested a historical countertruth, Parnell as the Great Tragedian, Yeats emphasized myth over history, contrasting transient cloud and bright star, its straight line representing the image of "saint or sage", recalling Parnell.[94] The star also recalled O'Grady's myth, which Yeats connected to the sacrifice of the god by the crowd, driven by "animal blood", later the blood of rats: "Brightness remains; a brighter star shoots down; / What shudders run through all that animal blood? / What is this sacrifice?''[95] These stanzas were supported by Yeats's notes to "The Vision of an Archer", and other mythical and mystical visions, evoking the falling star and violent death, "a star laid low".[96] Parnell was emotionally linked to these images – his beauty and power, ended by violent sacrifice.

The third stanza contained the lines printed in the introduction to *Fighting the Waves*; in this mythic context, they were abruptly concrete, recalling history and the names of past Irish martyrs. Parnell, the quarry dragged down by the bestial impulse, reinforced the earlier myths, making the devoured king a stronger image. The fourth stanza grew from these lines and Yeats's admission of his part in the collective guilt, and developed images of the guilty Irish as vituperative rats, betraying and devouring. Here, Yeats assumed the prominent position on the stage he had made, defiantly acknowledging his part in Irish guilt: "Come, fix upon me that accusing eye. / I thirst for accusation." This swept aside all attempts to blame the English for Parnell's betrayal; Yeats had made himself the scapegoat of the national guilt, perhaps hoping for a collective expiation. He also returned to his anger at past and present Irish rhetoric, rejecting all as false, motivated by "the contagion of the throng". Hearers and speakers were liars and rats, "animal blood" at its lowest, deserters of Parnell's ship. The final lines were, at first, typical Yeatsian renunciation: "Leave nothing but the nothings that belong / To this bare soul, let all men judge that can / Whether it be an animal or a man." It stripped away the non-essential, as he had done in "Sailing to Byzantium", "The Tower", and would do in "The Circus Animals' Desertion", leaving man, Yeats himself, as unaccommodated, Lear's bare, forked animal. Only when all mad and vile rhetoric was eliminated could the reader pronounce judgment on Parnell's "bare soul". The last line's choice, "animal or man", was not as simple as it appeared: had Parnell, too, been tainted by the crowd's contagion, or was he, when separated from it, forty years later, purified? Yeats's answer was obvious, for Parnell was never a man of the crowd, but it was unstated, for the judgment had to be public for Ireland to acknowledge its guilt.

"Forty Years Later" moved to Yeats's assessment of current Irish leaders by Parnell's standard, as he had done in "Modern Ireland", connecting them by the image of the devoured heart and its inspiration for the devourer – keeping Parnell's spirit perpetually alive, if the eater was worthy.[97] First on Yeats's list was Eamonn de

Valera, then President of Ireland, who had "impressed" Yeats "by his simplicity and honesty" although they "differed throughout . . .". De Valera would have been worthy; had he "eaten Parnell's heart / No loose-lipped demagogue had won the day, / No civil rancour torn the land apart." Yet the heart's value had been dissipated, as de Valera had not inherited Parnell's spiritual power, and Yeats saw the result as disastrous. He continued his declining list of political men with William Cosgrave, first President of the Irish Senate, who would have satisfied the land's imagination and saved Kevin O'Higgins, and ended with Eoin O'Duffy, the Blue Shirt leader, who was dismissed with "Had even O'Duffy – but I name no more – ."[98] Yeats had been disillusioned quickly with the Blue Shirts, but even O'Duffy, inspired by Parnell, would have been an improvement. All the men of Yeats's list were essentially different from Parnell; affected by the collective imagination, they lacked his "Anglo-Irish solitude".[99] At their best, they epitomized the crowd's animal nature, not solitary heroism, which Yeats depicted by a mythic vision of "Jonathan Swift's dark grove", through which Parnell had "passed, and there / Plucked bitter wisdom that enriched his blood".[100] Swift symbolized a solitary Irish intellect, embittered by his perceptions of vice and folly – Parnell was his descendent, not necessarily in ideology or intellect, but in his bitter solitude and end. At the poem's end, the star had fallen, the heart had been devoured, but no rebirth was possible, because of the limited men who followed Parnell; his energy and heroic potential had been lost in the crowd's rage, and none could match what had been lost. Although W.H. Auden satirically suggested that Yeats saw himself as Parnell's self-crowned successor, ". . . Yeats has helped himself to Parnell's heart",[101] Yeats understood Parnell's bitter wisdom, but could not have saved the nation from its own contagion.

When "Parnell's Funeral" was published, Yeats had written a necessary historical commentary.[102] For the most part, it was a reworking of "Modern Ireland", focusing on the historical events that had formed the modern Irish mind, with the "Four Bells" and heroic individualists – Swift, Berkeley, Wilde, Shaw, Moore, Parnell – in evidence as history or familiar as the personal past. Its fourth section began with a recollection of Parnell's funeral. Although Yeats had not attended, "in my sensitive and timid youth, I hated crowds and what crowds implied", he had heard Maud Gonne's tale of the falling star: "was it a collective hallucination or

an actual event?'' As in ''Modern Ireland'', he referred to
O'Grady's myth, and added his own substantiating recreation: ''I
think of the symbolism of the star shot with an arrow. . . . I ask if the
fall of a star may not upon occasion, symbolise an accepted
sacrifice.'' Although the promised rebirth had not come, perhaps
Parnell's sacrifice would be followed by purification or release. His
summary of the split omitted individual portraits but noted
representative works – Joyce's scene remained, abridged – and
characterized the violence in mythic terms: ''. . . an initiation like
that of the Tibetan ascetic, who staggers half dead from a trance,
where he has seen himself eaten alive and has not yet learned that the
eater was himself''. This recalled the devoured heart, the cult of
martyrdom where men were simultaneously priest and victim, and
the memory of Parnell in *A Vision* as the god who was a sacrifice to
himself. Yeats's final section returned to a familiar opposition: the
tragedian Parnell, with bloodied hands, opposed to the comedian
O'Connell, representing ''democratic bonhomie''. However, in
Yeats's desire to make the contraries appear simultaneous, he made
it appear that O'Connell had died during the split, not eighteen
years before Parnell's birth: ''As we discussed and argued . . .
O'Connell . . . left the scene and the tragedian Parnell took his
place.''[103]

Even with commentary, much of ''Parnell's Funeral'' might have
been cryptic. Yeats had reworked elements familiar to him, but it
was not a direct celebration of Parnell, rather Yeats's images and
feelings on the occasion of the funeral and on the impossibility of
surpassing Parnell in modern Ireland: his most direct evocation of
Parnell as hero would come in his ballad.

In 1934, Yeats encountered his final play on the subject, W.R.
Fearon's *Parnell of Avondale*, an artistic failure, less well-known than
Robinson's *The Lost Leader*. Yeats's sole comment on it, in a
September letter, suggests he knew its limitations: ''. . . a new play
about Parnell now has to be produced, in its performance perhaps
revised''.[104] The play, dedicated to Yeats, was the work of a
passionate Parnellite, and was indistinguishable from history, simply
a dramatized rendering of important events in Parnell's life, political
and private, from 1880 to 1891. He had selected material from
O'Brien's and Mrs Parnell's biographies, and turned it into an
accurate, sympathetic, and dull play, adding only snatches of
dialogue to counteract Parnell's natural reticence and broad stage
effects. The play was valuable as a failure – a negative example

of the purely historical approach, as opposed to a mythic approach to history.

In *Dramatis Personae*, Yeats's continuation of his autobiography, completed in 1935, there was only one notable reference to Parnell, recalling Yeats's emphasis in his speech on divorce. Parnell had been Protestant Ireland's "last great figure" on a list of "immense prestige, Burke, Swift, Grattan, Emmet, Fitzgerald, Parnell, almost every name sung in modern song . . .".[105] Although this lineage was no longer effective, Parnell's place was unimpeachable. In the September preface to the first Cuala *Broadside*, signed by Yeats and F.R. Higgins, he commented on the history and endurance of the Irish political ballad, remembering Parnell as one of those subjects to which "the popular mind goes back", a prelude to Yeats's ballads of the next years.[106]

Although Yeats firmly refused to involve himself in international politics, he could still rouse himself to an intense emotion and activity for Irish concerns – in this case, a political and moral issue almost fifty years old. The stimulus was Henry Harrison's *Parnell Vindicated: The Lifting of the Veil* and its new evidence on Parnell's liaison with Katharine, the result, Yeats's angry excitement and "Parnell ballad". Young Harrison had been one of Parnell's most fervent supporters in his last battles, had assisted Mrs Parnell after her husband's death, and had heard her story unaltered by her son's bias. The book, published in 1931, was his collection of reliable personal testimony establishing that Parnell's behaviour had been honourable. In Parnell's words, "If this case is ever fully gone into . . . you may rest assured it will be shown that the dishonour and the discredit have not been on my side."[107] Harrison was more reliable than Mrs Parnell, less cautious than O'Brien; although Yeats knew him slightly, he had not read the book in 1931 and might never have done so had not Harrison written to him, five years after its publication, asking his help "to make it known in Dublin".[108] Aware of Yeats's past interest in Parnell, Harrison felt he would share his reverent "amazement" at Parnell as "a demi-god – such vision, such simplicity, such concentrated passion". In the summer of 1936, Harrison visited Yeats, having first sent him a copy of the book and of R.C.K. Ensor's *England 1870 – 1914* to refer to; their discussion so excited Yeats that it provoked a relapse of ill-health.[109] Out of this meeting, the violent emotions it stirred, and Yeats's reading of *Parnell Vindicated*, came a vigorous ballad, a note on the meeting, and a revitalized emphasis upon Parnell as the betrayed hero.

Vindication was the book's primary motive; not a definitive biography, it carefully refuted the lies that had marked Parnell as the guilty destroyer of a marriage. Throughout, Harrison emphasized mythic characteristics Yeats had encouraged: Parnell as solitary and proud, opposed by the mob, the moral man, hounded by the pack yet fighting with intense courage. To this, he added a personal vulnerability, revealing Parnell's devotion to Katharine beneath the legendary aloofness. Parnell's heroism was central to the book, as Harrison described his "dominance", "sheer personal force", and a "pride which was described as not less than the pride of Lucifer, a personal dignity to which both friend and foe have borne tribute, and a simple directness of thought and speech and manner . . .". His vindication proved Captain O'Shea's assumed innocence false, for Parnell and Katharine had been "lovers from 1880 – 1890," and Harrison's evidence about O'Shea ". . . fell far short of proof that he was, or could have remained, in ignorance of the fact. And if he was not in ignorance, then he was acquiescent, and, above all, he was not deceived."[110] Far from simply being aware of his wife's relations with Parnell, O'Shea had "connived at and been accessory" to her love affair and "sex union", as Katharine told Harrison:

> Of course he knew. I do not mean that I or anybody else told him in so many words, except once. . . . There was no bargain; there were no discussions; people do not talk of such things. But he knew, and he actually encouraged me in it at times. I remember especially one particular occasion, very early in the affair, when he wanted to get Mr. Parnell's assent to something or other and he was urging me to get this assent, he said, 'Take him back with you to Eltham and make him all happy and comfortable for the night, and just get him to agree.' His air, his manner, made his meaning unmistakable to me. He knew too, of course, that Mr. Parnell was staying with me when he was not. How could he fail to know? Do you think it would have been possible to bind my children to secrecy? Would he not have heard it from the children when he saw them on Sundays? or the servants, if he cared to ask? I do not know exactly when he first learned of our love – we felt no obligation to tell him – but it cannot have been long before he knew it all. It was then, that was the only time, that I blurted the whole thing out, that I loved Parnell with my whole soul, loved him as I had never loved the husband whom I was defying.[111]

O'Shea had been silent to retain his political advantage and his share of the legacy expected at the death of Katharine's wealthy and elderly "Aunt Ben". Harrison proved him a blackmailer, liar, and panderer, ready to permit Katharine to obtain a divorce with the charges against himself, so that she could honourably marry Parnell – for twenty thousand pounds. This infamy angered and excited Yeats, but Harrison also offered him mythic evidence of Parnell's romantic heroism, such as the gallant gesture which was further evidence of O'Shea's connivance, in Katharine's recollection:

> One day Captain O'Shea came down to Eltham to discuss some important matter with Mr. Parnell and the three of us dined together. As the night drew on, I retired before the others, and my door was still standing open when Captain O'Shea, who was the second to retire, came upstairs. He spoke to me, and the discussion of our evening's debate began afresh and, in the course of it, he entered my room and the door closed. Suddenly, the door was banged violently open and Mr. Parnell stalked in, his head held high and his eyes snapping; he said not a word but marched straight up to me, picked me up, threw me over his shoulder and turned on his heel; still without a word, he marched out of the room across the landing and into his own room, where he threw me down on the bed and shut the door.[112]

Yeats, who had proudly written that the Irish had always been "good lovers of women", would have delighted in this.[113]

His reawakened interest took shape in a ballad, to satisfy Harrison's request that he "write something in verse or prose to convince all Parnellites that Parnell had nothing to be ashamed of in her love". Writing to Dorothy Wellesley, he enclosed a first draft and explained it: "You will understand the first verse better if you remember that Parnell's most impassioned followers are now very old men." The combination of age and passion shared by Harrison, "an old decrepit man", and Yeats made the ballad no longer reflect a defiant young man's current political issue, for all the actors were dead or dying. Based on Harrison's evidence, it also evoked a hero who had long passed, to make Parnell memorable to newer generations, another Protestant victim of Catholic duplicity. The ballad form was also the most appropriate shape to have Parnell's love and heroism sung into the public memory, although the historical footnote was needed because of the issue's historical remoteness. Although the Parnellites were aged, they could still revitalise heroic myth in an atmosphere of shared whiskey, legend, and song, united as an Irish community praising their "lovely man".

The first stanza concentrated on the extreme age of the Parnellites, asked to "stand upright", however briefly, as a communal salute to their leader one last time before their collective demise, which hovered over the stanza; it was also a memory of Yeats's meeting with Harrison, for Yeats was in his wheelchair. In the second stanza, Yeats gave reasons for their praise, sketching a simple heroic portrait, from the "hunted man", an echo of Goethe, appealing to the collective identity – the poor and farmers – depicting Parnell as the valiant Irish king who defeated his enemies. Its simple diction, "fought", "saved", "good", did not admit any qualification: Parnell was the Irish saviour, not the man who spoiled the nation's chances for Home Rule. His love, as well, was not for another man's wife, but for a worthy "lass". The final reason, which began the third stanza, was Parnell's magnificent durability as a heroic image that had inspired "every man that sings a song", whether Yeats, ballad-makers, or hearers; he had given Yeats "precisely that symbol he may require for the expression of himself". Neither time nor rumour could efface his heroism or pride, a "lovely", ennobling trait, and the stanza ended with an affirmation of the community's devotion to his noble image: "So pass the bottle round." It had been neither funeral nor wake, but a collective celebration of virtues. In the final stanza, Yeats attacked his chosen enemies: the clergy, the political betrayers, and the Captain, making emotionally fitting myth from simplified history. In that "tragic history", he saved O'Shea for last, indicting him with "sold" and "betrayed". Finally, the last four lines reaffirmed the strength and truth of myth. The "lies of history" were the most durable, and collective knowledge, "the verdict sung above the glass," would outlast historical fact. Yeats's verdict was the triumphant statement of Parnell's unblemished public and private honour, his love of Ireland equal to and inextricable from his love for Katharine: "Parnell loved his country / And Parnell loved his lass."[114]

Although polished, Yeats's final version of the ballad was equally intense. "Stand about" became "gather round", more active; "A hunted man" became "our chosen man", stressing the hero chosen by the community, not the victim, and "a verdict on that history" became "stories that live longest", a clearer tribute to the powers of myth.[115] Forceful and simple, it was the culmination of Yeats's poetic efforts on behalf of Parnell's heroic myth. Discarding all extraneous material, the ballad's scope was intentionally narrow, its references unambiguous; although the British had been guilty, its function was to re-establish Parnell's heroic honour. "Mourn – And Then Onward!" had been written to fill an external need; "To a Shade" was truer to Yeats's voice, but its emphasis was on Yeats's current enemies, rather than Parnell's lasting heroism, and "Parnell's Funeral" might have mystified a reader who expected a heroic elegy.

This final version appeared in the 1937 *Broadside*, and in *Essays 1931 – 1936*, at the end of Yeats's "historical footnote", titled "Parnell". In it, Yeats retold the story of his meeting with Harrison, briefly sketched *Parnell Vindicated*, and discussed the hypocrisy which had ruined Parnell and other Victorians, Wilde among them. This mild, ruminative essay directed the reader to Harrison's book and provided commentary in much the same way that Yeats had written a prose commentary to "Parnell's Funeral". In November 1936, Yeats wrote to Ethel Mannin, enraged by his reading of William J. Maloney's *The Forged Casement Diaries*, which proved that the British had ruined Casement as they had Parnell, on a larger scale: presenting forged diaries, they had made Casement appear sexually "degenerate", and, through the resulting scandal, had prevented the reprieve of his execution. Amidst his rage, Yeats mentioned his acts on Parnell's behalf, viewing himself as a conscious man of action:

> I have lately written a song in defence of Parnell (about love and marriage less foul lies were circulated), a drinking song to a popular tune and will have it sung from the Abbey stage at Xmas. All my life it has been hard to keep from action, as I wrote when a boy, – 'to be not of the things I dream'.[116]

In a January 1937 letter to Dorothy Wellesley, he enclosed three short poems which gave "the essence of my politics (the second contains an actual saying of Parnell's)".[117] Slightly revised, they became "The Great Day", "Parnell", and "What Was Lost"; they showed Yeats's despair at the illusion of political progress. The poems damned all sides, for neither revolutionary, democrat, or autocrat could improve the people's lot. Even Parnell knew his efforts were useless, making the outlook bleak, for it Parnell could

not free the Irish from slavery, what lesser man could? "What Was
Lost" was less despairing, but Yeats looked on the future with
dread, for progress and victory were illusions, and his leader was "a
lost king", as in "The Black Tower" and in Joyce's Christmas
dinner, perhaps an echo of Parnell as the king he had tried to
reinstate in the Irish memory. Loyally English, Wllesley was
saddened and offended by Yeats's vehement "old street ballad" on
Parnell arid those on Casement; although she thought the Parnell
ballad "excellent", it would spread "yet more hatred for centuries".
Yeats replied several days later, soothing her fears of eternal political
hatreds:

> The Parnell Ballad is on a theme which is here looked upon as
> ancient history. It no more rouses anti-English feelings than a
> poem on the battle of Trafalgar rouses anti-French feelings.
> There are reasons why Gladstone is not loved in Ireland but that
> is a long story. The Irish reader of the *Broadsides* would [not]
> consider the Parnell ballad political. It is a song about a
> personality far removed from politics of the day.[118]

This was partly to placate her, but it was true to the ballad, for Yeats
had not attacked England as the enemy; ideally, his Irish reader
would have seen it as a celebration of heroism.

In May, Yeats was "writing introductions for a new American
collected edition of my work", which was never published. In "A
General Introduction for my Work", he described Parnell as one of
the "great political predecessors" on a list that included Swift;
although they had "stepped back into the tapestry", they were still
alive in memory. At the end of "An Introduction for my Plays",
Yeats revealed his pleasure in active heroism, his passionate
celebration of men such as Parnell: "I delight in active men, taking
the same delight in soldier and craftsman . . .".[119]

In July, he sent the first draft of "A Model for the Laureate" to
Dorothy Wellesley; the first version, "A Marriage Ode", dealt with
the abdication of King Edward VIII, but the shades behind the
poem were also Parnell and Katharine.[120] The reference was not
specific, for Parnell did not officially abdicate his throne for love –
but, had he abandoned Katharine, he might have been a triumphant
leader. Yeats, however, valued human love more than political
devotion to any office or ideology. If political man, "For reason of
the State / Should keep their lovers waiting", ruin followed, and no

"decent man" would abandon his love for "Those cheers that can be bought or sold, / That office fools have run, / That waxen seal, that signature."[121] "Politics", which Yeats sent to Wellesley in May and June 1938, was his most blunt version of that choice between love and politics, which could "benumb mankind".[122] Here, he followed the Parnell principle, prizing love above all; devotion to Katharine, although politically self-destructive, was the act of a wise gentleman, who knew what was valuable.

Parnell's shade was still in Yeats's thought in the mid-1938 *On the Boiler*, in his description of the relationship between the ideal leader and the masses:

> . . . the Lord Mayor, a good, amiable, clever man . . . thinks, like English royalty, that his duty is to make himself popular among the common people. . . . The whole State should be so constructed that the people should think it their duty to grow popular with King and Lord Mayor instead of King and Lord Mayor growing popular with them; yet, as it is even, I have known some two or three men and women who never, apart from the day's natural kindness, gave the people a thought, or despised them with that old Shakespearian contempt and were worshipped after their death or even while they lived.[123]

The ideal was Parnell's aristocratic contempt for the mob, his justifiable unwillingness to lower himself, as did the Lord Mayor, to a degraded democratic ideal: Parnell would have made the masses rise to his level, and Yeats's pride in his behaviour had not altered.

Yeats's admiration for Parnell had been slow to materialize, complicated by his distaste for politics and the vituperative split. When Parnell was alive, it was difficult for Yeats to separate the political man and the hero, and when Yeats was vigorously battling partisanship after Parnell's death, he found it difficult not to regard Parnell as a distraction, happily gone. After the split had ended, and Yeats could blame the Irish hatred of thought on other sources, he developed Parnell's heroic image completely. Like Wilde, Parnell was an aristocrat victimized by the ignoble; however, his love for Katharine seemed heroically romantic to Yeats, as Wilde's affections did not. Thus, Parnell became an enviable model in public and private. He was also a political image for Yeats, his strong will turned to nationalism; in him, Yeats found an Irish champion, representing all possibilities, uncrowned King or persecuted scapegoat, an image for Yeats to emulate as a Senator, the lone Protestant voice against the Catholic mob.

Parnell was also ideal mythic material for Yeats, for he had triply inflamed the Irish imagination in their initial reverence, their fierce ire, and their guilty mourning. Yeats's "Parnell", like one of John Butler Yeats's paintings, had gone through many revisions: Lady Gregory had seen him as Moses, and Yeats saw reflections of Christ, Cuchulain, Swift, and Dionysius. Finally, Yeats merged the "Parnell" figure with his own, whether asserting aristocratic pride or rejecting unworthy modern Ireland. In ways not apparent in Wilde's case, Yeats almost wished to become Parnell, to assume that cold mastery, to be passionate yet self-controlled – to wear the hero's mask yet look out of it with the artist's eyes.

Parnell and Wilde, through much of Yeats's life, stood as two different directions for his energies, or as two choices, service of an international aesthetic ideal or a nationalist one. Neither figure entirely triumphed in his imagination, for he delighted in vacillation between equally valid contraries. In his art, he thought of a national heroic ideal – Parnell, Cuchulain, the men of the Rising, and, in his politics, he looked for ways to make Irish culture and imagination more artistic.

5 Swift: "The tomb of Swift wears it away"

Parnell and Wilde, although emotionally satisfying heroes, were incomplete; Yeats needed an image combining art and nationalism, which he found in Jonathan Swift, poet and Drapier. Much critical consideration of Yeats and Swift has emphasised Yeats's last years, when Swift emerged frequently in his poetry, drama, and prose, yet Yeats's earlier thoughts on Swift, although vacillating, were frequent, and are essential to an understanding of the roles Swift played in his life.[1]

Yeats's first reference to Swift in print, however indirect, was positive – although Swift was less important than William Carleton in this 1890 letter: "The 'Irish Established Church' has only once been satirised since Swift by a man of genius; that man was William Carleton." In his 1891 article on Irish rakes and duellists, Swift appeared in Yeats's description of an Anglo-Irish gentry who had not as yet ". . . listened to the terrible raillery of Swift".[2]

Remembering this period in the first draft of his autobiography, Yeats wrote that he was often at a disadvantage because of his ignorance of history and many authors, Swift among them. However, his May 1893 lecture on "Nationality and Literature", to the National Literary Society, showed his familiarity with a famous passage from the second book of *Gulliver's Travels*, here used to praise art's wasteful virtues and damn Irish utilitarianism:

> . . . I venture into criticism of the fundamentals of literature, and into the discussion of things which, I am proud to say, have never made two blades of grass grow where one did before . . .[3]

Late that year, defending Richard Ashe King in "The Silenced Sister", Yeats summoned Swift again, as a desirable alternative to rhetorical excess; he preferred "the plain and honest speaking" of

Swift and Berkeley.[4] His memory of the violent debates at the Irish Literary Society revealed a developing awareness of Swift's political writings:

> I remember some judge resigning from the committee after some speech of mine. . . . I had, a romantic in all, a cult of passion. In the speech that made the judge resign I had described the dishonest figures of Swift's attack on Wood's half-pence and, making that my text, had argued that, because no sane man is permitted to lie knowing[ly], God made certain men mad, and it was these men – daimon-possessed as I said – who, possessing truths of passion that were intellectual falsehoods, created nations.[5]

Although Yeats uncharacteristically equated lying and insanity, he was familiar with the *Drapier's Letters* and saw Swift as a creator of myths, the modern Irish nation, and a hero in his "cult of passion".

In his preface to the 1895 *A Book of Irish Verse*, however, Yeats excluded Swift the artist: "English-speaking Ireland had meanwhile no poetic voice . . . and Swift was but an Irishman by what Mr. Balfour has called the visitation of God, and much against his will . . .".[6] Attempting to establish an Irish literary tradition, Yeats was wary of Swift's poetry, for an acceptance of it would have made Irish art seem dependent on an English tradition. He continued to exclude Swift in his controversy with Edward Dowden, who had proposed insufficiently Irish books as "our national literature". *Gulliver's Travels*, although "admirable", was no substitute to Yeats for pure Irish art.[7] In July, remembering this controversy, Yeats defined Irish literature, consciously excluding less authentic writers, such as Swift:

> Some of my countrymen include among national writers all writers born in Ireland, but I prefer, though it greatly takes from the importance of our literature, to include only those who have written under Irish influence and of Irish subjects.[8]

In "The New Irish Library", one year later, Yeats reviewed Richard Ashe King's *Swift in Ireland*, perhaps remembering King as his ally in controversy in his praise of the book. It was broad and thus fragmentary, but Yeats was neither knowledgeable enough to detect its inadequacies nor sufficiently curious about Swift to read the volumes a comprehensive study required. King began by portraying Swift as un-Irish: ". . . a man less Irish in blood, character, temperament and sympathy it would be hard to point to . . . he was more English than the English themselves in his detestation", and by quoting from the *Holyhead Journal*:

Remove me from this land of slaves,
Where all are fools and all are knaves;
Where every knave and fool is bought,
Yet kindly sells himself for naught;
Where Whig and Tory fiercely fight,
Who's in the wrong, who's in the right;
And when their country lies at stake,
They only fight for fighting's sake,
While English sharpers take the pay
And then stand by to see fair play.

In "temperament and in character", Swift was "yet more un-Irish" for he did not fit the Celtic characteristic proposed by Henri Martin, the race's "readiness always to react against the despotism of fact". However, Swift was essentially Irish in his political service to a nation he owed no loyalty, fighting "cant, baseness, injustice and oppression". Swift was comprehensible only in terms of paradox, of the divided self, personally and politically:

Such was his horror of the hypocrisy of goodness that he became a kind of devil's hypocrite, and affected a Satanic cynicism amply belied by his private life and by the faithfulness, the affectionateness, the tenderness of his friendships . . . the humanity of his acts are in continual contradiction with the inhumanity of his words . . . in estimating Swift's motives for throwing himself into the cause of our country, his continual hypocrisy of inhumanity must not be lost sight of . . . what is all this fury against oppression and corruption and injustice but inverted love of fair and pure and just dealing?[9]

Love was the basis of Swift's apparent hatred, and disappointment in mankind, not misanthropy, explained his rage. This was the antithesis of the accepted portrait of mad hatred and terrible rage; although King depicted Swift as "a good hater; to smite the enemy hip and thigh was more to him than to fly upon the spoil", his defence of Ireland grew from a heroic love.[10] This love also coloured his relations with Stella and Vanessa; to King, Swift's reserve signified an overmastering love, and his unwillingness to marry his beloved Stella had justifiable cause, his "horror of poverty and dependence in his youth, and horror of impending madness in his manhood", which Yeats would remember in *The Words upon the Window-Pane*.[11]

In King's book, Yeats read of Swift's letter to Bolingbroke, where he feared a death "like a poisoned rat in a hole", his pamphlet, "On the Contests and Dissensions in Athens and Rome", Swift's encouragement of the universal adoption of Irish manufactured goods, Swift's definition of good writing, "proper words in proper places", and Swift's fable of the Spider and Bee – all essential fragments which he would return to in varied contexts. Referring to the *Drapier's Letters*, King recalled an anecdote of Swift's bravery and magnaminity which seemed to Yeats a paradigm of these qualities:

> He employed his butler, Robert Blakeley, to copy the "Letters" and to convey them to the printer, and he summarily dismissed him on his absenting himself from the Deanery one evening without leave. He was not going, he said, to keep a servant who was emboldened to neglect his duties by the consciousness of having his master in his power. "Strip off your livery, begone from the Deanery instantly, and do the worst to revenge yourself that you dare to do!" The man, more hurt by the suspicion which caused his dismissal than by the harshness of the dismissal itself, revenged himself by an inviolable secrecy as to the reason of his discharge. When the danger had blown over Swift sent for Blakeley, and summoned at the same time all the other Deanery servants to whom he thus re-introduced his late butler: – "This is no longer your fellow-servant, Robert, the butler, but Mr. Blakeley, verger of St. Patrick's, a post which his integrity has obtained him."[12]

Although Yeats rewrote this, he never forgot the gesture. King also showed Swift as a victim, a heroic failure, appropriate to Yeats's myth:

> . . . Swift, in spite of his great power and great efforts, had failed in everything, and in nothing more utterly, as it seemed, than in his single-handed struggle for the deliverance of Ireland. Can

there be a doubt that the consciousness of what he was, the reflection of what he ought to have achieved for himself and for his country, and the contemplation of the comparatively beggarly result of all his lifelong struggles, at once hastened and aggravated the malady which makes the last chapter of Swift's biography the most terrible reading in literary history?[13]

Swift's tragic end became another martyrdom – not public, like Wilde's or Parnell's – a mortification of the self through age, despair, and mental decay. Appropriately, King's book also contained Swift's epitaph, which epitomized grandeur and self-laceration in a few lines.

Finally, King made Swift much like Parnell, a resemblance that grew with time, as he saw Swift's travails, perhaps unconsciously, in terms reminiscent of "Mourn – And Then Onward!": ". . . remember only his championship of our cause, his tears as of blood for our sufferings, and his lonely and weary and hopeless, but Titanic, struggle for our deliverance". More specifically, Swift was Parnell's spiritual ancestor:

It is not the extravagant compliment it seems, to rank Swift with the Prophets who were defeated in their life-time and because of their greatness, only to triumph finally, through the spirit and the doctrine they bequeathed; for politically and in Ireland he was the Moses of his day. If he left his people in the Wilderness he showed them the way out of Egypt and the way into Canaan. To his example Ireland owes – and it is no small debt – her Protestant leaders, Lucas, Flood, Grattan and Parnell; to his initiative she owes the system of inert, dogged and solid resistance to oppression; and to his teaching she owes the lessons, that we must be self-respecting to be respected, self-reliant to be prosperous and self-dependent to be free.[14]

Yeats's review of the book praised King and his vivid portrait: it was "useful and readable", "witty and wise", and "a beginning of that scholarly criticism of men and things which is needed in Ireland even more perhaps than creative literature". Even its limitation revealed Yeats's interest in Swift's art: "it does not contain enough of purely literary criticism, and makes no serious endeavour to consider the values of Swift's writings taken apart from the light they throw upon his actions and opinions . . .". Swift's life and art were noble illustrations of a Wildean aesthetic:

> The recognition of the expression of a temperament as an end
> in itself, and not merely as a means towards a change of opinion,
> is the first condition of any cultivated life, and there is no better
> text than Swift for preaching this . . . he revealed in his writings
> and in his life a more intense nature, a more living temperament,
> than any of his contemporaries. He was as near a supreme man as
> that fallen age could produce . . . he has given the world an
> unforgettable parable by building an over powering genius upon
> the wreckage of the merely human faculties . . . and it is because
> the most ignorant feel this in some instinctive way that his throne
> is unassailable.[15]

Although Yeats separated Swift from his background, and that
century's reliance on logic over intuition, and saw Swift's writing as
occasionally inferior to Sir Thomas Browne's, he regarded Swift as
a member of his own party – an impassioned artist and heroic
belligerent, not a utilitarian nationalist – another man whose image
could turn Ireland away from faction and reform.

In "Rosa Alchemica" and "The Tables of the Law", both
published in 1897, Swift became a character in Yeats's fiction. In the
first, as the narrator dreamed of his alchemical work, Yeats
established a Dublin background through the house "my ancestors
had made almost famous through their part in the politics of the city
and their friendships with the famous men of their generations . . .".
After Michael Robartes's sudden arrival broke this reverie, the
narrator remembered that past's most famous man, leading the way
"up the wide staircase, where Swift had passed joking and railing
. . .". This was Yeats's first use of an explicitly Swiftian locale with
historical and emotional echoes, as in *The Words upon the Window-
Pane*. In the second tale, Owen Aherne used Swift as a countertruth
to Christ's "commandment of love": "Jonathan Swift made a soul
for the gentlemen of this city by hating his neighbour as himself."[16]
This might seem severe, even from the conservative Aherne, but
Swift, vital to a city, was orthodoxy's powerful rejoinder, Christ's
worthy opposite.

At this time, Yeats began spending his summers at Coole,
receiving Lady Gregory's protection and encouragement; perhaps
in its library, well-supplied with eighteenth-century classics, he
absorbed more direct knowledge of Swift's art. Her recollections

show Yeats publicly defending him as a characteristically Irish hero and artist:

> At another meeting of the Irish Literary Society a lecture by Stephen Gwynn on Irish Humour: ". . . Gwynn's lecture, rather good, was chiefly to prove how little humour there is in Ireland . . . Yeats made a fighting speech . . . and did not agree with Gwynn that Swift was un-Irish, as wherever he was born his humour was the humour of insult, which is so much in the Irish nature. 'The humour of insult has given us Swift, Mitchel, Tim Healy; the humour of servility has given us Handy Andy . . . Tim Healy is only divided from Jon Swift by an abyss of genius.' "[17]

This altered Aherne's notion of Swift's transfiguring hatred into an aggressive wit which supported a national pride, a defiant independence. As a heroic personality from the legendary past, Swift reappeared in Yeats's fiction. In *The Speckled Bird*, the autobiographical novel which Yeats worked on intermittently from 1896 to 1902, Swift appeared in the "De Burgh" version, probably written in 1900, in Yeats's description of a library, resembling Coole's, which had, as its pride, ". . . fine editions of the classics and of Bolingbroke and Berkeley and Swift and Johnson and of the *Spectator*, reminding one of the active days of a class long fallen into intellectual indolence". When Yeats revised the manuscript, his last phrase drew an even more pointed contrast between Swift's time and the present: ". . . when the Irish gentry had still destinies that had need of thought and preparation".[18]

The indirect effects of King's book were still apparent; having read of Swift's "A Proposal for the Universal Use of Irish Manufacture", Yeats adopted a similar approach in his Emmet lecture of February 1904; although it lacked Swift's vehemence, it was indebted to his example:

> When a man believes in his own nation . . . his belief very soon has a practical outlet in many directions. Wherever the Gaelic League goes you will find in the shop windows, in out of the way country towns even, printed notices that goods of Irish manufacture can be got there.[19]

In three instances, in the same year, Yeats considered Swift's Irishness, and moved from flat negation to a temporary resolution.

Although he had apparently settled the question in his reply to Gwynn – Swift's character was Irish, his birthplace irrelevant – he kept returning to it, defending Swift against external nationalistic forces. In a May reply to Clement Shorter, who had suggested that the Irish movement owed much to others besides Yeats and Lady Gregory, and that much worthy Irish literature had nothing to do with their movement, Yeats was forced to dismiss Swift in defending her work:

> All is personal preference in the end, and Mr. Shorter . . . naturally prefers Swift, Burke, and Goldsmith, who hardly seem to me to have come out of Ireland at all. I . . . would give all those great geniuses for the first book that has retold the old epic fragments in a style so full at once of dignity and simplicity and lyric ecstasy, that I can read them with entire delight.[20]

Shorter had not mentioned Swift at all, which suggests that he was Lady Gregory's foremost rival in Yeats's mind; forced to choose between Swift and *Cuchulain of Muirthemne* and *Gods and Fighting Men*, Yeats chose the latter, but weakened even this mild dismissal as "personal preference". Considering national literature in *Samhain*, Yeats used Swift as an example of his dilemma in defining it:

> It is the work of writers who are moulded by influences that are moulding their country, and who write out of so deep a life that they are accepted there in the end. It leaves a good deal unsettled – was Rossetti an Englishman, or Swift an Irishman? – but it covers more kinds of National literature than any I can think of.[21]

Eventually, he would regard Swift as an Irish writer by this definition because his work for the Irish cause overshadowed all else. In another passage, Yeats excluded Goldsmith, Sheridan, and Burke, who "had become so much a part of English life, were so greatly moulded by the movements that were moulding England, that, despite certain Irish elements that clung about them, we could not think of them as more important to us than any English writer of equal rank".[22] Notably, Swift was excused from this dismissal; Yeats had made a temporary peace with him.

Yeats's conception of himself and the fierce role he wished to play also often took on Swiftian dimensions, as in a June 1906 letter to

Stephen Gwynn: "What Dublin wants is some man who knows his own mind and has an intolerable tongue and a delight in enemies."[23] In his 1909 preface to the first edition of Synge's *Poems and Translations*, he returned to Swift's epitaph as representative of the hero he had portrayed to Gwynn:

> . . . some man will speak a few simple sentences which never die, because his life gives them energy and meaning . . . is not that epitaph that Swift made in Latin for his own tomb more immortal than his pamphlets, perhaps than his great allegory? – 'He has gone where fierce indignation can lacerate his heart no more.'[24]

Yeats also wrote an unsuccessful Swiftian epigram in 1909, and worried about his own tendencies towards a fearful "violent madness at the root of every mind, waiting for some breaking of the leash", in his private journals. Part of it was his fear of "some nervous weakness" inherited from his mother, but he also felt a kinship with Swift as he aged, fearing an equal decline into bodily and intellectual decrepitude worthy of the Struldbruggs – here, he was concerned about his vexations: "The feeling is always the same: a consciousness of energy, of certainty, and of transforming power stopped by a wall, by something one must either submit to or rage against helplessly."[25] Although the feeling was his personal frustration, it was also the emotional background for Swift's trapped anguish in *The Words upon the Window-Pane*, "locked in" with his enemies.

In a June 1910 interview, Yeats again commended Swift's ferocious satire, the foundation of an Irish strain exemplified in Yeats's time by Timothy Healy. Almost two years later, speaking of Synge, he divided the Irish into two types. Goldsmith, "gentle, harmless – you might call saintly . . . that knows no wrong, and goes through life happy and untroubled, without any evil or sadness", represented one type, Swift, the other: "It is true that he had little or no Irish blood, but in bringing up he was an Irish product. And that type is terribly bitter, hostile, sarcastic."[26] Although happier, the first type lacked the pain needed for creation: ". . . only an aching heart / Conceives a changeless work of art".[27] Now the question of Swift's lineage was less relevant, as he represented a characteristic type. Another interview and several letters of January 1913 reveal his continuing presence in Yeats's thoughts. Although Yeats again preferred Sir Thomas Browne in the interview, Swift was a point of literary reference, as Yeats was reading Strindberg, "as terrible as Swift". He wrote to Lady Gregory, expressing his intention of seeing G. Sidney Paternoster's four-act play, *The Dean of St. Patrick's*: "I am going to Dublin next week for *Swift* as I think it is too important a play for both of us to miss . . .". He had read the play, based on Swift's refusal of Stella because of feared madness, several months before, and had written to Paternoster, expressing his pleasure, but when it was produced at the Abbey, he was less impressed. As he wrote to Lady Gregory, it was "an effective, slightly melodramatic piece of commercial drama," and Paternoster was "a typical London hack".[28] However unimpressive the play, Yeats had supported it because of a growing fascination with its subject.

No comments by Yeats upon Swift were recorded in the next seven years – reflecting the shifting emphases of his thought and perhaps of those who recorded it – until an October 1920 letter to John Quinn, mainly concerned with Yeats's tonsillectomy and the haemorrhage which made him prepare a dying speech. Perhaps this brought Swift to mind, because of the need to compose his epitaph; Yeats's comment, however, indicated his expanding reading – here, the *Journal to Stella*:

> I have been arranging the portraits in my study. Swift wrote to Stella once, 'I am bringing back with me portraits of all my friends,' meaning by that, doubtless, mezzotints.[29]

In the *Journal to Stella*, Yeats found evidence of Swift's private life and his love for Stella, the emotional foundation of *The Words upon the Window-Pane*; Swift's devotion was durable, although they were separated: "God Almighty bless and preserve dearest little MD. . . . Farewell, dearest MD, and love Presto, who loves MD infinitely above all earthly things, and who will."[30] The *Journal* eradicated the "gloomy Dean"; one could not read it and think Swift misanthropic. It also revealed a playful lewdness, as in his comment on an impending appointment: ". . . he has appointed me an hour . . . when I will open my business to him, which expression I would not use if I were a woman . . ." and his complaint on the cold: ". . . 'tis still terribly cold. – I wish my cold hand was in the warmest place about you, young women, I'd give ten guineas on that account with all my heart, faith; oh, it starves my thigh . . .".[31] Yeats found this aspect of Swift earthily attractive, and celebrated the sexually rakish Swift of folklore, sending his servant to fetch a woman, rather than the emotionally repressed celibate. The *Journal* solved no mysteries –

rather, it provoked them – but its wit and devotion made Yeats feel a closeness to Swift, a loving man at home in the world of power and politics, a friend and influence upon the great and wise, that he could not feel to other heroes.

1922 marked a new intensification of Yeats's interest in the Irish eighteenth century; as he recalled a decade later, he had begun to read Berkeley on the recommendation of the Rev. Jephson Byrne O'Connell, an "Irish Free State soldier, engaged in dangerous service for his Government", who had said that "all the philosophy a man needed was in Berkeley". From Berkeley, Yeats "went to Swift, whose hold on Irish imagination is comparable to that of O'Connell".[32] In a November lecture on the Irish dramatic movement, sent as a letter to the students of a California school, Yeats praised Swift's art, without mentioning Sir Thomas Browne:

> If I were your professor of literature . . . and were compelled to choose examples of fine prose for an Irish reading book, I would take some passages from Swift, some from Burke, one perhaps from Mitchel . . . and from that on find no comparable passages till *The Gaol Gate* and the last act of *Deirdre of the Sorrows*.[33]

His enthusiasm permeated the Senate; when Oliver St. John Gogarty presented a motion in November 1923 that Yeats should be officially congratulated on winning the Nobel Prize, he mentioned Swift as one of Yeats's heroic ancestors, and, in 1925, Yeats brought Swift into the acrimonious debate on divorce.[34] Althouth Swift did not appear in the 1925 *A Vision*, as he would in Yeats's revision of it, Donald T. Torchiana noted an article, "The Sphere of Women", in which Yeats felt "mightily obliged to be the Swift of his day and to outrage youth itself".[35]

In June 1926, Charles Edward Lawrence published a one-act play, *Swift and Stella*, in *The Cornhill Magazine*. It was an ineffective exploration of the relations among Swift, Stella, and Vanessa, after Vanessa had asked Swift why he had never married Stella (to which Lawrence's answer was that Swift and Stella were illegitimate brother and sister). However, Mary Fitzgerald has suggested that Yeats knew the play, and that its limitations, perhaps like those of Paternoster's play, inspired him in his later efforts on the same theme.[36] Yeats also wrote an introduction to Arland Ussher's translation of Brian Merriman's *The Midnight Court*, which led him to Swift's *Cadenus and*

Vanessa as its source. He also dismissed Sir Walter Scott's theory of a "constitutional infirmity" as reason for Swift's "emotional entanglement", preferring instead the Irish tradition:

> Some years ago a one-act play was submitted to the Abbey Theatre reading committee which showed Swift saved from English soldiers at the time of the *Drapier Letters* by a young harlot he was accustomed to visit. The author claimed that though the actual incident was his invention, his view of Swift was traditional, and enquiry proved him right. I had always known that stories of Swift and his serving-man were folk-lore all over Ireland and now I learned from country friends why the man was once dismissed. Swift sent him out to fetch a woman, and when Swift woke in the morning he found she was a negress.[37]

In August 1927, Yeats spoke of Swift with Arthur Power, the author of that one-act play, *The Drapier Letters*, which he now agreed to produce, as Power remembered:

> In the argumentative mood of youth I maintained that Irish wit was playful and fantastical but Swift's was typically English – a hammer blow to kill. But Yeats maintained that Swift was Irish by residence and environment and sympathy.
>
> 'His mother came from Leicestershire and his father from Yorkshire, and even if you accept that Sir William Temple was his father he was still English', I replied, for one was nothing if one was not obstinate.
>
> In the end, however, Yeats smiled and said with a sigh: 'Anyway we try and claim him for our own'.[38]

More firmly than ever, Yeats claimed Swift for Ireland because of those qualities which had defined national writing a quarter-century before. Power's play, however, was another matter. As he stated in the introduction, he had written it to find reasons for Swift's transformation from his hatred of Ireland to his heroic defence of it, and he found reasons in Swift's devotion to a "harlot", Mary-Bridget Cafferty, accidentally shot by a soldier who thought Swift was hidden behind her door. In her dying speech, she stated that the *Drapier's Letters* had been written for love of her, which had shown Swift the Irish were worthy of his efforts. This potentially dramatic idea might have seemed superfluous to Yeats, who knew Swift's love for Stella and his strenuous defence of human liberty for its own sake. Although not a powerful inspiration, the play contained one profound stimulus in the note Power attached to his list of characters: "The personality of DEAN SWIFT rules the play, but he does not appear actually on the stage."[39] Although Power may not have realized the difficulties this surmounted, Yeats did – as his play shows.

In this month, Yeats wrote the first poem which named Swift as an integral part, "Blood and the Moon". Although his note gave the poem's source as Kevin O'Higgins's assassination, O'Higgins was secondary to the majestic figures of eighteenth-century thought, combined with the image and reality of Thoor Ballylee, and Yeats's resulting reflections on the modern world and the incompatibility of wisdom and power. Swift was a powerful reminder of the world's decline, the most dramatic of Yeats's four figures. Appropriately, he was the first to appear on the winding stair, itself an echo of *A Tale of A Tub*, combining the tower's actual gyre and the ascending family tree of Irish intellect.[40]

Yeats began by calling down blessings upon his tower, as he had done in "To be Carved on a Stone at Thoor Ballylee". A "powerful emblem", it represented the "bloody, arrogant power" of "Soldier, assassin, executioner", but also the cherished intellectual past, as the great minds of the eighteenth century had climbed its stairs (echoing "Rosa Alchemica" and anticipating *The Words upon the Window-Pane*). Its arrogant pride mocked the modern world, "Half dead at the top", an image indebted to Swift; although Yeats's annotation was more practical, referring to the "waste room" at the tower's top, its source was in Edward Young's *Conjectures on Original Composition*:

> I remember, as I and others were taking with him an evening's walk, about a mile out of Dublin, he stopt short; we passed on; but perceiving he did not follow us, I went back; and found him fixed as a statue, and earnestly gazing upward at a noble elm, which in its uppermost branches was much withered, and decayed. Pointing at it, he said, "I shall be like that tree, I shall die at top."[41]

The decay was not only the modern world's, but the foreshadowing of personal decay. The tower was, as well, grounded in mythic history; as Yeats's "ancestral stair", it signified his pride at occupying the same ground as his heroes, being spiritually in contact with Swift through shared surroundings. The second and third stanzas revealed his closeness to Swift, the only figure identified by his mythic title, "the Dean"; Swift's portrait revealed the passionate tension Yeats would use in drama, based on King's depiction of inner conflict: "Swift beating on his breast in sibylline frenzy blind / Because the heart in his blood-sodden breast had dragged him down into mankind." These lines symbolized the poem's antimony, the opposition of prophetic wisdom and mortal pain, the moon's ethereal wisdom and passionate frustration. Swift's emotions were violent rage, the desire to escape Yeats had seen in Wilde and Parnell, as well as the heart's laceration; although his suffering had majestic scope, it was the futile strife of "a poisoned rat in a hole", a martyrdom beyond help, the other side of the masterful mind saving Ireland. The final reference to Swift was after the less passionate sketches of the three other heroic ancestors – *"Saeva indignatio,"*[42] the passion of his life and epitaph. Although tormented, he was fully realised in heroic rage, for only he combined the wisdom of the dead and the passionate power of the living: nearly two hundred years later, his wisdom shaped modern Ireland, and his passion had kept its frightening intensity.

In 1928, Yeats's interest in Swift found many contexts. In April, he praised Sean O'Casey's work: ". . . you moved us as Swift moved his contemporaries". Discussing the threat of censorship in September, Yeats opposed the familiar enemy, repressive Catholicism, in his comments on birth control: Swift's "Modest Proposal" ". . . at any rate, would make love self-supporting."[43] Bidding farewell to the Irish Senate, he remembered images from Swift's fable of the Spider and Bee from *The Battle of the Books*: "I am glad . . . to be out of politics. I'd like to spend my old age as a bee and not as a wasp."[44] Revising *A Vision*, he found Swift's shadow over much of the "System". In "Rapallo", four lines from "The Progress of Beauty" were commentary on modern art, proclaiming the interdependence of form and matter as well as his growing liking for Swift's poetry:

> Matter as wise logicians say
> Cannot without a form subsist;
> And form, say I as well as they,
> Must fail, if matter brings no grist.

In his new introduction, he used Swift for a self-deflating perspective on his enterprise: "This way of publishing introductions to books, that are God knows when to come out, is either wholly new, or so long in practice that my small reading cannot trace it." "To Ezra Pound" equated Oedipus's horror at his actions with the horror "that is in *Gulliver*", and saw Oedipus's rage as "noble . . . because it seemed to contain all life". Finally, in "Stories of Michael Robartes and his Friends", by "John Duddon", Swift was the prophet of impending disaster, founded upon his essay on "the dissensions of the Greeks and Romans".[45] In December, Yeats wrote to Lady Gregory, actively trying to merge Swift's political thought with his perceptions of the modern world: "I still read Swift, and have tried . . . the theory that we dislike the present Royalty because of the impression Swift made on the nation, when his enemies the Whigs brought their ancestors from Germany."[46] Swift's truths were still true for Yeats; his reading had continued, and Yeats was still applying Swift's perspectives to his own experiences.

1929 began with Yeats's intense interest in Swift satisfied only by incessant reading, as he wrote to T. Sturge Moore in January, referring to Rapallo, where he had been since the previous November:

> For my first weeks here I read nothing but Swift but he became too exciting for my blood pressure and so after some sleeplessness I took, on my wife's advice, to detective stories again. Swift's *Epitaph* and Berkeley's *Commonplace Book* are the greatest works of modern Ireland.[47]

Another letter to Moore, in late March, was based on the four lines of "The Progress of Beauty": "There are four lines of Swift that I find good guides, if one substitutes 'percept' for 'matter' and 'intellect' for 'form' – though that is to modernise, not to improve . . . ".[48] Swift's thought was an adaptable philosophical matrix, but Yeats could not improve on his poetry.

Between the end of 1929 and early 1930, Yeats rewrote Swift's epitaph, praising and publicizing it. Lady Gregory recorded two versions in her 1930 journals; she preferred the first, Yeats the second:

Jonathan Swift is at the goal
Savage indignation there
     Cannot lacerate his soul,
Imitate him if you dare,

World estranged man for he
Saved human liberty.

Jonathan Swift's in port,
Savage indignation there
Cannot lacerate his heart:
Imitate him if you dare.
World-besotted wanderer, he
Served human liberty.[49]

A page of Yeats's Rapallo notebook showed his attempts at a
suitable opening line:

Jonathan Swift is at the goal

Jonathan Swift's in port

Swift has found the final rest

Swift has sailed and found his rest

Swift has sailed into his rest[50]

This was Yeats's way to honour Swift and also practice writing his
own epitaph, a proper occupation for an ailing man. In early
versions, Swift's death was the "goal", escape from a tormented
life, although Yeats soon amended this to a nautical image, Swift
safe in "port", having "found his rest" after a long and stormy
voyage, full of "savage laceration", Yeats's direct homage to the
original. The "traveller" became world-estranged or world-
besotted, which applied to Swift as well as any who sought to
imitate him, with "if you dare" suggesting the dangers of such
heroic emulation. Swift, estranged from the world, happy only in
death, was perhaps too melodramatic for Yeats; "World-
besotted" applied equally to the traveller and Swift. The final
version, completed in September 1930, resounded with the click
of the closing box; its first line was again nautical, but more
appropriately than "port", which suggested only a temporary
stopover: "Swift has sailed into his rest". "Breast",
compromised between "heart" and "soul", and Yeats referred
specifically to the traveller of "Abi viator": "Imitate him if you

dare, / World-besotted traveller; he / Served human liberty.''[51]

When Yeats wrote an introduction to *Wild Apples*, Oliver St. John Gogarty's Cuala volume of poetry, he again placed Swift in a famous tradition, characteristically Irish and Protestant, the aristocratic Few:

> . . . I was asked why a certain man did not live at Boar's Hill, that pleasant neighbourhood where so many writers live, and replied, 'We Anglo-Irish hate to surrender the solitude we have inherited', and then began to wonder what I meant. I ran over the lives of my friends, of Swift and Berkeley, and saw that all, as befits scattered men in an ignorant country, were solitaries.[52]

Two letters of April 1930 show Yeats's immersion in Swift continuing. To T. Sturge Moore, he wrote of reading "daily Swift's *Letters* and his *Journal to Stella*", and, to Lady Gregory, he was more expansive:

> When I am not reading detective stories I am reading Swift, the *Diary to Stella*, and his correspondence with Pope and Bolingbroke; these men fascinate me, in Bolingbroke the last pose and in Swift the last passion of the Renaissance, in Pope, whom I dislike, an imitation both of pose and passion.[53]

Yeats had been ill for five months with Malta fever – and the combination of illness, delirium, detective fiction, and the intimacies of Swift's writings created the necessary atmosphere for his "Swift play", mysterious and personal.

In his memoirs, Sir William Rothenstein remembered a luncheon with Yeats and Ramsay MacDonald from this period:

> Yeats, who lately had been seriously ill, was weak-voiced, almost inaudible, but as he talked his voice grew stronger, and he kept the conversation going. . . . Yeats got on the subject of Berkeley and Swift, spinning theories of Swift's character, of Stella's and Vanessa's, and presently George Trevelyan joined us, and as Yeats proceeded, getting more and more eloquent as he went on, Trevelyan, attracted, eager to bring his fine Whig sense of accuracy to bear on Yeats's improvisations, tried vainly to break in, while Yeats, his right hand raised as it were, forbidding

interruption, grew ever more fantastic and inventive. He was trying, he said finally, to inspire the youth of Ireland with the national ideals found in Berkeley and in Swift. The poetry of the Irish movement had served its purpose and was dead. Berkeley learned his nationalism in the university, Swift in politics.[54]

The passionate wills and strong personalities in emotional conflict were mysteries unsolved by history; only mythic "improvisations" held plausible answers.

Sections of Yeats's 1930 diary, from April to November, were devoted to Swift, as if preparing himself for the play he would begin. The diary began on 7 April, a day of much activity, as his letters to Moore and Lady Gregory show, and he wrote in it many of the same things he had written them: he read Swift's correspondence and detective fiction. His second entry of the day used Swift to reject F.S. Oliver's view of history (in his *Endless Adventure*, which Yeats was then reading) as "a reasoned conflict of material interests intelligible to all":

> I think of Swift's account of Marlborough's demand to be made captain-general for life, of the Queen's fear that he had designs upon the throne, of Argyll's boast that he would fetch him from the midst of his army dead or alive. These men sat next one another, suspected one another, and planned we do not know what. History seems to me a human drama, keeping the classical unities by the clear division of its epochs, turning one way or the other because this man hates or this man loves . . . the drama has its plot, and this plot ordains character and passions and exists for their sake.[55]

Powerful men moved the world by personal impulse, and were more fascinating than historical generalities – it was Yeats's continual championing of intuition, the individual impulse, over logic and cold rationality. Several entries showed him considering Swift's political thought and literary style in comparison to other thinkers and writers. His "Discourse of the Contests and Dissensions between the Nobles and the Commons in Athens and Rome" had anticipated Burke's thought, and had "re-created conservative thought" for Anglo-Ireland: "Indeed the *Discourse* with its law of history might be for us what Vico is to the Italians, had we a thinking nation." Comparing Burke to Swift as stylists, Yeats praised Swift:

. . . no matter what Swift talks of, one delights in his animation and clarity. . . . Swift always thought in English and is learned in that tongue. The writers who seem most characteristic of his time, Pope in his verse for instance, and the great orators, think in French or Latin. How much of my reading is to discover the English and Irish originals of my thought, its first language, and, where no such originals exist, its relation to what original did. I seek more than idioms, for thoughts become more vivid when I find they were thought out in historical circumstances which affect those in which I live, or, which is perhaps the same thing, were thought first by men my ancestors may have known. Some of my ancestors may have seen Swift, and probably my Hugenot grandmother who asked burial near Bishop King spoke both to Swift and Berkeley. . . . I most approximate towards that expression when I carry with me the greatest possible amount of hereditary thought and feeling, even national and family hatred and pride. . . . I can hear Swift's voice in his letters speaking the sentences at whatever pace makes their sound and idiom expressive. He speaks and we listen at leisure.

Burke, whether he wrote a pamphlet or prepared a speech, wrote for men in an assembly, whereas Swift wrote for men sitting at table or fireside – from that come his animation and his naturalness.

Swift's writing thus reflected Yeats's ideal of Anglo-Irish aristocratic solitude – an individual man speaking to other individuals, rather than the commonplace expansiveness of oratory and rhetoric meant for mob ears. Here, most clearly, Yeats connected himself with the mythic past; reading Swift or even thinking of him was rediscovering his own link to a heroic Ireland. In another entry, responding to his son's question of which area Ireland excelled in, Yeats found his answer in Swift's intellectual power: "the thought of Swift, enlarged and enriched by Burke, saddled and bitted reality, and that materialism was hamstrung by Berkeley, and ancient wisdom brought back . . . modern Europe has known no men more powerful". Finally, Yeats returned to the "Discourse" to support his fears of collective rule; in democracy, Swift had seen "predatory instinct".[56]

On 1 June, Yeats wrote to Olivia Shakespear that he read Swift "constantly", and an entry of 19 June reflected this concentration on Swift's heroic image: "When I think of Swift, of Burke, of

Coleridge, or Mallarmé, I remember that they spoke as it were sword in hand, that they played their part in a unique drama, but played it, as a politician cannot though he stand in the same ranks, with the whole soul.''[57] Although he had once rejected the swordsman as heroic image in ''All Things Can Tempt Me'', he saw in Swift a belligerent defence of liberty, a hero realising himself in combat with the mob, as well as the choice of the warrior's role through conscious self-dramatization.[58] On 9 August, Yeats wrote of the ''Discourse'', now ''more important to modern thought'' than Vico, expressing an aristocratic fear of democracy and a cyclical view of the development of civilizations. A spiritual and intellectual aristocracy was essential: ''I think of Swift's own life, of the letter where he describes his hatred of this man and of that, and his hatred of all classes and professions. I remember his epitaph and understand that the liberty he served was that of intellect, not liberty for the masses but for those who could make it visible.''[59] The next day, Yeats was occupied with the question of ''pure thought'', which led to Swift as clergyman as well as philosopher:

> Did Swift deliberately set 'pure thought' aside? He advised his clergy to preach the mysteries of religion once or twice a year and then speak no more of what none can or should understand. He thought missionaries in China should say nothing about Christ's divinity and said that the first Christians thought it 'too high' for general understanding and so kept silent about it. He prayed much, had the Communion Service by heart, but he received dogma and ritual from the State and condemned Hugenot and Dissenter alike.[60]

Yeats admired Swift's assertion that there were mysteries beyond human comprehension, perhaps as another defence of intuition over logic. Mystery was essential, and attempts to comprehend it often debased it – although Yeats had attempted to make his ''System'' visible to those who could understand it, he had not lowered it to the commonest mind.

Yeats's September letter to Wyndham Lewis, gently rebuking Lewis for having satirised Edith Sitwell, took the opportunity to praise Swift, who needed no literal identification. In Sitwell's *Gold Coast Customs*, ''something absent from all literature for a generation was back again, and in a form rare in the literature of all generations, passion ennobled by intensity, by endurance, by wisdom. We had it in one man once. He lies in St. Patrick's now under the greatest epitaph in history".[61] Yeats's order was notable; having celebrated the political philosopher and prophet in his diary, he would now consider the passionate man first, his wisdom second. Before we note the beginnings of Yeats's "Swift play", we must note two entries in Yeats's diary that complement it. On 9 September, he returned to Swift's dread of "a return to public disorder", and his intellectual power – had Swift chosen to do so, he could have resolved the dilemma Berkeley posed and gone beyond Burke. Although incomplete, his vision was the most worthy: "We owe allegiance to the government of our day in so far as it embodies that historical being."[62] Finally, Yeats returned to that heroic gesture of which Richard Ashe King, Thomas Sheridan, and Samuel Johnson had written:

> . . . do I not communicate with the living mind of Swift still in that . . . moment when discovering that his life or liberty depended upon an unsatisfactory servant, he dismissed him that he might not through fear endure any man's negligence or insolence, & restored him & honoured him when all danger had passed.[63]

In "that eternal moment", Swift's "living mind" was alive, haunting Yeats; that memory could become "a conscious moral agent" in our lives, not only an act of heroic independence. Yeats had remembered the incident from King's description and would return to it as foundation for myth. Although we must leave his 1930 diary, rich in Swift, heroic models, and his eighteenth-century ancestors, to examine his most elaborate dramatization of Swift's myth, *The Words upon the Window-Pane*, we should not forget Swift and his butler, for this mental re-staging of a dramatic incident prepared Yeats for the play, summing up moral courage in heroic and dramatic terms.

In his diary, Yeats had made a proud witticism: "I know so much more about Swift than about the saints."[64] From the diary devoted to the public man, thinker, and writer, Yeats turned to public drama, where Swift "played a part with sword in hand". The play combined Swift and the saints, for it was more spiritual than corporeal, avoiding the limitations of a historical drama with powdered wigs. Swift's private life had fascinated Yeats because so much of it was hidden, and he had energetically conjectured on it; in his intense reading of Swift, Yeats's concurrent reading was detective fiction. This gave a unique cast to his thought, almost making John Corbet the play's private investigator, searching through the séance's tangled evidence for a solution to the emotional mysteries of the past. Swift was an ideal subject for drama, in ways Wilde and Parnell had not been. Although a historical figure, he had no surviving relatives to litigate against Yeats, and his private life had been lawful, neither homosexual nor adulterous. Its mystery was naturally dramatic, with an intensely private man revealing himself onstage. The idea of the medium, as well, gave consistent artistic licence, as Swift haunted the Abbey stage as he haunted Yeats, in a classically triangular confrontation, giving Yeats the opportunity to make the audience hear the voice he heard.

The diary entry of 13 September, referring to something "quite simple" which he would do, perhaps his "Swift play", suggests that it was almost finished, for he was adding details of stage business to it at this point. Before this, and his arrival at Coole in August, he had stayed at Oliver St. John Gogarty's house, and seen a rhymed couplet which had been cut into the window. At Coole, revising early stories, he would have re-read "Rosa Alchemica" with its references to Swift in an eighteenth-century house and "pieces of painted china" which had fallen, images which would reappear in the play. Late in October, it was finished, as he wrote to Olivia Shakespear; it had come rapidly to him, for its subjects, Swift and séances, were familiar and fascinating.[65]

Yeats's scenario began with the title *Jonathan Swift*, later *Swift*, as Yeats concentrated on him from the beginning. It was set in a great house, established in place and tradition, "a Georgian house near Dublin", and it opened in conversation between a young Englishman and an older Dubliner on Swift, more than on the séance to which they had come. Much of this dialogue was retained in the final version: the young man displayed an intimate knowledge of Swift, opposed to the older man's inexact generalities – his reference to Swift as a pagan, and his assumption that the poetry on the window-pane, which he had never looked at, was "something cynical". Yeats's favourite mythic landmarks appeared: the magicians's island of *Gulliver's Travels*, Swift's philosophical superiority to Rousseau, and his satire's opposition to "the uneducated mob". This concentrated on Swift in a way more suited to the imaginary dialogue of "Compulsory Gaelic" or *Intentions*; it was a philosophical, not dramatic, exposition of Yeats's views through the young man's corrections of the older man's misconceptions. Although the physical hallmarks of the play were present, the play was static – a quality which remained through Yeats's exposition of spiritualism for the audience's benefit. This, however, introduced the séance, with its theories of cyclical purgation, and the memory of the previous appearances of Swift's "horrid spirit", "connected with the house perhaps", which had spoiled two séances: "He would do nothing but pour out a lot of abuse, abusing some woman. He said the most awful things. Two of their members resigned." The medium and the members prepared for the séance by singing a hymn, and the medium's control, a little American Indian girl, "Silver Cloud", spoke. Swift's spirit appeared almost instantly, speaking through the medium: Vanessa's voice was heard, and the young man recognized both in their emotional conflict. Yeats did not work out the contrasting scene with Stella through dialogue and stage directions, but outlined it in a prose paragraph. As the séance ended, the young man asked the medium for information for his dissertation on Swift and Stella, and discussed theories of Swift's relationships dear to Yeats, rejecting the idea "of what the biographers call a physical defect" as "dead against the old Dublin tradition", asking the medium if she remembered "the story about the negress". At the scenario's end, the medium gave Swift's final outburst, except that the detail of dropping the saucer was added later.

Although Yeats transformed much from this to the final version, its basic elements were immediately present: Swift's relations with Vanessa and Stella, and his spirit speaking through the medium. Some necessary changes were made: his exposition on spiritualism was slowed down, for an audience unfamiliar with it, and "Silver Cloud" became "Lulu", to avoid her reference to Swift as a "big chief". In his first and second drafts, he established a firmer connection between Swift and the house: "In the early eighteenth century this house belonged to friends of Swift – it's mentioned in the Journal to Stella several times. Stella used to play cards here and Swift chaffed her about her losses."[66] The young man, now "John Corbet", perhaps a memory of Yeats's great-uncle Robert Corbet of Sandymount Castle, was given a reason for his interest in Swift and Stella: his essay for a Cambridge doctorate.[67] Yeats's second draft resembled the final version in its greater detail and completeness, and, in the final version, he reduced the static lectures on Swift and spiritualism, and clarified what had been obscure.

Although the play showed Swift in torment, it paid homage to his thought and presented him as the symbol of a greater age. Appropriately, it was finished at Coole and dedicated to Lady Gregory, for it honoured the departed heroic past and great houses such as Coole, where nobility and intellect were encouraged and sheltered. As Coole was to Lady Gregory, the house of *The Words upon the Window-Pane* was a shrine to Swift's memory, fierce intellect, and moral love of Stella.

Discussing Swift, Corbet and Dr Trench represented calm intellect, free from prejudice, and Corbet's speech was Yeats's praise at its highest:

> . . . in Swift's day men of intellect reached the height of their power – the greatest position they ever attained in society and in the State . . . everything great in Ireland and in our character, in what remains of our architecture, comes from that day; we have kept its seal longer than England.

In Trench's reply, he remembered the personal contrary to that achievement: Swift's "tragic life" and all of his friends, "banished and broken". Although Yeats later called Corbet's affirmation "the overstatement of an enthusiastic Cambridge student", he did this only to keep distance between himself and his character.[68] More than any other, Corbet spoke Yeats's thoughts on Swift, especially his praise of a lost golden age. Trench's comment balanced the political man with the emotional tragedy: had the play been purely about the philosophical struggle among the One, Few, and Many, there would have been nothing to dramatise. Swift's tragic mystery, the growing sense of loss, was the play's emotional foundation – as well as foreshadowing Mrs Henderson's final lines. Corbet explained Swift's tragedy, not simply as personal disappointment, but as his disappointment at the world's decline, agony to a perceptive man; his "ideal order" was no longer possible, and he saw the democratic "ruin to come", the motivation for his rage, madness, and art.

A counter-character, the Rev. Abraham Johnson, appeared, unable to appreciate Swift's spiritual tradition and irritably protesting against the hostile influence that had disturbed past séances. With the introduction of Johnson, Mrs Mallet, and Cornelius Patterson, dramatic images of Swift's Many, Yeats gently satirised their common weakness, ignorance, and self-centred assurance, showing their comic insignificance and unworthiness in their speech patterns and desires. Although Corbet, Trench, and Miss Mackenna did not share Swift's majesty, they were free from comic limitations. Mrs Mallet relied on her late husband's spirit for practical advice; Patterson, frivolously good-humoured, searched for a Heaven with dogs and horse-races; Johnson, emptily self-assured, pompously placed himself above the mysteries he was ordained to preach, and began most of his sentences with "I". Contemporary Dubliners all, they were unworthy of a heroic ideal.

In the séance, controlled by their shallow natures, Swift's spirit was only disruptive, interfering with their self-serving desires. This intensified as Yeats's dramatic tour-de-force began, with Mrs Henderson embodying Swift and Vanessa in heated dispute, his fury at her having written to Stella to find out if they were married. Here, Yeats's answers for Swift's celibacy emerged: "I was a man of strong passions and I had sworn never to marry. . . . I have something in my blood that no child must inherit. I have constant attacks of dizziness; I pretend they come from a surfeit of fruit when I was a child." Vanessa replied with Dryden's "Great wits are sure to madness near allied", which Yeats represented as part of the education given her by Swift. Placing her hands on her breast, she attempted to convince him that her body could purify his, her blood produce healthy children – and Mrs Henderson simulated the drama both within and outside herself. Swift's answer was characteristic in emotion and cadence: "Am I to add another to the healthy rascaldom and knavery of the world?" Vanessa's appeal, represented by her with breast, "white as the gambler's dice – white ivory dice" proposed a risky erotic love, balanced against Swift's certain knowledge of impending ruin for himself and the world. As her appeal intensified and grew more vindictive, Mrs Henderson's movements grew more convulsive; Swift's reponse, eloquent and despairing, appropriately took the form of prayer, the rational appeal of a man threatened by sensual and primitive "Nature", Rousseau's ideal:

O God, hear the prayer of Jonathan Swift, that afflicted man, and grant that he may leave to posterity nothing but his intellect that came to him from Heaven. [In Vanessa's voice.] Can you face solitude with that mind, Jonathan? [Mrs Henderson goes to the door, finds that it is closed.] Dice, white ivory dice. [In Swift's voice.] My God, I am left alone with my enemy. Who

locked me in with my enemy? [Mrs Henderson beats upon the
door, sinks to the floor and then speaks as Lulu.]

This violent activity took up three-quarters of the play, and we
might wonder where such a brief play could proceed from such
exhausting catharsis. With the hymn the participants sang to ''bring
good influence'', Stella's spirit appeared, the spiritual answer to
Vanessa's destructive sensuality. The meeting of Swift and Stella
was vastly different; because Stella did not speak, their dialogue was
not an irreconcilable conflict. Instead, she brought the serene solace
of mutual love without pleading or threatening. Her silence was
more powerful and noble than Vanessa's emotional force, and her
gentle love was evident in Swift's reflections of it and in her poetry
– the lines upon the window-pane, the play's moral standard,
consoling Swift, celebrating love joyously and willingly based on
purity over carnality, which could bring physical beauty, happiness,
and peace. In his loving concern for Stella, Swift effectively refuted
Vanessa's appeal, for spiritual love outlasted the erotic, and Stella's
''heart'' was more worthy than Vanessa's ''white dice''.

When Mrs Henderson awoke, she apologized for the seance's
''failure'', for only Corbet, and, to a lesser extent, Miss Mackenna,
understood and appreciated what they had seen. To him, it was
historical evidence; to her, it was passionate experience, as she
confessed, endearingly, ''That spirit rather thrilled me''. Although
the idea was Mrs Yeats's, a gesture revealed Yeats's mastery of
dramatic realism: Mrs Henderson's ''furtive glance'' at the money
each member put down, slyly counting the amounts. Corbet,
convinced that she was ''an accomplished actress and scholar''
whose theory of Swift's celibacy was ''the only plausible one'',
(perhaps Yeats's sole reservation about Corbet, who could not
accept the occult in terms beyond rational logic), wanted to make her
another source for his essay:

> . . . there is something I must ask you. Swift was the chief
> representative of the intellect of his epoch, that arrogant intellect
> free at last from superstition. He foresaw its collapse. He foresaw
> Democracy, he must have dreaded the future. Did he refuse to
> beget children because of that dread? Was Swift mad? Or was it
> the intellect itself that was mad?

His question, seeking a source for Swift's celibacy among cosmic, political, and personal reasons, was the play's philosophical centre, and, true to character, Mrs Henderson was bewildered by it: she did not know "anybody called Swift". Her echoes of Swift, becoming more pronounced, showed that his spirit had not departed. Convinced that the spiritual world had receded, that they were firmly in tangible, familiar reality, the audience watched as Mrs Henderson, alone on stage, made herself a cup of tea:

> How tired I am! I'd be the better of a cup of tea. [She finds the teapot and puts kettle on fire, and then as she crouches down by the hearth suddenly lifts up her hands and counts her fingers, speaking in Swift's voice.] Five great Ministers that were my friends are gone, ten great Ministers that were my friends are gone. I have not fingers enough to count the great Ministers that were my friends and thatare gone. [She wakes with a start and speaks in her own voice.] Where did I put that tea-caddy? Ah! there it is. And there should be a cup and saucer. [She finds the saucer.] But where's the cup? [She moves aimlessly about the stage and then, letting the saucer fall and break, speaks in Swift's voice.] Perish the day on which I was born![69]

The final line, magnificent far beyond the loss of a saucer, was the grim injunction from Job Swift supposedly reserved for his birthdays; here, as David R. Clark noted, it was the culmination of a constant, gradually intensifying pattern of loss:

> The house is decayed some of the sitters have lost loved ones; the medium is impoverished; the seance is a failure; the spirits lose the chance to speak, the sitters the chance to hear; Vanessa loses Swift; Stella loses money at cards as well as health and life; Swift loses Stella, his reason, his friends, his appearance; the world loses a great moment of its history; Mrs Henderson is tired out; a china saucer is shattered . . . the theme of enforced loss is reiterated by the word *gone* . . .". He has gone where fierce indignation can lacerate his heart no more." "Man with funny pin gone away." "Power almost gone." "Vanessa has gone, Stella has taken her place." "Bad old man gone." "Go away, go away!" "His brain had gone."[70]

To this, we add the loss of the ideal order Swift had hoped for, represented by a china saucer's fragility, and his voice, lamenting

". . . the great Ministers that were my friends and that are gone".
"Power almost gone" was a fitting subtitle, for the play was Swift's
eulogy, honouring his lost love and the lost hopes of the eighteenth
century. The decaying house was Swift's shrine; Stella's memory
made it sacred, as did the holy text of love etched in the window-
pane. Although the sitters did not understand, they, too, did him
homage, as did the audience, all gathered to participate in the
summoning of his passionate spirit as a commentary on the
diminished modern world. Against this magnitude, even the majesty
of his pain, rage, and frustration, we measured ourselves. His
rejection of Vanessa's sexuality was, in this context, noble –
remembering that Yeats was writing poems that celebrated sexuality
at this time, it might seem an uncharacteristic act to celebrate – but
Swift rejected the savage democracy it would bring. Self-indulgently
succumbing to her appeal, propagating mad or knavish children,
was hastening the ruin to come. Ironically, Stella's noble love was
incomprehensible to all at the seance except Corbet, Miss
Mackenna, and perhaps Trench. Like Swift's spirit, it was alien to
the modern world. The sitters would have understood Rousseau,
Vanessa, and the gospel of self-satisfaction, as they came to fulfill
specific personal wants. Their incomprehension was, however,
evidence of their limitations and their decay from the ideals Swift
represented.

Yeats's homage also required an acceptance of the less glorified
aspects of Swift's image – his pain, decay, despair, and rejection
were inextricable from his majesty, and Yeats presented equally
three images of him: the public man and thinker Corbet celebrated,
the man Vanessa loved, less majestic but not declining, and the
elderly, mad Dean Mrs Henderson saw: "His clothes were dirty, his
face covered with boils. Some disease had made one of his eyes swell
up, it stood out from his face like a hen's egg."[71] The homage was
to the hero, but it acknowledged the lacerated victim, whose pain,
although rending, was ennobling.

In the short time in which Yeats wrote the play, his comments on
Swift in his diary naturally lessened; yet, on 19 October, he referred
to him in an entry on order and personal power: ". . . Swift, who
almost certainly hated sex, looked upon himself, he says somewhere,
as appointed to guard a position . . .". Although initially startling,
it was the play's understandable outgrowth; Yeats could celebrate
moral, celibate devotion, but part of him rebuked Swift for having
denied Vanessa. "Guarding a position" was not only religious

orthodoxy; Swift, upholding a moral ideal, could not surrender to her. In the same entry, Yeats proposed that study of the eighteenth century could help modern Ireland:

> Preserve that which is living and help the two Irelands, Gaelic Ireland and Anglo-Ireland, so to unite that neither shall shed its pride. Study the great problems of the world, as they have been lived in our scenery, the re-birth of European spirituality in the mind of Berkeley, the restoration of European order in the mind of Burke. Every nation is the whole world in a mirror, and our mirror has been twice very bright and clear.[72]

We might wonder at the omission of Swift's name, but the answer was clear: although the Irish should study Berkeley and Burke, they should watch Yeats's play to understand Swift's intellectual glory.

The play opened at the Abbey on 17 November, and Yeats wrote to Olivia Shakespear that it had been "a much greater success than I ever hoped and beautifully acted". He was also writing an introduction to it, "a series of comments on various statements about Swift contained in it".[73] In a notebook which he had begun on 23 November, Yeats made notes for "Modern Ireland", and mentioned Swift's fable of the Spider and Bee and *Gulliver's Travels*, as well as envisioning Swift as an active political leader, the "De Valera" of the developing Protestant intellect at the end of the seventeenth century.[74] He also celebrated the Irish eighteenth century again, in "The Seven Sages". In it, seven elderly speakers, sympathetic to Yeats's view of the past, reminisced about their familial ties to that century's heroes. Swift's image was most powerful; after the first three sages boasted of ties to Burke, Grattan, Goldsmith, and Berkeley, the fourth outdid them with one sentence which made them change the subject: his ancestor "saw Stella once". The fifth and sixth sages spoke of the source of "our thought", "four great minds that hated Whiggery", which had overwhelmed the modern world: "A levelling, rancorous, rational sort of mind / That never looked out of the eye of a saint / Or out of drunkard's eye." Again, Swift's one line was sufficient: "The tomb of Swift wears it away." "It" was synonymous with safe and predictable modern logic, which could be defeated by Swift's image, memory, and epitaph.[75]

Yeats's introduction to *The Words upon the Window-Pane*, a philosophical consideration of Swift and spiritualism, was the violently emotional play's countertruth. The first essay of *Wheels and Butterflies*, it began generally, Yeats identifying those philosophical Dubliners, who "met in Cellars and Garrets", who would appreciate Swift's thought; they might become a new audience, turn to the "Discourse", and, through a new generation, Swift's thought could again reshape Ireland:

> What shall occupy our imagination? We must, I think, decide among these three ideas of national life: that of Swift; that of a great Italian of his day; that of modern England.

Modern England was not a plausible choice to a politically and philosophically aware Irishman, and Yeats had already termed Swift Vico's superior in his 1930 diary. First, however, he considered the play's genesis; it had come to him "as a reward, as a moment of excitement". Remembering O'Leary, Thomas Davis, and J.F. Taylor, Yeats urged a practical approach to an ideal: "we must serve with all our faculties some actual thing", no longer Davis's "personified ideal"; now, that "actual thing" was Swift's concept of the balanced State. With characteristic declarative overstatement, Yeats remembered his past willful ignorance, almost apologising for a tardy involvement: ". . . I turned from . . . Swift, because I acknowledged, being a romantic, no verse between Cowley and Smart's *Song to David*, no prose between Sir Thomas Browne and the *Conversations* of Landor". This was inaccurate, but the self-created myth of his late discovery was more dramatically in character with his conception of the play as a "reward". The present was a radical change from that feigned ignorance; now Yeats read Swift "for months together", for pleasure and inspiration, for himself and Ireland:

> I collect materials for my thought and work, for some identification of my beliefs with the nation itself, I seek an image of the modern mind's discovery of itself, of its own permanent form, in that one Irish century that escaped from darkness and confusion.

Swift had taken over his imagination; his fascination, bolstered by Swift's "nearness", was all-consuming:

> Swift haunts me; he is always just round the next corner. Sometimes it is a thought of my great-great grandmother, a friend

of that Archbishop King who sent him to England about the 'First Fruits,' sometimes it is Saint Patrick's, where I have gone to wander and meditate, that brings him to mind, and sometimes I remember something hard or harsh in O'Leary or in Taylor, or in the public speech of our statesmen, that reminds me by its style of his verse or prose. Did he not speak, perhaps, with just such an intonation?[76]

Swift's image was physically powerful and constant, especially in Dublin, and his verse was foremost, perhaps closest to his natural speech. Yeats referred to this attachment in crucial terms: "pride", "kindred", and "mythology". Swift was a proud ancestor and one Yeats was proud of, embodying the best personal and national character. The connection had no vanity, for Yeats did not advertise himself as Swift's spiritual descendent, but it brought "wisdom, pride, discipline". That "astringent eloquence . . . which created the political nationality of Ireland" in the fourth *Drapier's Letter* was more important to Yeats because he heard Swift's Irish voice in it.

Contemplating Swift's convictions, which had come from "action and passion", not mere political theory, Yeats turned to the "Discourse", Swift's "one philosophical work", which proposed a natural balance of the State among the One, the "executive", the aristocratic Few, who "have come to identify their lives with the life of the State", and the Many, who, when set to work in the State, became the dreaded mob:

> . . . every man Jack is 'listed in a party', becomes the fanatical follower of men of whose characters he knows next to nothing, and from that day on puts nothing in his mouth that some other man has not already chewed and digested. And furthermore, from the moment of enlistment thinks himself above other men and struggles for power until all is in confusion.

Although a tyranny was the predominance of the One, the Few, or the Many, the Many posed "the immediate threat":

> . . . the Many obsessed by emotion create a multitude of religious sects but gives themselves at last to one master of bribes and flatteries and sink into the ignoble tranquility of servitude.

Swift's rightful balance of power "seated in the whole body as that of the soul in the human body''[77] reflected a Unity of Being and of Culture. Like an individual, the State was not static; it was born, grew, died, and might be reborn in another form, in keeping with Yeats's historical cycles. Swift's fear of the virulent and easily dominated Many reflected Yeats's desire for an aristocratic rule, and Yeats also cherished Swift's idea of liberty, perhaps repressive in terms of modern democracy: individual liberty was less important than national liberty and national liberty came only through individual self-discipline. Looking back at Swift's age, Yeats remembered the greatness possible in a time of national balance, when political men were not demagogues:

> . . . Swift called himself a poor scholar in comparison with Lord Treasurer Harley. Unity of Being was still possible. . . . When Swift sank into imbecility or madness his epoch had finished in the British Isles . . . more than the 'great Ministers' had gone.[78]

Swift, a lost ideal, had been courageous beyond all human longing, possessing ''a fakir-like contempt for human desire'' no longer possible; to Yeats, he was timeless, ''as if at the edge of a cliff, time broken away from . . . [his] feet'', ''free at last from all pre-possessions'', able to touch ''the extremes of thought''.[79]

From this, Yeats considered the mysteries of Swift's personal life which had provoked his play: Scott's suggestion of a ''physical defect'', which Yeats found ''incredible'', Lecky's theory of ''dread of madness . . . of madness already present in constant eccentricity'', someone else's suggestion that Swift had contracted syphillis, and Shane Leslie's theory that the relationship between Swift and Vanessa was not platonic, and ''whenever his letters speak of a cup of coffee they mean the sexual act'', although Yeats confessed his boredom with their letters. He was certain of only two things: Swift's relationship to Stella was platonic love, and that there was no satisfactory solution to the mysteries, for Swift, ''though he lived in great publicity, and wrote and received many letters, hid two things which constituted perhaps all he had of private life: his loves and his religious beliefs''. Yeats's array of sources showed that he had consulted many authorities and quasi-authorities; whether he accepted or rejected their theories, the breadth of his investigation testified to his fascination, as he attempted to reconcile Swift's platonic love with ''a black woman at his side'' and ''the nameless barren women of the streets'', as if Swift's intellectual and passionate energy was incompatible with celibacy.[80]

He concluded the introduction's first section with his conversation with Sir Harold Williams, who would edit the standard edition of Swift's poetry:

> The other day a scholar in whose imagination Swift has a pre-eminence scarcely possible outside Ireland said: 'I sometimes feel that there is a black cloud about to overwhelm me, and then comes a great jet of life; Swift had that black cloud and no jet. He was terrified.' I said, 'Terrified perhaps of everything but death', and reminded him of a story of Dr Johnson's. There was a reward of £500 for the identification of the author of the *Drapier Letters*. Swift's butler, who had carried the manuscript to the publisher, stayed away from work. When he returned Swift said, 'I know that my life is in your hands, but I will not bear, out of fear, either your insolence or negligence.' He dismissed the butler, and when the danger had passed he restored him to his post, rewarded him, and said to the other servants, 'No more Barclay, henceforth Mr. Barclay.' 'Yes,' said my friend, 'he was not afraid of death but of life, of what might happen next; that is what made him defiant in public and in private and demand for the State the obedience a Connacht priest demands for the Church'. I have put a cognate thought into the mind of John Corbet . . . that the intellect of Swift's age, persuaded that the mechanicians mocked by Gulliver would prevail, that its moment of freedom could not last, so dreaded the historic process that it became in the half-mad mind of Swift a dread of parentage . . .[81]

Williams's view of "the gloomy Dean" was tempered by Yeats's now-mythic tale of Swift and his butler. The battle against restrictive logic resulted in Swift made "half-mad", suggesting Yeats's limited interest in purely medical explanations for Swift's decline; madness was as vital to Swift's folklore as the black woman at his side.

The final two sections of the introduction concentrated on the occult, with Swift almost peripheral, but Yeats's comment that "No character upon the stage spoke my thoughts", was unusual in the closeness of Corbet's thought and his own, even considering Corbet's naivete, overstatement, and academic predilections.[82] Following that, Yeats asked himself, rhetorically, had he allowed a character to speak his thoughts, what would that character have said? Our hopes of his revealing all, unhampered by Corbet's eager exaggerations, were unfulfilled, as Yeats turned to occult concerns without further reference to the question.

In July 1931, Swift still haunted Yeats, and he appeared several times in Yeats's introduction to *Bishop Berkeley*, by Joseph Hone and Mario Rossi, still vivid:

> . . . when we search our own experience whether of life or letters how many stand solidly? At this moment I but recall four or five intimate friends, an old woman that I never spoke to, seen at a public assembly in America, an image met ten years ago in a sudden blaze of light under my half closed eyelids, William Morris, and the half symbolic image of Jonathan Swift . . . these two images, standing and sounding together, Swift and Berkeley, concern all those who feel a responsibility for the thought of modern Ireland that can take away their sleep.

Yeats also remembered him as a mocker of abstraction, which Yeats had seen in *Gulliver's Travels*, and remembered the fable of the Spider and Bee.[83] Although Berkeley's life was occasionally intertwined with those of Vanessa and Swift, Yeats found nothing new in the biography, except for a remarkable conjunction of heroic names: "It is recorded that on an evening, Berkeley, Swift and the poet Parnell – three great names in modern Irish history – dined together in an alehouse."[84]

In the summer of 1931, Yeats met Mario Rossi, then writing a book on Swift with Hone, and helped him to get his "An Introduction to Swift" published. Before we note his involvement with Rossi, we must note his reference to Swift as a poetic landmark in an interview, when asked about the "present and future state of poetry": "The position of the young poet to-day is not unlike that of the young Swift in the library of Sir William Temple", for the new poetry was "a poetry of statement as against the old metaphor".[85] In "Ireland 1921 – 1931", published in January 1932, Yeats mentioned Swift twice in passing as an eighteenth-century thinker, on whose pattern he hoped Ireland would mould itself; he was an intellectually courageous predecessor, upon whom "blind old men" had turned their backs.[86]

Having read Rossi's essay in February 1932, he wrote to Hone, its translator:

It is sometimes profound, sometimes beautiful, sometimes

obscure through over concentration. . . . I feel a barrier of language between myself and Rossi, something therefore that seems inexpert.

It is not my Swift though it is part of the truth and may well be the beginning of a more profound Swift criticism. There was something not himself that Swift served. He called it 'freedom' but never defined it and thus has passion. Passion is to me the essential. I was educated upon Balzac and Shakespeare and cannot go beyond them. That passion is his charm.[87]

Although Yeats admired *Bishop Berkeley* and liked both Hone and Rossi, Rossi's view of Swift as an egotist was alien to him, and, when faced with the book itself, Yeats tried hard not to offend friends who had produced work of which he could not approve.

In a letter of September 1932, Yeats's commented on Swift's sense of defeat, and saw in it "the defeat of a European phase by an incoming phase which was successful because mechanical, commonplace & normal: – the iron was cooling".[88] Again representing a greater epoch, Swift had been replaced by the ordinary. In two versions of his commentary upon modern Ireland and the sources of "Parnell's Funeral", Yeats referred to Swift and his "dark grove". Before Parnell's death, in Yeats's historical scheme of four bells, "Ireland had produced three world figures and possibly a fourth": Berkeley, Burke, and Swift, "the first great modern mind to deny the value of life", perhaps a reference to Swift's prayer for Stella, rejecting earthly concerns. His other commentary, published with "Parnell's Funeral", praised the lost past, the first time in Irish history that the nation "possessed a cold, logical intellect. . . . An emotion of pride and confidence at that time ran through what there was of an intellectual minority," and referred to Swift's "well-known sermon", "Causes of the Wretched Condition of Ireland".[89]

Late in 1933, Yeats wrote to Rossi, attempting to connect their differing views on Swift:

. . . in Swift you are surely [?merely] concerned with the history of a manner or limitation of perception. Swift's absorption in the useful, (the contemporary decline of common sense), all that made him write *The Tale of a Tub*, compelled his nature to become coarse. The man who ignores the poetry of sex, let us say, finds the bare facts written up on the walls of a privy, or himself is

compelled to write them there. But all this seems to me of his
time, his mere inheritance. When a [man] of Swift's sort is born
into such dryness, is he not in the Catholic sense of the word its
victim? A French Catholic priest once told me of certain holy
women. One was victim for a whole country, another for such
and such a village. Is not Swift the human soul in that dryness, is
that not his tragedy and his genius? Perhaps every historical phase
may have its victims – its poisoned rat in a hole . . .[90]

The holy "victim" came form *The Trembling of the Veil*, in his
memory of those saints who "did really cure disease by taking it
upon themselves. As disease was considered the consequence of sin,
to take it upon themselves was to copy Christ". Swift as a soul in
dryness was also his revision of Coleridge's "Swift was *anima
Rabelaisii habitans in sicco* – the soul of Rabelais dwelling in a dry
place."[91] The paradox of Swift's "coarse nature" and apparent
celibacy made Yeats uneasy; he could explain it only by portraying
Swift as martyr to the age's aberrations, reversing Rossi's criticism
of his unhealthiness.

Hone and Rossi's *Swift, or the Egotist* was published in 1934, as was
the Cuala edition of *The Words upon the Window-Pane*; Yeats inscribed
a copy of the latter, "I wrote this play as a help to bring back a part
of the Irish mind which we have been thrusting out as it were
foreign. Now that our period of violent protest is over we claim the
Anglo-Irish eighteenth century as our own."[92] As Rossi's guide and
mentor, Yeats was familiar with the book, and was mentioned in it
twice – in reference to his introduction to *The Words upon the
Window-Pane* and to Swift's poetry.[93] Although Yeats encouraged
any new work on Swift, he gently disagreed with Rossi's point of
view, as an undated fragment showed: "You have made me for the
first time understand Gulliver. . . . I do not accept your description
of Swift as an egotist yet that description has led you to certain truths
of great value: I think of him rather as a solitary, who felt no need to
explain or justify his religious conviction just because he was a
solitary."[94] Yeats never specified what Rossi's "truths" were; if he
had made Yeats understand Gulliver for the first time, then Yeats
had never understood *Gulliver's Travels* at all. Rossi's portrait of the
egotist was the antithesis of Yeats's:

> . . . the egotist . . . does not calculate, for his selfishness is too
> profound to let him imagine the possibility of opposition from

others. He is assured that others must in the last resort depend on himself, and therefore he takes no pains to affirm himself. So Swift fled when he could not have his way, as he did in his love with Vanessa, in his politics after the final clash between Harley and Bolingbroke, and when Stella was near death. The egotist easily tires of effort. . . . From Swift's assertion that he loathed humanity and yet loved Jack, William, and Tom, we are not to suppose that he loved them for what they were, nor indeed that he had even *knowledge* of them as they were. He loved them in so far as they surrendered to his whim, he loved them for being a sort of extension of himself, other bodies of his overlapping self. He disliked humanity because it was a number of extraneous selves; the egotist cannot identify himself with a mass. He identifies himself with individuals in so far as they are his servants.

Neither was Swift, obsessively selfish, a writer, to Rossi:

This man was never a writer, a literary man, a poet – call it what you will, no appropriate definition of him as a writer will be found. He really wrote for a purpose. And even with no end at all, but he is never caught writing for the pleasure of writing; he is never interested in itself. When he had nothing in view he did not write. There was indeed nothing in his soul which compelled him to express himself, he had no pleasure in expressing what he felt – and truly he never expressed what he did feel. His work is mainly objective; for himself, he had nothing to say.

Gulliver's Travels was Swift's autobiography; Gulliver was Swift and Swift's "hero", "the only complete, sane, and normal man in an abnormal world." It was Swift's "desperate philosophy", and he "saw in Stella the Yahoo".[95] It is difficult to imagine Yeats's agreement with these views, so uncharacteristic of his heroic myth and portrait of Swift.

In March 1934, Swift was part of Yeats's early versions of the Blue Shirt marching songs; they were to "build in the mind" what "Molyneux and Swift began", in the image of a growing tree of wisdom; they were to "finish the work" that "Swift, Grattan, Burke / Began".[96] In *Dramatis Personae*, his references to Swift were slight, resembling those to Parnell, with Swift's name a major one on the list of worthy Protestants.[97] Typically, Yeats absorbed Swift's knowledge into his writings, as in Swift's definition of good written style, "Proper Words in proper Places", which he had read in Richard Ashe King, Samel Johnson, and "A Letter to a Young Gentleman, Lately Entered into Holy Orders". In broadcasts and letters from March 1934 to August 1938 to Margot Ruddock and Dorothy Wellesley, Yeats took over the formula completely, revising it to "the natural words in the natural order", which was "an escape from artificial diction", producing "music".[98] Swift himself had best described this act of literary osmosis:

> If a rational Man reads an excellent Author with just Application, he shall find himself extremely improved, and perhaps insensibly led to imitate that Author's Perfections; although in a little Time he should not remember one Word in the Book, nor even the Subject it handled: For, Books give the same Turn to our Thoughts and Way of Reasoning, that good and ill Company do to our Behaviour and Conversation; without either loading our Memories, or making us even sensible of the Change.[99]

In the 1935 *Broadside*, he remembered Swift as a precursor of his vivid ballads: ". . . Swift's political lampoons were still sung in the Coombe when Sir Walter Scott visited Ireland . . .".[100] Writing to Dorothy Wellesley in December 1936, on Roger Casement, he celebrated Swift's *saeva indignatio*:

> You say that we must not hate. You are right, but we may, & sometimes must be indignant & speak it. Hate is a kind of 'passive suffering' but indignation is a kind of joy. 'When I am told that somebody is my brother protestant', said Swift, 'I remember that the rat is a fellow creature'; that seems to me a joyous saying. We that are joyous need not be afraid to denounce.

No longer corrosive, Swift's indignation was an inspiring and purifying joy, battling injustice as in the Casement ballads:

> I am fighting in those ballads for what I have been fighting all my life, it is our Irish fight, though it has nothing to do with this or that country. Bernard Shaw fights with the same object. When somebody talks of justice, who knows that justice is accompanied by secret forgery, when an archbishop wants a man to go to the

communion table, when that man says he is not spiritually fit, then we remember our age old quarrel against gold-brayed and ermine & that our ancestor Swift has gone where 'fierce indignation can lacerate his heart no more', & we go stark, staring mad. . . . It is not our business to reply to this & that, but to set up our love and indignation against their pity & hate . . .[101]

Modern injustice made Yeats remember a history of amorality, and those offenses brought back his ancestor's sacred memory and creed.

In a June 1937 letter to Oliver St. John Gogarty, Yeats noted the solution to a mystery which had indirectly given rise to his play; he had identified the "Mary Kilpatrick" of the verses cut into a window in Gogarty's house.[102] In "A General Introduction for My Work", the Spider and Bee were again symbols, and Swift, like Parnell, was a "great political predecessor" who had stepped back into the historical tapestry. Finally, as Yeats spoke of himself, torn between hatred of the English and love of their art, Swift represented an Irish passion, again approaching insanity: "This is Irish hatred and solitude, the hatred of human life that made Swift write *Gulliver* and the epitaph upon his tomb, that can still make us wag between extremes and doubt our sanity."[103] In the essay, Yeats had summoned Swift three times: as a writer whose fable provided a symbolic structure, as a worthy political ancestor, and as a passionate Irish figure; to Yeats, an understanding of Swift was essential to an understanding of his life's work.

Swift's influence was equally widespread in the 1938 *On the Boiler*, Yeats's equally blunt commentary upon the declining world. "Why Should Not Old Men be Mad", although untitled, took emotional power from Swift's example and from his comment in the pamphlet on Irish manufacture Yeats had read in King's book: "The Scripture tells us that 'oppression makes a wise man mad', therefore, consequently speaking, the reason why some men are not mad is because they are not wise."[104] In "Private Thoughts", Yeats credited Swift with perceiving history as "human drama", which Yeats, "philosophical, not scientific", agreed with, for "observed facts do not mean much until I can make them part of my experience".[105] Finally, Yeats quoted from the "Ode to Temple", and, in "Ireland after the Revolution", Swift's name was part of Yeats's acclamation of Irish glory:

. . . although the Irish masses are vague and excitable because they have not yet been moulded and cast, we have as good blood as there is in Europe. Berkeley, Swift, Burke, Grattan, Parnell, Augusta Gregory, Synge, Kevin O'Higgins, are the true Irish people, and there is nothing too hard for such as these. If the Catholic names are few history will soon fill the gap. My imagination goes back to those Catholic exiled gentlemen of whom Swift said that their bravery exceeded that of all nations.[106]

Swift was also indirectly apparent in Yeats's interest in eugenics as a way to stop the gradual, even inevitable decline of mind and body – as in Swift's celibacy in *The Words upon the Window-Pane*, a conscious rejection of risky breeding. Eugenics would prevent a race of mad knaves, Yahoos, the Many, and keep a physical and cultural aristocracy alive, instead of the ". . . growing cohesiveness, the growing frenzy, everybody thinking like everybody else . . .".[107] Swift exemplified the grandeur from which we had degenerated, and stood as a warning against democracy.

Over more than forty years, Swift was much to Yeats: passionate hero, satirist, poet, political activist and philosopher, and eminent representative of the Irish eighteenth century's daring and clear thought. Impassioned and passionate, Swift was the tormented man of tantalizing personal mysteries, who loved greatly but was apparently celibate, who could reject Vanessa yet contract syphillis from prostitutes. His enigma fascinated Yeats, and its unanswered questions provoked him to create his own answers in myth. Swift's passion was intellectual as well, as a fervent member of Yeats's gallant Anglo-Irish Protestant lineage, and his political philosophy reinforced Yeats's, in the need for a balanced government and an aristocratic rule that expressed the national spirit. He saw the impending ruin, and, as Dean and Drapier, fought it vigorously, whether it was represented by Wood's half-pence or the self-destructive Irish fancy for English products. Contemplation of that ruin made him melancholy, but also made him protect the despised Irish race from persecution and oppression – a love of humanity which expressed itself in rage at their stupidity. To Yeats, he was the ideal artist and patriot, proving the inextricability of nationality and literature, for his art, the *Drapier's Letters*, had saved a nation. Without stating it, Yeats hoped to become to Ireland what Swift had been – his name would be alongside Swift's on the lists of the heroic Protestant aristocracy – and to receive the thanks of a grateful nation. Yeats had read in Sheridan's life of Swift, for example, the welcome Swift had received on his October 1729 return to Ireland:

> . . . upon notice that the ship in which he sailed was in the bay, several Heads of the different corporations, and principal citizens of Dublin, went out to meet him in a great number of wherries engaged for that purpose, in order to welcome him back . . . boats adorned with streamers, and colours, in which there were many emblematic devices, made a fine appearance; and thus was the Drapier brought to his landing-place in a kind of triumph, where he was received and welcomed on shore by a multitude of his grateful countrymen, by whom he was conducted to his house amid repeated acclamations, of *Long live the Drapier.* The bells were all set a ringing, and bonfires kindled in every street.[108]

As the Drapier, "the Dean" to the nation, the man Walpole could have arrested only with the help of ten thousand men, he gained "such an ascendancy over his countrymen, as perhaps no private citizen ever attained in any age or country . . . the first and greatest man in the kingdom".[109] More than Parnell, he was an uncrowned Irish king. As a writer, he combined Yeats's ideals of art and nationalism, surpassing Wilde; as a political man, he surpassed Parnell. In Yeats's later years, Swift's figure took on added depth, reflecting Yeats's fears that he would also die feeble or mad; only by fully mastering Swift's enigma could Yeats conquer the threat Swift's example posed. By practising upon Swift's epitaph he could write his own; by emulating Swift's heroism, he could become fully realised as poet and patriot too. Ultimately, the thought of Swift at the height of his intellectual passion and power was a heroic image to which Yeats could find no equal.

6   Swift's Poetry

In a letter to Donald T. Torchiana, Yeats's friend Oliver Edwards remembered a meeting with Yeats in 1934 or 1935 that is strong evidence of Yeats's acknowledged debt to Swift's poetry: ". . . Yeats told me about himself and Swift's verse. He said . . . 'I get my later manner from Swift.' And he proceeded to read . . . a Sir William Temple poem of Swift's — beginning . . . 'But [?] what does our proud ignorance learning call? ending at the words '. . . and nauseate company.' "[1] The "later manner", characteristic of Yeats's mature poetry, was based on Swift's "animation and naturalness" and the relentless directness praised by Goldsmith: Swift ". . . owes his title to the name of poet not so much to the greatness of his genius, as to the boldness of it".[2] Yeats knew Swift's poetry more thoroughly than he admitted, and its influence was quietly pervasive. Reading his comment in a later letter to Dorothy Wellesley, " 'When I am told that somebody is my brother protestant,' said Swift, 'I remember that the rat is a fellow creature'; that seems to me a joyous saying", we almost automatically assume its source was in the prose Yeats knew.[3] However, Yeats had remembered the poem, "On the Words – *Brother Protestants and Fellow Christians*, so familiarly used by advocates for the Repeal of the *Test Act* in Ireland, 1733":

> And thus Fanatic Saints, tho' neither in
> Doctrine, or Discipline our Brethren,
> Are *Brother Protestants and Christians*,
> As much as *Hebrews and Philistines*:
> But in no other Sense, than Nature
> Has made a Rat our Fellow-Creature.[4]

Perhaps the first lines of Swift's poetry Yeats encountered were from the *Holyhead Journal*, included in King's 1896 *Swift in Ireland*.[5] His verse provided a means to express rage and indignation, and Yeats learned to put into his poetry his anger at the same apathy, immorality, and foolishness that had enraged Swift. "Slave", "knave", "fool", and, later, "dolt", essential invective for Swift, became Yeats's: Ireland became "my fool-driven land", he regretted having "ranted to the knave and fool", and characterized theatre business as "the day's war with every knave and dolt".[6] This was no coincidental adoption of eighteenth-century invective; Swift's words stood for particular types of vice and folly, English or Irish, personal or national.

In later years, Yeats commented upon other Swift poems, *Cadenus and Vanessa* and "The Progress of Beauty" among them, but the most impressive was the third section of the "Ode to the Honourable Sir William Temple", an early ode which he commended to many – Edwards, Sir Harold Williams, Stephen Gwynn, Mario Rossi and Joseph Hone – as well as quoting it in *On the Boiler*:

> But what does our proud Ign'rance Learning call,
>   We oddly *Plato's* Paradox make good,
> Our Knowledge is but mere Remembrance all,
>   Remembrance is our Treasure and our Food;
> Nature's fair Table-book our tender Souls
> We scrawl all o'er with old and empty Rules,
>   Stale Memorandums of the Schools;
>   For Learning's mighty Treasures look
>   In that deep Grave a Book,
>   Think she there does all her Treasures hide,
> And that her troubled Ghost still haunts there since she dy'd;
>   Confine her Walks to Colleges and Schools,
>   Her Priests, her Train and Followers show
>   As if they all were Spectres too,
>   They purchase Knowledge at the Expence
>   Of common Breeding, common Sense,
>   And at once grow Scholars and Fools;
>   Affect ill-manner'd Pedantry,
>   Rudeness, Ill-nature, Incivility,
>   And sick with Dregs of Knowledge grown,
>   Which greedily they swallow down,
> Still cast it up and nauseate Company.[7]

To Rossi and Hone, Yeats characterised this as a youthful satire of pedantry: ". . . the third stanza . . . is truly inspired, as W.B. Yeats thinks, possibly because Swift was really moved against the learning which he lacked and the learned who despised him. Poetry was for him a way of rebellion against 'school', a finding of a path in the world by means which his teachers disparaged".[8] More intriguing, however, were Swift's bold sensory images, vehement and intertwined. Treasure, grave, and food returned violently in the final lines, as what had been buried or digested turned to vomit, treasure to excrescence. Although Yeats rejected Swift's early inversions, his audaciously blunt vocabulary was triumphant: "scrawl", "stale", "common sense", "rudeness", "dregs", and "nauseate". A revolting pretense to learning was made incarnate in vomiting; this vivid directness rescued Swift from a poetic tradition Yeats saw as arid and made him a contemporary.

The effect of those Swift poems Yeats did not cite was even more powerful, beginning with the 1910 *The Green Helmet and Other Poems*, which showed, in varying degree, a Swiftian influence, from the "knave or dolt" of "Against Unworthy Praise",[9] to Yeats's unsuccessful attempt to assimilate Swiftian ferocity in an epigram, "To a Poet, who would have me Praise certain Bad Poets, Imitators of His and Mine":

> You say, as I have often given tongue
> In praise of what another's said or sung,
> 'Twere politic to do the like by these;
> But was there ever dog that praised his fleas?[10]

The image of parasitism was modelled on Swift's view of the poetic world as a jungle where great poets were preyed on by their inferiors, appropriate to Hobbes's view of Nature as "a State of War":

> . . . search among the rhiming Race,
> The Brave are worried by the Base.
> If, on *Parnassus'* Top you sit,
> You rarely bite, are always bit:
> Each Poet of inferior Size
> On you shall rail and criticize;
> And strive to tear you Limb from Limb,
> While others do as much for him.
>
>   The Vermin only teaze and pinch
> Their Foes superior by an Inch.

So, Nat'ralists observe, a Flea
Hath smaller Fleas that on him prey
And these have smaller Fleas to bite 'em,
And so proceed *ad infinitum*:
Thus ev'ry Poet in his Kind,
Is bit by him that comes behind;
Who, tho' too little to be seen,
Can teaze, and gall, and give the Spleen;[11]

Without Swift's expansive development of images, Yeats merely sounded querulous, although he had attempted to condense the idea for effect.

In the 1914 *Responsibilities*, the portrait of Dublin as "the blind and ignorant town" echoed Swift's "this thankless Town", as Yeats made poetry into forceful personal speech, whether attacking, accusing, or hoping to reform an offender, Walpole or William Martin Murphy. Yeats's belligerence was less savage than Swift's, for Yeats still hoped for reform through enlightenment, but later disillusionments made his anger more violent, less forgiving.[12] His advice to Lady Gregory, "To A Friend Whose Work has Come to Nothing", "Be secret and take defeat / From any brazen throat", "Be secret and exult", and to reject her opponents as unworthy, not "honour bred", owed much to Swift's consolation of Patrick Delany, "To a Friend who had been much abused in many inveterate Libels". Swift encouraged fearless defiance, not secret exultation, but both poems were founded on the vast gulf between the victim and attackers, and both poets characteristically saw the noble suffering at the hands of the common:

The greatest monarch may be stabb'd by night,
And fortune help the murd'rer in his flight;
The vilest Ruffian may commit a rape,
Yet safe from injured innocence escape:
And calumny, by working under ground,
Can, unreveng'd, the greatest merit wound.

What's to be done? shall wit and learning chuse,
To live obscure, and have no fame to lose?
By censure frightened out of honour's road,
Nor dare to use the gifts by heav'n bestow'd;
Or fearless enter in thro' virtue's gate
And buy distinction at the dearest rate.[13]

"To a Shade", Yeats's memorial to Parnell, reflected Swift's use of the ironic parenthesis, undermining the value of what surrounded it: "If you have revisited this town, thin Shade, / Whether to look upon your monument / (I wonder if the builder has been paid)." In "Verses on the Death of Dr. Swift", his female friends received the news of his death at their card game, and continued with enthusiasm undiminished:

> "The Dean is dead, (*and what is Trumps?*)
> "Then Lord have Mercy on his Soul.
> "(Ladies I'll venture for the *Vole*.)
> "Six Deans they say must bear the Pall.
> "(I wish I knew what *King* to call.)[14]

In the 1917 *The Wild Swans at Coole*, "To a Young Beauty" explicitly echoed Swift's aristocratic disdain: "There is not a fool can call me friend" was indebted to "To Doctor D – L—Y on the Libels Writ against him":

> 'Till Block-heads blame, and Judges praise,
> The Poet cannot claim his Bays;
> On me, when Dunces are satyrick,
> I take it for a Panegyrick.
> *Hated by Fools*, and *Fools to hate*,
> Be that my Motto, and my Fate.[15]

Frightening lines from "Nineteen Hundred and Nineteen", published in the 1928 *The Tower*, although based on an actual incident, took their inspiration from Swift's equally nightmarish vision:

> Now days are dragon-ridden, the nightmare
> Rides upon sleep: a drunken soldiery
> Can leave the mother, murdered at her door,
> To crawl in her own blood, and go scot-free;

Although Swift's "On Dreams" encompassed many murders, its atmosphere was similarly violent, and its title would have attracted Yeats to it:

> The drowsy tyrant, by his Minions led,
> To regal Rage devotes some Patriot's Head.

With equal Terrors, not with equal Guilt,
The Murd'rer dreams of all the Blood he spilt.

The Soldier smiling hears the Widows Cries,
And stabs the Son before the Mother's Eyes.
With like Remorse his Brother of the Trade,
The Butcher, feels the Lamb beneath his blade.[16]

Yeats's nightmare took place in historical reality, but a terrifying cruelty linked the two visions; their shared foundation was also Swift's definition of a soldier, "a *Yahoo* hired to kill in cold Blood as many of his own Species, who have never offended him, as possibly he can".[17]

Swift's shade was especially prominent in the 1933 *The Winding Stair and Other Poems*, in Yeats's evocations and tributes – "Blood and the Moon", "The Seven Sages", and "Swift's Epitaph" – and his influence was tangible in "The Choice" and two Crazy Jane poems. "The Choice", Yeats's comment on the opposition of the perfected life and the perfected work, recalled "The Progress of Poetry", Swift's mocking version of the same tension between personal satisfaction and artistic excellence. Swift had burlesqued the poet as a goose. Her belly full, she was inert and mute; when hungry, she flew, sang, created. Although Yeats's voice differed from Swift's, their views of the situation did not: art and starvation, material success and creative stagnation, were interdependent.[18] D.E.S. Maxwell saw antecedents to "Crazy Jane Talks with the Bishop" in Swift's scatological verses, but these, to him, revealed Swift's "unbalanced view of love", and disillusioned Strephon's "Celia shits" was the source of "A woman can be proud and stiff / When on love intent; / But love has pitched his mansion in / The place of excrement."[19] Yet, in "The Lady's Dressing Room", Swift suggested what Yeats would have seen as an acceptance of the contraries; if Strephon "would but stop his Nose", he could see "Such gaudy Tulips rais'd from Dung". As in Crazy Jane's vision, human beauty emerged from physical mire, "stinking Ooze", the body's "foul rag-and-bone shop". Spiritual love needed physical reality for unity and wholeness, as in "Crazy Jane on the Day of Judgment": "Love is all / Unsatisfied / That cannot take the whole / Body and soul."[20]

Swift's influence in *Last Poems* was varied. His "Shall I repine" was obscure, but it echoed in Yeats's rejection of the traditional lament on the collapse of beloved things in "Lapis Lazuli": Yeats's prescription for behaviour in the face of catastrophe, "Gaiety transfiguring all that dread," for "All things fall and are built again, / And those that build them are gay," echoed Swift's cheerful acceptance:

> If neither brass nor marble can withstand
> The mortal force of Time's dystructive hand
> If mountains sink to vales, if cityes dye
> And lessening rivers mourn their fountains dry
> When my old cassock says a Welch divine
> Is out at elbows why should I repine?[21]

The worn cassock was deliberately mundane amidst cosmic decay, far less artistic than Yeats's carved stone, but both poets looked to gaiety as a salvation. Yeats's impressive meditation on himself, "The Circus Animals' Desertion", looked back on Swift's images, recreated in Yeats's final lines:

> A mound of refuse or the sweepings of the street,
> Old kettles, old bottles, and a broken can,
> Old iron, old bones, old rags, that raving slut
> Who keeps the till. Now that my ladder's gone,
> I must lie down where all the ladders start,
> In the foul rag-and-bone shop of the heart.

His vivid catalogue of street debris, the antithesis of "pure mind", came from "A Description of a City Shower", where "the swelling Kennels" bore "Filth of all Hues and Odours":

> Sweepings from Butchers Stalls, Dung, Guts, and Blood,
> Drown'd Puppies, stinking Sprats, all drench'd in Mud,   [22]
> Dead Cats and Turnip-Tops come tumbling down the Flood.

Although Swift had meant his final triplet as a satire on modern poetic fashion, Yeats was affected far more by its violently graphic images.[23]

Although "Under Ben Bulben" had no specific Swiftian antecedent, it owed much to his epitaph and poetic self-dramatisations. In his epitaph, Swift had avoided unseemly self-praise by portraying himself as passion-lacerated, emphasising the pain of his attempts rather than his successes; his example taught Yeats well how to die in poetry, with "no conventional phrase": "Cast a cold eye / On life, on death. / Horseman, pass by!" These lines were descended from Yeats's earlier rewriting of Swift's epitaph, as he had omitted a crucial section – Swift's instruction to the traveller to go and imitate his defence of liberty, which emerged here, as the horseman was instructed to cast a cold eye at the evidence of Yeats's death and to hurry on. That "cold eye" was also a Swiftian legacy; in his introduction to *The Words upon the Window-Pane*, Yeats had written of Swift's ". . . fakir-like contempt for all human desire; 'take from her', Swift prayed for Stella in sickness, 'all violent desire whether of life or death' ".[24] It represented a freedom from the intricacies of emotion which enabled one to act heroically – in shunning human desire or public glorification. Yeats's epitaph, shaped by a Swiftian model – his heroism, thought, and poetry – was fitting tribute to the endurance of Swift's image in Yeats's mind, intensely alive even amidst the self-contemplation of "Under Ben Bulben".

Although Yeats's developing art drew upon many Swiftian echoes, a comparison of the two poetic canons reveals vast differences. Yeats was less an occasional poet and far less an actively political one; he took his verse far more seriously, never dismissing it as "trifles".[25] The witty wordplay that delighted Swift and his friends gave Yeats less joy; we cannot imagine Yeats and Lady Gregory exchanging riddles and anagrams by mail. Yet, although Yeats borrowed from Swift's poetry with great selectivity, often recreating what he found, the echoes made his "later manner" possible. The echoes also show that Ezra Pound was not the only poet whose work altered Yeats's, for Swift was always a vivid example for his concreteness, directness, and boldness. Yeats also adopted Swift's role when appropriate – to lash fool and knave, to comment scathingly on public vice and folly, to reveal moral lapses, and, ultimately, to become a public poet. Swift's was only one transfiguring influence on Yeats's poetry, but his was an affecting, impressive, and often neglected one.

Appendix: Roger Casement: "They . . . blackened his good name"

In the nineteen-thirties, the figure of Roger Casement, although on a lesser scale than Parnell, also provoked Yeats into mythic ballads. Actively campaigning for Irish independence through German help during the First World War, Casement did little to stir Yeats's imagination, as Sir William Rothenstein remembered:

> . . . Casement . . . was full, too, of the wrongs of Ireland. 'As long as he only bothers about present conditions,' said Yeats, 'it doesn't matter; but Heaven help him if he fills his head with Ireland's past wrongs.'[1]

Casement's fanatic hatred of England and reverence for Germany made others uneasy, and they doubted the effectiveness of his plans. John Butler Yeats, who had met him at John Quinn's, liked him, but noted that he "is about sick with grief over 'poor Kaiser' ".[2] Writing to Quinn, AE described Casement as "a romantic person of the picturesque kind, with no heavy mentality to embarass him in his actions."[3] However, when he was sentenced to death for treason, Yeats signed a petition on his behalf at Maud Gonne's urging, and wrote Eva Gore-Booth that "the argument for clemency is so strong that the government cannot disregard this argument . . ."[4]

When he was executed, however, Casement was not much more to Yeats than the unnamed sixteenth man of "Sixteen Dead Men". To Maud Gonne, although his death was "a national loss", it was "a less terrible blow" than other deaths – and, like her, Yeats's imagination had been captured by other martyrs of 1916: even John MacBride was mentioned in "Easter 1916", and Casement was not.[5]

152

Yeats's involvement with Casement's image began only in March 1933, when Patrick McCartan, an American doctor and ex-I.R.B. man whom Yeats had met on his American tour, asked his help in obtaining a prominent author's introduction to William J. Maloney's book, *The Forged Casement Diaries*. At this time, Yeats probably had no special knowledge about the diaries: they purported to be Casement's, they apparently chronicled his homosexual activities in graphic detail, and they had been circulated by the British government when he was imprisoned to stir public revulsion and discourage a reprieve. The diaries discredited the only hero of 1916 that the British had to explain: to the British public, the others were rebellious Irish nonentities, whereas Casement was *Sir* Roger Casement, K.C.M.G. After Casement's death, Maloney and others had uncovered evidence that the diaries were forged, created purely to ruin Casement. The case echoed the Parnell and Wilde histories: the Pigott forgeries superimposed on the public outcry against Wilde's homosexuality, as if the British had sought a foolproof combination with which to discredit Casement.

Yeats had not read Maloney's book, but he offered McCartan a letter of introduction to Shaw; letters of May and June 1934 between Yeats and McCartan detailed Shaw's interest. In September, Yeats received Maloney's manuscript, although when he wrote to McCartan in October, he had done no more than "look at the chapter headings" before he sent it to Mrs Shaw, because he "did not want to delay it". In late November, Yeats was again an intermediary in the correspondence between McCartan, Maloney, Shaw, and a cousin of Casement's, but that was the end of his activity on the subject until November 1936, by which time Maloney's book had found a publisher – without Shaw's introduction – and Yeats had read it.[6] *The Forged Casement Diaries* thoroughly documented the various British efforts to discredit Casement. From November 1914 on, the Foreign Office spread rumours to British newspapers that Casement was mad, and, from June 1916, "evidence" from the forged diaries began to appear in the press, as the government hoped to add "degeneracy" to his offences:

> . . . the various ways in which the special theme of this diary was disclosed by the British press after Casement's capture . . . ranged from plain terms like "sexual perversion" and "unnatural vice"

used by Nevinson in the *Manchester Guardian*, to the conventional euphemism, "a charge which is not specified", or an "unspecified charge", adopted by the nicer newspapers.[7]

Although the charge of homosexuality was the most sensational, it was not the only one, but a part of an interlocking puzzle designed to alienate all possible supporters:

> To offset Germany's declaration of friendship for Ireland, Casement was said to be mad for seeking it; or, alternatively, to have sought it as a German agent: and as proof he had not acted for Ireland, Irish loyalists were brought forward to repudiate both him and the pledge he had got. . . . The reputed resentment aroused in the Irish soldiers by Casement's efforts to enlist them, destroyed the moral effect of the move to form an Irish Brigade. And . . . the primary object of the degeneracy story was to secure popular sanction for the hanging.[8]

Thus, the attack was a comprehensive fraud, which Maloney saw as part of a tradition of British political forgery and wartime propaganda; it was far more effective than the Pigott letters, for Casement was discredited by a falsified document displaying ". . . the ravings of the victim of perversion", and was thus executed.[9] Maloney's conclusion was inescapable: ". . . the British Government . . . forged, planted, published, authenticated, and used this atrocity diary to destroy their Irish enemy . . .".[10] Once dead, Casement could not clear his name; he had died another victim of British "diplomacy" in his pursuit of Irish independence.

Yeats's reaction to this evidence was intense and violent, as seen in his November 1936 letter to Ethel Mannin:

> I am in a rage. I have just got a book published by the Talbot Press called *The Forged Casement Diaries.* It is by a Dr. Maloney I knew in New York and he has spent years collecting research. He has proved that the diaries, supposed to prove Casement 'a Degenerate' and successfully used to prevent an agitation for his reprieve, were forged. Casement was not a very able man but he was gallant and unselfish, and had surely his right to leave what he would have considered an unsullied name. I long to break my rule against politics and call these men criminals, but I must not. Perhaps a verse may come to me, now or a year hence.[11]

He mentioned, as well, that he had just completed a ballad on Parnell: *Parnell Vindicated* and *The Forged Casement Diaries* enhanced and intensified one another. Although Casement had not achieved heroic ends, he had been another Irish victim of English dishonour. Yeats's rage quickly overwhelmed his restraint; he had written a ballad on Casement by the end of the month, and had described it to Dorothy Wellesley:

> Yesterday was a most eventful day. . . . I sent off a ferocious ballad written to a popular tune, to a newspaper. It is on 'The Forged Diaries of Roger Casement' a book published here, & denounces by name —— and —— for their share in abetting the forgeries. I shall not be happy until I hear that it is sung by Irish undergraduates at Oxford. I wrote to the editor saying I had not hitherto sent him a poem because almost [all] my poems were unsuitable because they came out of rage or lust. I heard my ballad sung last night. It is a stirring thing . . . better written than my 'Parnell' because I passed things when I had to find three rhymes & did not pass when I had to find two.[12]

After the Parnell model, it would be sung into the Irish memory, celebrating heroism and publicising English evil. Before its publication, however, letters passed among Yeats, Mannin, and Wellesley: Yeats angrily gleeful at the outrage his ballad would cause, Mannin pleased, but Wellesley made unhappy because of another attack on her government. Writing to Mannin, Yeats enclosed a copy of the ballad, as well as an explanation of his politics: although he had refused to assist her in her international political crusades, he was still enraged at past Irish controversies:

> If my rage lasts I may go on in still more savage mood . . . Some day you will understand what I see in the Irish National movement and why I can be no other sort of revolutionist – as a young man I belonged to the I.R.B. and was in many things O'Leary's pupil. Besides, why should I trouble about communism, fascism, liberalism, radicalism, when all, though some bow first and some stem first but all at the same pace, all are going down stream with the artificial unity which ends every civilisation? . . . My rage and that of others like me seems more important – though we may but be the first of the final destroying horde. I remember old O'Leary saying 'No gentleman can be a socialist though he might be an anarchist.'[13]

Any ideology was incompatible with his aristocratic individualism, the personal ideal of the solitary hero, cast in the O'Leary mould.

By 1 December, Wellesley had replied to Yeats's excited and angry 28 November letter, with shock and agitation, even a reprimand of Yeats's extravagant behaviour: "Please please don't insist on this savage attack on —— at Oxford. Let us find out the facts first. If you were God Almighty I would say the same to you."[14] In his reply, three days later, Yeats attempted to establish the background of the forgeries, explain his impulse, and soothe her offended loyalties – still sensitive because of his recent Parnell ballad:

> I could not stop that ballad if I would, people have copies, & I don't want to. —— belongs to a type of man for whom I have no respect. Such men have no moral sense. They are painted cardboard manipulated by intreaguers. If he had been a man he would before circulating those charges against Casement have asked 'was the evidence shown to Casement?' & have learned that Casement denied the charges & asked in vain to be shown the evidence. I was present when the Editor of *The Times* spoke of making the same charges in *The Times*. He did not do so, probably because of the infuriated comment of Roger Fry & myself. . . . However I hate 'Leagues of Nations' & Leagues of all kinds & am not likely to be just.
>
> [A discussion of the well-known Casement charge follows.]
>
> But the Casement evidence was not true as we know – it was one of a number of acts of forgery committed at that time. I can only repeat words spoken to me by the old head of the Fenians years ago. 'There are things a man must not do to even save a nation.'

> By the by my ballad should begin
>> 'I say that Roger Casement
>> Did what he had to do
>> But died upon the scaffold
>> But that is nothing new.'
>
> I feel that one's verse must be as direct & as natural as spoken words. The opening I sent you was not quite natural.
>
> No I shall not get the ballad sung in Oxford: that was but a 'passing' thought because I happen to know a certain wild student who would have been made quite happy by the task – the idea amused me.

We will have no great popular literature until we get rid of the moral sycophants. Montaigne says that a prince must sometimes commit a crime to save his people, but that if he does so he must mourn all his life. I only hate the men who do not mourn.

Forgive all this my dear but I have told you that my poetry all comes from rage or lust.[15]

Far from being simply a defence of rage, Yeats based his attack on a morality which the English had again violated in pursuit of political expedience – that was more important than any ideological agreement with Casement.

On 7 December, he wrote to Wellesley, repenting of some of his "blind rage", excusing Gilbert Murray but not Alfred Noyes. He had "lost the book & trusted to memory", and was "full of remorse . . . full of shame". Unintentionally, acting on invalid evidence, he had almost blackened a man's reputation as the British had ruined Casement's. His letter of 9 December to her ended with a contrite postscript: "O my dear, O my dear do write. I feel I am in such disgrace. Do burn that letter about ——."[16] One day later, he wrote to her, commenting on Ethel Mannin's reaction to the corrected ballad: ". . . she writes approving of what she supposes to be my hatred of England. It has shocked me for it has made me fear that you think the same. I have written to my correspondent. 'How can I hate England, owing what I do to Shakespeare, Blake & Morris. England is the only country I cannot hate' ".[17] In his letter to Mannin, he had identified his true enemy and cause for fear; no nation, but a ruthless amorality: "I am alarmed at the growing moral cowardice of the world, as the old security disappears – people run in packs that they may get courage from one another and even sit at home and shiver. You and I, my dear, were as it were put naked into the midst of armed men and women and we have both found arms and kept our independence."[18] Ten days later, he wrote to Wellesley, noting the physical effects of the Casement poem, for rage and remorse had taken their toll: "I had a black fortnight the result of nervous strain writing the Casement poem you have seen & another you have not – beating the paste-board men – & some other odds and ends."[19] On 23 December, he wrote to her, linking himself, Shaw, Swift in "our Irish fight" against ecclesiastical and governmental immoralities:

. . . both in England & Ireland I want to stiffen the back bone of the high hearted and high-minded & the sweet hearted & sweet-minded, so that they may no longer shrink & hedge, when they face rag merchants like ——.[20]

In a letter of a few days later to her, he wrote of having been ill from "exhaustion (overwork, mental strain)," and numbered its causes, with "Casement forgeries (rage that men of honour should do such things)" first.[21] Although the ballads and correspondence might have purged his rage, he could not resign himself to this dishonourable behaviour. Three weeks later, he mentioned to her that the Casement ballad would be part of his first radio broadcast of poems "sung & recited", for the "Foreign Office has forgotten its crimes".[22] However, he quickly turned from joyous indignation to melancholy, a week later: "Something happened to me in the darkness some weeks ago. It began with those damned forgeries – I have the old Fenian conscience – death & execution are in the day's work but not that."[23] If ostensibly honourable men could do these things, what could one rely on? Rage was necessarily succeeded by a despairing horror at the universal amorality, treachery based on lies. The previous slanders of Wilde and Parnell had been based on fact, however interpreted; Yeats's belief in the diaries's fraudulence enraged, depressed, and sickened him.

The first Casement ballad was finally published in De Valera's *Irish Press* on 2 February, 1937, with a subtitle crediting Maloney's book and note giving the tune to which it should be sung, to fix it in the Irish mind. It was titled simply "Roger Casement", and turned from Yeats's philosophical despair at amorality to a simple narration of Casement's tale, as Yeats had gathered ageing Parnellites around him to retell Parnell's saga. Its style was assertively colloquial: Casement's death was "nothing new", his enemies had "turned a trick by forgery", and were finally told to "speak your bit in public".[24] It was permeated by a sense of his heroic martyrdom and his enemies's dishonour; in its first stanza, Yeats saw Casement's act as an inevitable response, based on a heroic sense of duty. Reflecting on Casement's death at enemy hands, Yeats reminded his readers of the historical pattern, without having to list Irish heroes martyred by the British. Having introduced the forgeries, spread worldwide by a perjurer, Yeats ended the third stanza with "And that is something new", the depth of British dishonour. The fourth stanza mentioned Sir Cecil Arthur Spring-Rice, the British ambassador to the United States, who Yeats believed had spread the forgeries and blackened

Casement's name. In the next stanza, Yeats departed from his fairly simple rendering of historic legend to exhort the slanderers to atone. In the first printing, it was "Come Alfred Noyes and all the troup / That cried it far and wide, / Come from the forger and his desk, / Desert the perjurer's side."[25] When Noyes wrote to the *Irish Press*, Yeats accepted his disclaimer and made his attack communal: "No matter what the names they wear." In the final version, he was even more colloquial: "Come Tom and Dick, come all the troop." Thus, Yeats had placed Casement in the heroic tradition, explained the wrong done him, asked those responsible to explain and apologize publicly, and ended with Casement, "this most gallant gentleman", a mythic image to counterattack homosexual degeneracy, "That is in quicklime laid", sharply contrasting his heroism and his ignoble burial in Pentonville Prison, as well as remembering the story of the quicklime thrown in Parnell's eye, another humiliating offense to an Irish hero.

Yeats's direct accusation had been tempered by remorse; thus, this ballad differed from his efforts on Parnell's behalf, but Yeats's emotions were equally intense, as Hone remembered:

Meeting W.B.Y. just after his "Roger Casement", I was astonished by the ferocity of his feelings. He almost collapsed after reading the verses and had to call for a little port wine. Afterwards he admitted having wronged Alfred Noyes and others, who were named in the first version as persons who had spread stories about Casement's private life for political ends.[26]

On 8 February, Yeats wrote to Wellesley, commenting on the grateful Irish reaction to the ballad, and noting a characteristic British evasion:

On Feb. 2 my wife went to Dublin shopping & was surprised by the defference everyone showed her in buses & shop. Then she found what it was – the Casement poem was in the morning paper. Next day I was publicly thanked by the vice-president of the Executive Counsil, by De Valera's political secretary, by our chief antiquarian & an old revolutionist, Count Plunket, who calls my poem 'a ballad the people much needed.' De Valera's newspaper gave me a long leader saying that for generations to come my poem will pour scorn on the forgers & their backers. The only English comment is in *The Evening Standard* which points out my bad rhymes & says that after so many years it is impossible to discuss the authenticity of the diaries. (The British Government has hidden them for years.)

Politics as the game is played to-day are so much foul lying.[27]

Three days later, writing to Mannin as "an old Fenian", Yeats returned to Casement as indicative of the larger issue of modern political dishonour:

. . . I see nothing but the manipulation of popular enthusiasm by false news – a horror that has been deepened in these last weeks by the Casement business. My ballad on that subject has had success . . . I shall return to the matter again, in a new ballad. These ballads of mine though not supremely good are not ephemeral, the young will sing them now and after I am dead. In them I defend a noble-natured man, I do the old work of the poets but I will defend no cause. Get out of the thing, look on with sardonic laughter.[28]

His defence of a noble individual, not an ideology, encouraged and permitted himself to remove himself from the conflict, a self-imposed exile into art, with its immunity to dishonour. Between the publication of "Roger Casement" and this time, Alfred Noyes had written to the *Irish Press*, responding to Yeats's use of his name as one of Casement's slanderers. While working for the News Department, attached to the British Foreign Office, in 1916, Noyes had been shown a typed copy of Casement's alleged diary, assumed it genuine, and wrote on it as part of a British propaganda article against the Easter Rising, denouncing the rebels and Casement, as their leader, in particular; his "own written confessions about himself" were unprintable, because they were "filthy beyond all description", touching "the lowest depths that human degradation has ever touched. Page after page . . . would be an insult to a pig's trough to let the foul record touch it".[29]

Because of Noyes's explanation and disclaimer, in which he acknowledged that he had accepted the diary as genuine – had it been a forgery, it was "an unspeakably wicked fabrication", and he could imagine "no more wicked imposture, and no more detestable crime",[30] Yeats wrote to the *Irish Press*, enclosing an amended version of the ballad, with Noyes's name omitted, and restated his charges against others:

I accept Mr. Alfred Noyes' explanation and I thank him for his noble letter. I, too, think that the British Government should lay the diaries before some tribunal acceptable to Ireland and to England. He suggests that Dr. G.P. Gooch, a great expert in such matters, and I should be 'associated with such an enquiry.' I have neither legal training nor training in the examination of documents, nor have I the trust of the people. But I thank him for his courtesy in suggesting my name.

I add a new version of my song. Mr. Noyes' name is left out: but I repeat my accusation that a slander based on forged diaries was spread through the world and that, whatever the compulsion, 'Spring-Rice had to whisper it'. He was an honourable, able man in the ordinary affairs of life; why then did he not ask whether the evidence had been submitted to the accused? The British Government would have been compelled to answer.

I was dining with the wife of a Belgian Cabinet Minister after Casement's condemnation, perhaps after his execution, somebody connected with *The Times* was there; he said they had been asked to draw attention to the diaries. I said it was infamous to blacken Casement's name with evidence that had neither been submitted to him nor examined at his trial. Presently, Roger Fry, the famous art critic, came in, and the journalist repeated his statement, and Roger Fry commented with unmeasured fury. I do not remember whether *The Times* spoke of the diaries or not.

Had Spring-Rice been a free man he would have shared my indignation and that of Roger Fry.[31]

Spring-Rice, the British government, and *The Times*, were all partners in treachery; had all the slanderers written contritely to the *Irish Press*, it would not have brought Casement back.

On 18 February, Yeats wrote to Dorothy Wellesley, commenting on the stir his actions had provoked:

Shaw has written a long, rambling, vegetarian, sexless letter, disturbed by my causing 'bad-blood' between the nations; & strange to say Alfred Noyes has done what I asked him. . . . Public opinion is excited & there is a demand for a production of the documents & their submission to some impartial tribunal. It would be a great relief to me if they were so submitted & proven genuine. If Casement were a homo-sexual what matter! But if the British Government can with impunity forge evidence to prove

him so no unpopular man with a cause will ever be safe.
Henceforth he will be denied his last refuge – Martyrdom.[32]

The "commotion" was exciting, but Yeats's comment on
Casement's sexuality was not simple liberalism – had the
documents been genuine, the British government would have been
less vicious. Wellesley, unfortunately, was convinced that Yeats's
furor was unnecessary, as her interpretation of the facts exonerated
her government. The Casement scandal was "the invention of some
underling, War hysteria, . . . *after* he was convicted of high
treason".[33]

A day later, on 20 February, Yeats wrote to Ethel Mannin,
announcing the end of his political activity: "Here is an anonymous
subscription for your labour poor-box – not for politics – I am
finished with that for ever. It was sent me by the *Irish Press* as pay-
ment for my Casement ballad and I do not want to take money for
that poem."[34] Casement's gallantry required an equal nobility, but
when Mannin wrote back, wondering what she was to do with the
money, Yeats replied, his gallantry mixed with irony: "Give it to
your gardener – that is the best possible use for it."[35] In his August
speech at a banquet of the Irish Academy of Letters, Casement was
part of "that great pictured song" he had seen in his visit to the
Municipal Gallery; he had become art and myth: ". . . the events of
the last thirty years in fine pictures: a peasant ambush, the trial of
Roger Casement, a pilgrimage to Lough Derg, event after event:
Ireland not as she is displayed in guide book or history, but, Ireland
seen because of the magnificent vitality of her painters, in the glory
of her passions".[36]

Yeats's final statement on Casement was his second ballad;
although written between October 1936 and January 1937, it was
not published in the *Irish Press*, but in the 1938 Cuala *New Poems*, as
"The Ghost of Roger Casement".[37] It concentrated on Casement's
actively avenging image, as if the ghost of Parnell Yeats had sent
from Dublin in "To a Shade" had returned in Casement's shape,
not to be turned away again. In the contrast between its refrain,
"The ghost of Roger Casement / Is beating on the door," and the
present political situation, Yeats saw British weakness and
deterioration. The sea's roar contained "mockery" because "John
Bull" no longer ruled the waves: ". . . this is not the old sea / Nor
this the old seashore," perhaps an awareness of the old relations
between England, Ireland, and Germany, and their alteration in

1937. In the second stanza, Yeats revised three lines from the first Casement ballad: "A dog must have his day, / And whether a man be rich or poor / He takes the devil's pay," making a scathing portrait of British politics, where the dog and "John Bull" were equal partners in empty rhetoric and expedience: ". . . he knows how to say, / At a beanfeast or a banquet, / That all must hang their trust / Upon the British Empire, / Upon the Church of Christ". In "hang their trust", there was an echo of Casement's fate at the hands of Yeats's traditional enemies. English conduct outside England, in colonial India, was also fraudulent: ". . . there's no luck about a house / If it lack honesty". England, ruined by fraud, was the wreckage of one of the great houses he had written about; Yeats drew the decline of a great tradition into active dishonesty. In the final stanza, England's decline from ancestral majesty – continuous from the first line – was completed, as was England's symbolic history. From the "inheritance" and the "milk" "John Bull" had sucked, Yeats, as genealogist, looked into the Empire's heritage of slander: "I poked about a village church / And found his family tomb / And copied out what I could read / In that religious gloom; / Found many a famous man there; / But fame and virtue rot." At the poem's close, Yeats, as in Parnell's case, rallied the "beloved and bitter men" in angry community to "raise a shout", to participate in noble indignation and to spread the legend of British infamy as the British had slandered Casement. "Draw round" echoed "Come gather round me": if enough noble men protested as an enlightened community, they could stop fraud.[38] Initially, the ballad appeared only a deflation of England, linked to Casement by title and refrain, but his powerful ghost accused the English of treachery.

Yeats's spirited defence of a man he did not especially like or feel confident of, making Casement worthy of his intense personal and poetic energy, when he knew that his energy could not last much longer, may seem incongruous, but it made Yeats's defence especially powerful, resembling Swift's advocacy of a people he detested in a nation he could not wait to leave. Casement, like Wilde and Parnell, had suffered unjustly, and had been victimised by the dishonourable. Yeats saw this as an ominous infringement on a solitary man, and protested in indignant art and letters. Casement's value as an Irish political leader became as irrelevant as Parnell's specific political strategies or Wilde's poetry: what was important was the tableau of the lone hero attacked by the mob.

List of Abbreviations

Artist   *The Artist as Critic: Critical Writings of Oscar Wilde*, ed. Richard Ellmann (New York: Random House, 1969).

Auto   *The Autobiography of William Butler Yeats* (New York: Collier, 1974).

Correspondence   *The Correspondence of Jonathan Swift*, ed. Harold Williams (London: Oxford U.P., 1963–5).

E&I   Yeats, *Essays and Introductions* (New York: Collier, 1961).

Explorations Yeats, *Explorations*, selected by Mrs Yeats (New York: Collier, 1973).

JBY Letters   John Butler Yeats, *Letters to his Son W.B. Yeats and Others*, ed. Joseph Hone (London: Faber and Faber, 2nd edn, 1944).

Letters   *The Letters of W.B. Yeats*, ed. Allan Wade (New York: Macmillan, 1955).

Memoirs   Yeats, *Memoirs*, ed. and transcribed by Denis Donoghue (New York: Macmillan, 1973).

Moore   *W.B. Yeats and T. Sturge Moore: Their Correspondence 1901–1937*, ed. Ursula Bridge (New York: Oxford U.P., 1953).

Mythologies   Yeats, *Mythologies* (New York: Collier, 1969).

Poems   *The Poems of Jonathan Swift*, ed. Harold Williams (London: Oxford U.P., 2nd edn, 1958).

Prose   *The Prose Writings of Jonathan Swift*, ed. Herbert Davis *et al.* (London: Blackwell, 1939–69).

Tynan   *W.B. Yeats's Letters to Katharine Tynan*, ed. Roger McHugh (New York: McMullen Books, 1953).

UP I, II   Yeats, *Uncollected Prose*, I, ed. John P. Frayne (New York: Columbia U.P., 1970) and *Uncollected Prose*, II, eds John P. Frayne and Colton Johnson (New York: Columbia U.P., 1976).

V. Plays	*The Variorum Edition of the Plays of W.B. Yeats*, ed. Russell K. Alspach (New York: Macmillan, 1966).
V. Poems	*The Variorum Edition of the Poems of W.B. Yeats*, eds. Peter Allt and Russell K. Alspach (New York: Macmillan, 1957).
WBY I&R I, II	*W.B. Yeats: Interviews and Recollections*, ed. E.H. Mikhail (New York: Barnes & Noble, 1977).
Wellesley	*Letters on Poetry from W.B. Yeats to Dorothy Wellesley* (London: Oxford U.P., 1940, rpt. 1964).
Yeats	Joseph Hone, *W.B. Yeats 1865–1939* (New York: Macmillan, 1943).

Notes

1 Introduction

1. *E&I*, 114.
2. William Makepeace Thackeray, *English Humourists of the Eighteenth Century*, rpt. in part in *Jonathan Swift: A Critical Anthology*, ed. Denis Donoghue (Baltimore: Penguin, 1971) 117.
3. T.S. Eliot, "Yeats", in *Yeats: A Collection of Critical Essays*, ed. John Unterecker (Engelwood Cliffs, N.J.: Prentice-Hall, 1963) 62–3.
4. *Auto*, 19.

2 Wilde: ". . . Oscar ruled the table"

1. *Auto*, 5; *V. Poems*, 478–9, "A Dialogue of Self and Soul".
2. *E&I*, 428.
3. William Martin Murphy, *Prodigal Father: The Life of John Butler Yeats (1839–1922)* (Ithaca, N.Y.: Cornell U.P., 1979) 133; refer to letters from JBY to Matthew Yeats, 20 and 22 Nov. 1883.
4. Rupert Hart-Davis, ed., *The Letters of Oscar Wilde* (London: Hart-Davis, 1962) 152n.
5. *Yeats*, 5, 25; *Tynan*, 61, 25 July, 1888; Richard Ellmann, *Eminent Domain: Yeats Among Wilde, Joyce, Pound, Eliot, and Auden* (New York: Oxford U.P., 1970) 12, 128n; Anna, Comtesse de Brèmont, *Oscar Wilde and his Mother: A Memoir* (London: Everett & Co., 1911, rpt. 1972: Haskell House, New York) 76. See also Mary Helen Thuente, *W.B. Yeats and Irish Folklore* (Totowa, N.J.: Barnes & Noble, 1981) 62–4 for an evaluation of the Wildes as folklorists.
6. *E&I*, 266.
7. *Yeats*, 64. See also *Auto*, 90.
8. *Auto*, 91.
9. Ibid., 90.
10. George W. Russell, *Letters from AE*, selected and ed. by Alan Denson (London: Abelard-Schuman, 1961) 109–10, to George A. Moore, c. 6 Apr. 1916.
11. Coulson Kernahan, *In Good Company: Some Personal Recollections of Swinburne, Lord Roberts Watts-Dunton, Oscar Wilde, Edward Whymper, S.J. Stone, Stephen Phillips* (1917; rpt. 1968, Freeport, N.Y.: Books for Libraries Press) 211.
12. *Letters*, 102–3, to Katharine Tynan, 24 Jan., 1889; 107, to Tynan, 31 Jan., 1889.

13. *Artist*, 134.
14. Ibid., 131. See also *Letters*, 114, to Katharine Tynan, end of Feb.–8 Mar., 1889, for another reference to Wilde and "Faery book".
15. *Artist*, 150–1.
16. Yeats, *Letters to the New Island*, ed. Horace Reynolds (Cambridge: Harvard U.P., 1934, rpt. 1970) 76–7.
17. Ibid., 90.
18. *Letters*, 151, to Katharine Tynan, 28 February, 1890; *Letters to the New Island*, 206, 130.
19. *Letters*, 170, to Katharine Tynan, [in week ending June 27, 1889.]
20. *UP I*, 199, 202.
21. Ibid., 203–4.
22. Ibid., 250; John Butler Yeats, *Letters From Bedford Park: A Selection of the Correspondence (1890–1901) of John Butler Yeats*, ed. William Martin Murphy (Dublin: Cuala Press, 1972) 8, from JBY to Lily, 10 June, 1894.
23. *Letters of Oscar Wilde*, 365. See *UP I*, 354n, for an example of this criticism.
24. *UP I*, 354, 355.
25. Hesketh Pearson, *Oscar Wilde: His Life and Wit* (London: Methuen, 1954) 305, 318; see also *Yeats*, 116–7. For Maud Gonne's tale, see Conrad A. Balliet, "Micheal MacLiammoir Recalls Maud Gonne MacBride," (*Journal of Irish Literature*, VI, 2, May 1977, 48.)
26. *Letters of Oscar Wilde*, 523, 6 Apr., 1897.
27. *JBY Letters*, 55, 16 Sept., 1898.
28. *UP II*, 257.
29. *V. Poems*, 204, "Adam's Curse".
30. Allan Wade, ed., *A Bibliography of the Writings of W.B. Yeats* (London: Hart-Davis, 1951; 2nd edn., rev., 1958) 30. The play ran from 29 Mar. to 12 May, 1894.
31. *Explorations*, 197–8.
32. Richard Ellmann, *Golden Codgers: Biographical Speculations* (New York: Oxford U.P., 1973) 40n.
33. *Moore*, 8–9, to T. Sturge Moore, 6 May, 1906.
34. *Letters*, 524, to JBY, 17 Jan., 1909.
35. *Memoirs*, 151, Journal entry 34, 26 Jan., 1909.
36. *Artist*, 393.
37. *Auto*, 311; see also *Memoirs*, 139, Journal entry 4, 14 Jan., 1909.
38. *WBY I&R I*, 66.
39. *E&I*, 338–9.
40. *WBY I&R I*, 89–90. See also *WBY I&R II*, 295, for Hugh Lunn's 1941 memories of this interview.
41. *WBY I&R I*, 93.
42. Charles S. Ricketts, *Self-Portrait: Taken from the Letters and Journals of Charles Ricketts, R.A.*, collected and compiled by T. Sturge Moore, ed. by Cecil Lewis (London: Peter Davies, 1939) 195–6, Journal of 29 May, 1914.
43. *Memoirs*, 12–3; *Letters*, 602, to JBY [*c*. Nov. – Dec. 1915]
44. *Memoirs*, 21–2.
45. Ibid., 22.
46. Vincent O'Sullivan, *Aspects of Wilde* (New York: Holt, 1936) 21.
47. *Memoirs*, 79.
48. Ibid., 89.

49. *WBY I&R II*, 395, 396, 398; see also *WBY I&R I*, 112, 107–8.
50. *Auto*, 55, 87.
51. Ibid., 102.
52. Ibid., 88, 90, 91, 93.
53. Ibid., 192, 193.
54. Ibid., 195.
55. Yeats, *A Vision* (New York: Collier, 1966, rpt. 1975) 98.
56. Ibid., 147–8.
57. *Letters*, 467, to Sydney Cockerell, 22 Jan., 1906. A. Norman Jeffares, *W.B. Yeats: Man and Poet* (New Haven: Yale U.P., 1949) 143.
58. *A Vision*, 148–9.
59. Ibid., 150–1.
60. Ibid., 154.
61. Ibid., 255.
62. Oscar Wilde, *The Happy Prince and Other Fairy Tales*, introduction by W.B. Yeats (Garden City, N.Y.: Doubleday, 1923) ix – xvi. Yeats's introduction was also reprinted in *Oscar Wilde: The Critical Heritage*, ed. Karl Beckson (New York: Barnes & Noble, 1970) 396–9.
63. *E&I*, 93. Lady Augusta Isabella Gregory, *Seventy Years: 1852–1922*, ed. Colin Smythe (New York: Macmillan, 1974) 350. Lady Gregory, *Lady Gregory's Journals*, I, ed. Daniel J. Murphy (New York: Oxford U.P., 1978) 520; 4 Apr., 1924; 602; 10 Nov., 1924.
64. *UP II*, 440.
65. *WBY I&R I*, 182; *WBY I&R II*, 301.
66. *Letters*, 764–5, to Olivia Shakespear, 2 July, 1929. *Yeats*, 425; letter to Mrs. Yeats, 3 Mar., 1932. *Letters*, 798, to Olivia Shakespear, 30 June, 1932.
67. *V. Poems*, 834.
68. *Letters*, 826–7, to Olivia Shakespear, 7 Aug., 1934.
69. *V. Poems*, 840, revised slightly on 857; rpt. in *V. Plays*, 1010, 1311, 1312.
70. Yeats, ed., *The Oxford Book of Modern Verse: 1892–1935* (New York: Oxford U.P., 1936, rpt. 1947) vi – viii.
71. *Explorations*, 452–3, rpt. in *V Poems*, 626–7.
72. *Auto*, 165–6.

3   Yeats and Wilde's Art

1. Wilde, *Poems* (Garden City, N.Y.: Doubleday, 1923) 246.
2. Ibid., 24, 25.
3. Ibid., 71, 173.
4. *V. Poems*, 64. *Poems*, 40, 49.
5. *Poems*, 245.
6. Ibid., 297, 105.
7. See David R. Clark, *Lyric Resonance* (Amherst: U. of Mass. Press, 1972) 57–65, "Some Irish Poems".
8. Personal interview with Richard Ellmann, 14 Mar., 1980, at the Graduate School and University Center of the City University of New York.
9. Ibid.
10. *Tynan*, 47, 14 Mar., 1888.
11. *UP I*, 204.

12. *A Vision*, 68, 197, 210, 70.
13. Ibid., 24–5, dated "November 23, 1928, and later".
14. Wilde, *The Picture of Dorian Gray*, ed. Isobel Murray (London: Oxford U.P., 1974) 106, 128.
15. Ibid., 178–9.
16. Ibid., 216. William Rothenstein, *Since Fifty: Men and Memories 1922–1938* (New York: Macmillan, 1940) 328–9.
17. *Dorian Gray*, 39.
18. Ibid., 17, 78.
19. Ibid., 218. Lady Gregory, *Seventy Years*, 334. Her source was the meeting of the Irish Literary Society, probably in February 1897; Yeats was replying to speeches on Clarence Mangan by T.W. Rolleston and J.F. Taylor.
20. *Dorian Gray*, 4, 175, 142–3, 110.
21. Ibid., 41. *V. Poems*, 678–9.
22. *Dorian Gray*, 100.
23. *V. Poems*, 392–4, 632. In her essay, "Yeats, Pearse, and Cuchulain", (*Eire – Ireland*, XI, 4, Winter 1976, 51–65), Joan Towey Mitchell attributed "terrible beauty" to a line from Pearse's *An Ri (The King)*: "the terrible beautiful voice that comes out of the heart of battle". The play was produced at the Abbey on 17 May 1913, at Yeats's invitation. Maureen Murphy, extending the argument in " 'What Stood in the Post Office / With Pearse and Connolly?': The Case for Robert Emmet", (*Eire-Ireland*, XIV, 3, 1979, 141–3), convincingly showed that Yeats's "And what if excess of love / Bewildered them until they died?" stemmed from Pearse's frequent quotation of the line attributed to St. Columcille, "If I die it shall be from the excess of love I bear the Gael." With such evidence, it may appear difficult to support *Dorian Gray* as the source of "terrible beauty", but several factors favour it. First, the phrase appeared in English in the novel. Although Yeats first read it in 1891, and Pearse's play was chronologically closer to the Rising, given Yeats's startlingly accurate ability to quote Wilde's phrases precisely, even late in his life, it might well have remained in his mind. The phrase, depicting an inartistic tragedy, was perhaps closer to Yeats's ambivalence about the Rising than was Pearse's more patriotic statement. Finally, in the process of reclaiming ideas from himself, Yeats, in his *Autobiography*, referred to the singular tenor of Wilde's "The Doer of Good" as its "terrible beauty", (190) which suggests a strong link in Yeats's memory between the phrase and Wilde. The search for the ancestry of "terrible beauty", however, shows no abating. D.H. MacMullan has suggested a source in O. Henry's "A Story in Santone", in "an awful pulchritude is born". ("Yeats and O. Henry", *Times Literary Supplement*, 28 Nov., 1968, 1339.) In reply, Austin Clarke found a more plausible source in an unidentified LeFanu poem, which described a "fearful spirit that was sometimes seen in Munster": "With a terrible beauty the vision accurst . . .". (*TLS*, 12 Dec., 1968, 1409.)
24. Wilde, *The Soul of Man Under Socialism and Other Essays* (New York: Harper, 1970) 241.
25. Ibid., 247, 258.
26. Ibid., 250–1, 252, 253.
27. *Explorations*, 111.
28. *UP II*, 479–80.
29. *The Soul of Man Under Socialism*, 255–6.

30. Wilde, *De Profundis* (New York: Vintage, 1964) 80, 86.
31. Ibid., 99, 100, 110–11, 114.
32. Ibid., 116.
33. Ibid., 115.
34. *Dorian Gray*, 181.
35. *Wellesley*, 47.
36. *Auto*, 91. D.H. Lawrence reshaped this idea in *The Man Who Died.*
37. Ellmann, *Golden Codgers*, 95.
38. *Letters*, 645, to Lady Gregory, 14 Jan., 1918.
39. Ellmann, *Eminent Domain*, 130.
40. *Mythologies*, 147–56.
41. *V. Poems*, 318, 319. See also Conrad A. Balliet, " 'The Dolls' of Yeats and the Birth of Christ," *Research Studies*, 38 (1970) 54–7.
42. *V. Poems*, 402.
43. Ibid., 436.
44. Ibid., 437, 438; see also "Wisdom", 440.
45. Ibid., 483.
46. Ibid., 483.
47. Ibid., 499.
48. Ibid., 619; *Explorations*, 437.
49. Ibid., 510, "Crazy Jane on the Day of Judgment".
50. Ibid., 625.
51. *V. Plays*, 783, 785.
52. *A Vision*, 178.
53. *V. Plays*, 910, 916, 918, 930.
54. Ibid., 944.
55. Ibid., 1049.
56. *A Vision*, 273. I have concentrated solely on *A Full Moon in March*, because, as Yeats acknowledged, *The King of the Great Clock Tower*, which had "a character too many," was a lesser play. See *V. Plays*, 1311.
57. *A Vision*, 250, 245.
58. *V. Plays*, 1311.
59. Marilyn Gaddis Rose, "The Daughters of Herodias in *Herodiade, Salomé*, and *A Full Moon in March,"* *Comparative Drama*, 1, no. 3 (1967) 173.
60. *V. Plays*, 989.
61. *V. Poems*, 513, "Crazy Jane Talks With the Bishop".
62. Rothenstein, *Since Fifty*, 242.
63. *E&I*, 227.
64. *Oscar Wilde: Interviews and Recollections*, ed. E.H. Mikhail (New York: Barnes and Noble, 1979) I, 115.
65. *Letters*, 280, to Fiona MacLeod [? early Jan. 1897.]
66. *Explorations*, 96.
67. Wilde, *Lady Windermere's Fan and A Woman of No Importance* (Garden City, N.Y.: Doubleday, 1923) 201. Yeats knew this exchange; see *UP I*, 354–5, for his reference to it.
68. Wilde, *The Importance of Being Earnest and An Ideal Husband* (Garden City, N.Y.: Doubleday, 1923) 198, 297.
69. Ibid., 51, 137–8.
70. Ibid., 63–4. See also George Bornstein, "A Borrowing From Wilde in Yeats's *The King's Threshold,"* *Notes and Queries*, 18 (1971) 421–2.

71. *Artist*, 293, 294, 300, 304.
72. *UP I*, 309.
73. *Artist*, 303. Although this was convincing to Yeats, Wilde's plays did not renounce realism as thoroughly as this would suggest.
74. Ibid., 319.
75. Ibid., 296. Note the aristocratic rejection of art that concerned itself with social problems.
76. *Explorations*, 451.
77. *Artist*, 305, 302.
78. *WBY I&R I*, 54.
79. *E&I*, 254.
80. *Artist*, 313.
81. Ibid., 311. See also *Mythologies*, 333–4, *Auto*, 181, *A Vision*, 244.
82. See *Explorations*, 88, *E&I*, 101, and *UP II*, 251, among many other instances.
83. *Artist*, 307.
84. *V. Plays*, 264, 265. Bornstein, "A Borrowing From Wilde in Yeats's *The King's Threshold*", 422.
85. *V. Poems*, 610.
86. Ibid., 564.
87. Ibid., 319. Malcolm Brown, in *The Politics of Irish Literature: From Thomas Davis to W.B. Yeats* (Washington: U. of Washington Press, 1973), has suggested "An Acre of Grass" as a "Decay of Lying" poem, to Yeats's discredit. (361–2).
88. *V. Poems*, 638, 640.
89. *Artist*, 308.
90. *Explorations*, 93.
91. *Artist*, 319.
92. *V. Poems*, 611, "The Statues".
93. *Artist*, 391, 393; see also *Dorian Gray*, 142–3.
94. *Artist*, 432.
95. *V. Poems*, 370.
96. *Artist*, 320–1, 324, 323.
97. *V. Poems*, 263.
98. *Artist*, 423, 432. A slight possibility exists, because the essay was published in May 1885, that Yeats got his notion of the contraries from this before his Blake work with Edwin Ellis in 1891.
99. Ibid., 361, 359.
100. Ibid., 362.
101. Ibid., 375.
102. Ibid., 389, 391.
103. Ibid., 407.
104. Ibid., 386.

4   Parnell: "A proud man's a lovely man"

1. Mrs Parnell noted that the one book she saw Parnell read seriously was *Alice in Wonderland*. Although his ancestor, Thomas Parnell, was Swift's friend and was praised by Dr Johnson for his poetry, his talent did not descend to Charles. See F.S.L. Lyons, *Charles Stewart Parnell* (New York: Oxford U.P.,

1970) 16 and John, Viscount Morley, *Recollections* (New York: Macmillan, 1907) I, 241.

2. *Prodigal Father*, 31. The source is a fragment of a letter from JBY to Edward Dowden, c. 1912. *JBY Letters*, 276, to WBY, 28 May, 1921; 219, to WBY, 24 Feb., 1916. John Butler Yeats, *Further Letters of John Butler Yeats*, ed. Lennox Robinson (Dublin: Cuala Press, 1920, rpt. Shannon: Irish U.P., 1971) 69–70, 19 Oct., 1917.

3. John Devoy, *Devoy's Post Bag*, ed. William O'Brien and Desmond Ryan, 2 vols (Dublin: Fallon Press, 1948–53) II, 237–8, rpt. in Brown, *Politics of Irish Literature*, 312.

4. Maud Gonne MacBride, *A Servant of the Queen* (London: Victor Gollancz, 1938) 92, 166, 167.

5. Katharine Tynan Hinkson, *Twenty-five Years: Reminiscences* (New York: Devin-Adair, 1913) 328–9, 372–3, 383. Her regard for Parnell had a romantic, even erotic worship to it, typical of other women of the time: see Mary Gladstone's diaries in F.S.L. Lyons's *Parnell*, 423, 450, for one example. Delia, in Virginia Woolf's *The Years*, exemplified this adoration.

6. *Auto*, 171–2.

'7. *Prodigal Father*, 140. *Auto*, 94.

8. *Tynan*, 85, Feb. (after 22nd), 1889; 87–8, Feb. (end of)–8 Mar., 1889. Mrs Katharine O'Shea, *Charles Stewart Parnell: His Love-Story and Political Life* (London: Cassell, 1914) II, 129.

9. *UP I*, 145–6. See also *Auto*, 238, and *UP I*, 146, n. 7.

10. *Letters to the New Island*, 112. *UP I*, 185.

11. *Yeats*, 81. Hone dated the publication of *Representative Irish Tales* as 1890; Thomas Flanagan, in "Yeats, Joyce, and the Matter of Ireland", (*Critical Inquiry*, Autumn 1975, 44–5), dated it as 1891. The edition in the possession of the New York Public Library has an anonymously pencilled "1891" on the title page. (*Representative Irish Tales, Compiled and with an Introduction by W.B. Yeats*, First Series, New York and London: G.P. Putnam's sons: The Knickerbocker Press, 15–6.)

12. Lyons, *Parnell*, 476. Joyce Marlow, *The Uncrowned Queen of Ireland: The Life of 'Kitty' O'Shea* (New York: Saturday Review Press, Dutton, 1975) 259.

13. Lyons, *Parnell*, 492, rpt. from Morley, *Recollections*, I, 259–60. *Parnell*, 494–5, rpt. from Morley, *The Life of William Ewart Gladstone* (London: 1911) III, 329.

14. Richard Ellmann, *Yeats: The Man and the Masks* (New York: Dutton, 1948) 100. Conor Cruise O'Brien, "Passion and Cunning in the Politics of W.B. Yeats", in A. Norman Jeffares and K.G.W. Cross, eds, *In Excited Reverie: A Centenary Tribute to William Butler Yeats* (New York: Macmillan, 1969) 217n.

15. *Letters*, 163–4, to John O'Leary, 22 Jan., 1891.

16. *UP I*, 206–7.

17. Lyons, *Parnell*, 601. "Passion and Cunning in the Politics of W.B. Yeats", 219. *V. Poems*, 737–8.

18. *Letters*, 179, to Lily Yeats, 11 Oct., 1891.

19. *Memoirs*, 63–5. *Letters*, 222, to T. Fisher Unwin, [? November 1892.]

20. *UP I*, 309.

21. Ibid., 367–9.

22. *Explorations*, 235.

23. *Memoirs*, 109–10.

24 *Seventy Years*, 335, 329–31.
25 *UP II*, 91. Yeats's reference to the "Celt's futile revolt against the despotism of fact" was a phrase he had read in Richard Ashe King's 1896 *Swift in Ireland*. Ian Fletcher, ed., *The Complete Poems of Lionel Johnson* (London: Unicorn Press, 1953) 30–2. *Twenty One Poems Written by Lionel Johnson*, selected by William Butler Yeats (Dundrum, Ireland: Dun Emer Press, 1904; rpt. Shannon: Irish U.P., 1971) 15–7.
26. Ellmann, *Yeats: The Man and the Masks*, 111; see also *Memoirs*, 114, for details of the procession, which Yeats believed was "the immediate cause of the reunion of the Irish party".
27. Barton R. Friedman, "Yeats, Johnson, and Ireland's Heroic Dead: Toward A Poetry of Politics", (*Eire – Ireland*, 7, iv, 1972) 39.
28. *Seventy Years*, 341, *c.* 1 Mar., 1899.
29. See Conor Cruise O'Brien, *Parnell and his Party* (New York: Oxford, 1957, corrected 1964, rpt. 1974) 364, and F.S.L. Lyons, *The Fall of Parnell 1890–1* (London: Routledge and Kegan Paul, 1962) 343.
30. R. Barry O'Brien, *The Life of Charles Stewart Parnell*, 2 vols (London: 1898, rpt. New York: Haskell House, 1968) I, 102. See *A Vision*, 124, for echoes of this incident, although the specifics are clearly different.
31. O'Brien, *Parnell*, II, 178.
32. Ibid., II, 366, 367.
33. *UP II*, 148, 150.
34. I am referring to the revised version; however, both versions are compared in *UP II*, 184–96. Yeats, "The Literary Movement in Ireland," in Lady Gregory, ed., *Ideals in Ireland* (London: Unicorn Press, 1901, rpt. New York: Lemma Pub. Corp., 1973) 87, 88.
35. *Ideals in Ireland*, 90, 101.
36. *Explorations*, 79. *Mythologies*, 337. *Moore*, 154, 17 April, 1929.
37. *Letters*, 333, to the Editor of the *United Irishman*, 20 Jan., 1900.
38. *UP II*, 288.
39. *Explorations*, 115.
40. *UP II*, 306–7.
41. Ibid., 315, 320.
42. Ibid., 321. Yeats's image of Parnell's sale to the enemy echoed O'Brien's biography (II, 278); in the meeting of the Irish party on 1 Dec., 1890, in Committee Room 15, John Redmond, supporting Parnell, had observed, "When we are asked to sell our leader to preserve the English alliance, it seems to me that we are bound to inquire what we are getting for the price we are paying", and Parnell had interrupted, "Don't sell me for nothing. If you get my value you may change me to-morrow."
43. *UP II*, 327, 326.
44. *Explorations*, 28.
45. Ibid., 147–8.
46. Robert Hogan and Michael J. O'Neill, eds., *Joseph Holloway's Abbey Theatre* (Carbondale, Ill.: Southern Illinois U.P., 1967) 58, entry of 26 Apr., 1905.
47. *V. Plays*, 463.
48. *WBY I&R I*, 54–5.
49. *E&I*, 259.
50. *V. Poems*, 591, "What Was Lost".
51. *Joseph Holloway's Abbey Theatre*, 103–4, rpt. in *UP II*, 361. *UP II*, 362. See also

WBY I&R II, 391–2, for another view of Yeats and *The Piper*.

52. *Memoirs*, 163, Journal entry 55, 6 Feb., 1909; 195, Journal entry 111, 21 Mar., 1909; 212–3, Journal entry　146, 5 Apr., 1909.

53. *Letters*, 555, to JBY, 24 Nov., 1910. Lady Gregory, *Our Irish Theatre* (New York: Putnam's, 1912) 95. Lady Gregory, *Irish Folk-History Plays, Second Series* (New York: Putnam's, 1912) 195, 183. The mob always presented itself to the artistic eye as bestial: to Lady Gregory, they were great cats; to Yeats (from Goethe), they were hounds; to Joyce, wolves; and even Barry O'Brien titled one of his last chapters in his biography of Parnell "At Bay". (II, 257).

54. *WBY I&R I*, 82.

55. Yeats, ed. and intro., *Selections from the Writings of Lord Dunsany* (Dundrum: Cuala Press, 1912, rpt. Shannon: Irish U.P., 1971) n.p., Section I of Yeats's introduction.

56. *V. Poems*, 819, 287.

57. Ibid., 289.

58. Ibid., 292, 293.

59. Ibid., 818.

60. See *Memoirs*, 39, 47, 49, 50, 55.

61. *JBY Letters*, 184–5, to WBY, 2 June, 1914; 211, to Susan Mitchell, 20 Sept., 1915.

62. Mrs O'Shea, *Charles Stewart Parnell*, I, x, 175; II, 78–9.

63. Ibid., II, 233.

64. Ibid., II, 36.

65. Ibid., I, 164, 173.

66. Ibid., II, 143–4.

67. Yeats, "Thomas Davis," in *Davis, Mangan, Ferguson?: Tradition and the Irish Writer* (Dublin: Dolmen, 1970) 15, 16–7.

68. Morley, *Recollections*, I, 238. *A Vision*, 124.

69. *Letters*, 635, to Lady Gregory, 16 Dec., 1917. See also Frank O'Connor, *My Father's Son* (New York: Knopf, 1969) 192–3.

70. *WBY I&R I*, 121–2.

71. *Lady Gregory's Journals*, ed. Murphy, 338; 13 Apr., 1922; 344; 15 Apr., 1922.

72. *Auto*, 132, 156.

73. *Lady Gregory's Journals*, ed. Murphy, 387; 20 Aug., 1922. *Seventy Years*, 128.

74. *A Vision*, 97, 100, 101, 121.

75. Ibid., 122, 123.

76. Ibid., 170, 123.

77. Ibid., 154, 123–4.

78. Ibid., 127.

79. Ibid., 124.

80. *Auto*, 156.

81. Donald R. Pearce, ed., *The Senate Speeches of W.B. Yeats* (Bloomington, Indiana: U. of Indiana Press, 1960) 11.

82. Ibid., 89.

83. *UP II*, 451.

84. *V. Poems*, 460. See also A. Norman Jeffares, *A Commentary on the Collected Poems of W.B. Yeats* (Stanford, Cal.: Stanford U.P., 1968) 312.

85. *Senate Speeches*, 92, 94, 97–9, 101–2. The final comment on the Catholic orthodoxy that opposed Yeats so comprehensively came in his 25 June, 1925 letter to L.A.G. Strong, speaking of the typist who "wept because put to type

a speech in favour of divorce I was to deliver in the Senate''. *Letters*, 709.
86. *Letters*, 701, to Lady Gregory, 13 Jan., 1924. *Auto*, 378.
87. *Explorations*, 343, 336.
88. Ibid., 372–3. For other references to *Hysterica passio*, see Ricketts's *Self Portrait*, 195–6; *Memoirs*, 179; *Mythologies*, 278; *Wellesley*, 86.
89. *V. Poems*, 437–8.
90. Robert Hogan and Michael J. O'Neill, eds, *Joseph Holloway's Irish Theatre*, 3 vols, (Dixon, Cal.: Proscenium Press, 1968–1970) II, 17–18, 18 Sept., 1932.
91. Yeats, "Modern Ireland: An Address to American Audiences, 1932–1933, ed. and transcribed by Curtis Bradford, *Massachusetts Review*, 5 (1964) I, 256–8.
92. Ibid., 259, 262–4, 266.
93. Patrick Holland has suggested that only the first part of "Parnell's Funeral" could have been completed by mid-April 1933, and the second part dates from between August 1933 and 1934. See his "From Parnell to O'Duffy: The Composition of 'Parnell's Funeral' ", *Canadian Journal of Irish Studies*, 2, no. 1 (1976) 15–20.
94. *Mythologies*, 340, 361.
95. *V. Poems*, 541. Was Yeats, consciously or not, echoing Nashe's "A Litany in Time of Plague", which he had remembered in other contexts?
96. *Auto*, 388–92.
97. Both F.A.C. Wilson and Peter Ure have suggested a source for the eating of Parnell's heart in the *planh* of the thirteenth-century troubadour poet, Sordello di Goito, for his master, Sir Blacatz, which Yeats would have known through Ezra Pound's translation of it. See Wilson, " 'Parnell's Funeral', II", *Explicator*, 27 (1969), Item 72, and Ure's "A Source for Yeats's 'Parnell's Funeral' ", *English Studies*, XXXIX (1958) 257–8.
98. *Letters*, 806, to Olivia Shakespear, 9 Mar. 1933. *V. Poems*, 542, 543.
99. *Explorations*, 308, 325.
100. *V. Poems*, 543.
101. "Letter to Lord Byron", 1936, quoted in *Eminent Domain*, 100.
102. Late in May 1934, Yeats sent Patrick McCartan a copy of the first part of "Parnell's Funeral", then titled "Somebody at Parnell's Funeral", and his commentary, "An Irish Historical Note", dated April 1934. See John Unterecker, ed. *Yeats and Patrick McCartan: A Fenian Friendship*, Dolmen Press Yeats Centenary Papers, no. 10 (Dublin: Dolmen, 1965) 364–8.
103. *V. Poems*, 834, 835.
104. Roger McHugh, ed., *Ah, Sweet Dancer: W.B. Yeats and Margot Ruddock* (New York: Macmillan, 1971), 20, to Margot Ruddock (Collis) 24 Sept., 1934.
105. *Auto*, 280–1, 285.
106. Yeats and F.R. Higgins, eds, *Broadsides: A Collection of Old and New Songs* (Dublin: Cuala, 1935, rpt. Shannon: Irish U.P., 1971), "A Foreword on Anglo-Irish Ballads by W.B. Yeats and F.R. Higgins", n.p., section I.
107. Henry Harrison, *Parnell Vindicated: The Lifting of the Veil* (New York: Richard R. Smith, 1931) 9.
108. *E&I*, 486.
109. Two letters from Harrison to Yeats, of 20 July and 23 July, 1936, exist; copies are available in the William Butler Yeats Archives at the State University of New York at Stony Brook. *Yeats*, 449.

110. *Parnell Vindicated*, 17–18, 163.
111. Ibid., 221, 123–4.
112. Ibid., 127–9, 125–6.
113. *Auto*, 368.
114. *Wellesley*, 93–4, rpt. in *Letters*, 862–3; see *V. Poems*, 586–7. *Explorations*, 147–8.
115. *V. Poems*, 586–7.
116. *Letters*, 867–8, to Ethel Mannin, 15 Nov., 1936.
117. *Wellesley*, 123; on envelope, 28 Jan., 1937. Although mythically appropriate, Parnell's "actual saying" has not been traced.
118. *Letters*, 880, to Dorothy Wellesley, 6 Feb., 1937. *Wellesley*, 127, to WBY, 19 Feb., 1937; 130, 26 Feb., 1937.
119. *Letters*, 888, to Edith Shackelton Heald, 18 May, 1937. *E&I*, 517, 530.
120. See Richard Ellmann, *The Identity of Yeats* (New York: Oxford U.P., 1954, rpt. 1968) 293; Jeffares, *Commentary*, 477, *Wellesley*, 141–2.
121. *V. Poems*, 597–8. "Those cheers that can be bought or sold" echoed Yeats's 1900 essay on Queen Victoria's visit. See *UP II*, 211, 213.
122. *Wellesley*, 163–4, 24 May, 1938; 164–5, 10 June, 1938. *V. Poems*, 631.
123. *Explorations*, 409–10.

5   Swift: "The tomb of Swift wears it away"

1. In his essay, "*The Words upon the Window-Pane* and Yeats's Encounter with Jonathan Swift", rpt. in *Yeats and the Theatre*, eds Robert O'Driscoll and Lorna Reynolds (Niagara Falls: Maclean-Hunter Press, 1975), Douglas N. Archibald suggests that Yeats's encounters began in 1926 and 1927 (178–80). Donald T. Torchiana, in his *Yeats and Georgian Ireland* (Evanston, Ill.: Northwestern U.P., 1966) states that Yeats's involvement was primarily a product of his last two decades. (xi) Only Adele M. Dalsimer's "Yeats's Unchanging Swift", (*Eire–Ireland*, 9, ii, 1974, 65–89), reverses this limiting tendency by examining the visible foundations of Yeats's interest in Swift.
2. *UP I*, 167, 201.
3. *Memoirs*, 68. *UP I*, 268. The passage Yeats paraphrased can be found in *Prose*, III, 135–6.
4. *UP I*, 308.
5. *Memoirs*, 84.
6. Yeats, ed., *A Book of Irish Verse* (London: Methuen, 1920) xviii.
7. *UP I*, 352.
8. Ibid., 360.
9. Richard Ashe King, *Swift in Ireland* (London: T. Fisher Unwin, 1895) 1–8.
10. Ibid., 50.
11. Ibid., 30.
12. Ibid., 130–1.
13. Ibid., 197–8.
14. Ibid., 194, 204. The Mosaic analogy had been used by Gladstone and Parnell themselves; see F.S.L. Lyons, "The Parnell Myth in Literature", in Andrew Carpenter, ed., *Place, Personality, and the Irish Writer* (New York: Barnes & Noble, 1977) 70–1.
15. *UP I*, 407–8.

16. *Mythologies*, 267–8, 271, 301.
17. *Memoirs*, 117, 102, and Lady Gregory, *Coole* (Dublin: Cuala, 1931, rpt. Shannon: Irish U.P., 1971), *Seventy Years*, 334–5.
18. Yeats, *The Speckled Bird*, ed. William H. O'Donnell (Toronto: McClelland and Stewart, 1976) xxxviii–lix, 148, 8.
19. *UP II*, 324–5.
20. Ibid., 328.
21. *Explorations*, 156.
22. Ibid., 159.
23. Ellmann, *Yeats: The Man and the Masks*, 179, letter of 13 June, 1906 to Stephen Gwynn.
24. *E&I*, 307–8.
25. *Memoirs*, 156–7, 235–6.
26. Torchiana, *Yeats and Georgian Ireland*, 123n. *WBY I&R I*, 86.
27. *V. Poems*, 421, "My Table".
28. Donald T. Torchiana and Glenn O'Malley, eds, "Some New Letters from W.B. Yeats to Lady Gregory," *Review of English Literature*, 4 (1969) 11, 13, 17, 20–1. See also "Out of a medium's mouth: the Writing of *The Words upon the Window-Pane*", Mary Fitzgerald, *Colby Library Quarterly*, XVII, no. 2, June 1981, 62n.
29. *Letters*, 664, to John Quinn, 30 Oct., 1920. Yeats's source was the *Journal to Stella*, ed. Sir Harold Williams (London: Oxford, 1948, rpt. 1963) II, 628–9.
30. *Journal to Stella*, II, 414.
31. Ibid., I, 41, 181.
32. *UP II*, 489. The identification is from *Yeats and Georgian Ireland*, 222–3n.
33. Robert O'Driscoll, ed., *Theatre and Nationalism in Twentieth-Century Ireland* (Toronto: U. of Toronto Press, 1971) 84, "Two Lectures on the Irish Theatre by W.B. Yeats". Yeats dated his manuscript November 1922. (212n35).
34. *Senate Speeches*, 154, 99.
35. *Yeats and Georgian Ireland*, 153n.
36. Mary Fitzgerald, "Out of a medium's mouth: the Writing of *The Words upon the Window-Pane*", 63–70.
37. *Explorations*, 281–2n. See also Mackie L. Jarrell, " 'Jack and the Dane': Swift Folklore in Ireland", rpt. in *Fair Liberty Was All His Cry*, ed. A. Norman Jeffares (New York: St. Martin's Press, 1967) 311–41, and Lady Gregory, *The Kiltartan Books: Containing the Kiltartan Poetry, History, and Wonder Books by Lady Gregory* (Gerrards Cross: Colin Smythe, 1971) 94–5.
38. *WBY I&R I*, 191.
39. Arthur R. Power, *The Drapier Letters* and *Her Ladyship – The Poet – and the Dog: Two One-Act Plays* (Dublin: Talbot Press, 1927) 22, 6. *The Drapier Letters* was produced at the Abbey on 22 Aug., 1927. See *Joseph Holloway's Irish Theatre*, I, 26, for his adverse reaction.
40. *V. Poems*, 831. In his dedication to Lord Somers, Swift, in search of panegyric-writers, goes ". . . to several other Wits of my Acquaintance, with no small Hazard and Weariness to my Person, from a prodigious Number of dark, winding Stairs . . .". *A Tale of A Tub*, ed. A.C. Guthkelch and D. Nichol Smith (London: Oxford U.P., 1958, rpt. 1968) 24.
41. *V. Poems*, 480, 831. Archibald, "*The Words upon the Window-Pane* and Yeats's

Encounter with Jonathan Swift'', 176.

42. *V. Poems*, 480–2. King, *Swift in Ireland*, 145. The phrase came from a letter of Swift's to Bolingbroke, *Correspondence*, V, 383.

43. *Letters*, 741, to Sean O'Casey, 20 Apr., 1928. Notwithstanding Yeats's praise, the letter was a rejection of *The Silver Tassie*. *UP II*, 483.

44. *Yeats and Georgian Ireland*, 143.

45. *A Vision*, 4n, 8, 27–8, 50. Swift's comment on introductions came from *Prose*, IV, 57.

46. *Yeats and Georgian Ireland*, 133.

47. *Moore*, 141.

48. Ibid., 147, 149–50.

49. Lady Gregory, *Lady Gregory's Journals 1916–1930*, ed. Lennox Robinson (New York: Macmillan, 1947) 266.

50. Courtesy of the William Butler Yeats Archives, from a Rapallo notebook begun in 1928. (Reel 29, vol. 7, 247.)

51. *V. Poems*, 493. A variant, published in *The Dublin Magazine* of Oct.–Dec. 1931, represented an earlier stage of composition.

52. Oliver Gogarty, *Wild Apples*, with a Preface by W.B. Yeats (Dublin: Cuala, 1930, rpt. Shannon: Irish U.P., 1971) n.p., Section II of Yeats's Preface.

53. *Moore*, 160, 7 Apr., 1930. *Letters*, 773, to Lady Gregory, 7 Apr., 1930.

54. Rothenstein, *Since Fifty*, 241–2. His recollection of this luncheon was undated, but reference to Yeats's ''serious illness'' places it in close proximity to his recovery from Malta fever.

55. *Explorations*, 289–90. Torchiana, in *Yeats and Georgian Ireland*, 135–6n, has noted that one of Yeats's few place-markers in his edition of Swift was found in Swift's description of Marlborough's fall, from *History of the Last Four Years of the Queen*. Yeats's specific source, however, can be found in *Prose*, VIII, 114–5, ''Memoirs, Relating to The Change which happened in the Queen's Ministry in the Year 1710''.

56. *Explorations*, 292–8.

57. *Letters*, 776, to Olivia Shakespear, 1 June, 1930. *Explorations*, 301.

58. *V. Poems*, 267.

59. *Explorations*, 313–5.

60. Ibid., 317. See *Prose*, IX, 162, 165, 73, 77, 262, for Yeats's sources of Swift's thoughts on religion.

61. *Letters*, 776, to Wyndham Lewis, tentatively dated as September 1930.

62. *Explorations*, 318.

63. *Yeats and Georgian Ireland*, 136.

64. Ibid., 131.

65. *Explorations*, 322. Fitzgerald, ''Out of a medium's mouth'', 71–3. Curtis Bradford, *Yeats at Work* (Carbondale, Ill.; Southern Illinois U.P., 1965) 218. *Letters*, 777.

66. Bradford, 219, 221, 224–6, 229. See Samuel J. Rogal, ''Keble's Hymn and Yeats's *Words upon the Window-Pane*'', *Modern Drama*, 16 (1973) 87–9, for his discussion of the hymn's importance.

67. *Yeats*, 7–11. Swift's *Correspondence* also refers favourably to a Francis Corbet, who eventually succeeded him as Dean of St. Patrick's''. (III, 71).

68. *V. Plays*, 941–2. *Explorations*, 347.

69. *V. Plays*, 942, 949–51, 954–6.

70. David R. Clark, *W. B. Yeats and the Theatre of Desolate Reality* (Chester Springs,

Pa.: Dufour Editions, 1965) 74.

71. *V. Plays*, 955. Yeats got his information on Swift's last days from Johnson's life of Swift and the *Correspondence*. For Johnson's version, see *The Lives of the Most Eminent English Poets*, III, "Swift", 25–6 (Chicago: Stone and Kimball, 1896); for the latter, see *Correspondence*, V, 207, 213–4; for a reference to the "great Ministers", see IV, 546.

72. *Explorations*, 334, 337. His source was "Thoughts on Religion", *Prose*, IX, 262.

73. *Letters*, 779. Even Joseph Holloway liked the play; see *Joseph Holloway's Irish Theatre*, I, 69.

74. *Yeats and Georgian Ireland*, 140, 154–5.

75. Ellmann, in *The Identity of Yeats*, dated its completion as 30 Jan., 1931. (291) *V. Poems*, 486–7.

76. *Explorations*, 343–5; see also *V. Poems*, 787.

77. *Explorations*, 345, 8, 351–2.

78. Ibid., 358. See *Prose*, IX, 28.

79. Ibid., 359–60.

80. Ibid., 360–2. For Shane Leslie's conjectures, see *The Skull of Swift* (London: Chatto and Windus, 1928) 187–9, 194, 196–9, 200, 202.

81. Ibid., 362–3. In *Yeats and Georgian Ireland*, 121n, Torchiana identified the "scholar" through Mrs. Yeats's information. Yeats's footnote to 362, as printed, indicated that he was familiar with the versions of the story of Swift and his butler previously told by Dr. Johnson and Thomas Sheridan. For Johnson's, see *The Lives of the Most Eminent English Poets*, III, 18–9, and Mary Fitzgerald's "Out of a medium's mouth", 73. For Sheridan's version, see Thomas Sheridan, *The Life of the Rev. Dr. Jonathan Swift* (London: C. Bathurst *et al.*, 1784; rpt. New York: Garland Pub. Corp., 1974) 244–6.

82. *Explorations*, 363.

83. *E&I*, 397, 398, 399–400, 409.

84. Joseph Hone and Mario M. Rossi, *Bishop Berkeley* (New York: Macmillan, 1931) 89.

85. *WBY I&R II*, 200.

86. *UP II*, 489, 490.

87. *Letters*, 791, to Joseph Hone, 14 Feb., 1932. Rossi's essay was published as "Essay on the Character of Swift", in the September 1932 *Life and Letters*.

88. *Yeats and Georgian Ireland*, 133.

89. Ibid., 102. *V. Poems*, 833. In May 1933, Sir Harold Williams spent an afternoon with Yeats, discussing Swift. In August 1960, Williams wrote to Torchiana, describing the afternoon, and he has graciously allowed me to reprint the relevant portions of that letter: "The afternoon . . . is chiefly memorable to me for listening to a continuous monologue, the most of which I do not now clearly remember. . . . I do remember him praising the Rossi and Hone biography of Swift which was then in the course of preparation. I picked up sufficient courage to cast doubts on it, in which I was certainly justified.

   If you will turn to page xiv of the Introduction to my edition of Swift's *Poems* you will note that Yeats called my attention to certain lines in one of the early odes."

90. *Letters*, 818–9, fragment to Mario M. Rossi [in the last months of 1933.]

91. *Auto*, 221. See also *A Vision*, 159. Denis Donoghue, ed., *Jonathan Swift: A Critical*

Anthology (Baltimore: Penguin, 1971) 112, rpt. from *Table Talk* (1830), published in H.N. Coleridge, ed., *Specimens of the Table Talk of Coleridge* (1874) 98.

92. Mary Fitzgerald, "Out of a medium's mouth", 61.
93. Mario M. Rossi and Joseph M. Hone, *Swift, or the Egotist* (London: Victor Gollancz, 1934) 45, 77.
94. *Yeats*, 424.
95. *Swift, or the Egotist*, 17, 18, 20–1, 310, 319, 320, 351, 326.
96. *Yeats and Georgian Ireland*, 163.
97. *Auto*, 280, 258.
98. See King, 61; Johnson, 34; *Prose*, IX, 65. *UP II*, 498; *Ah, Sweet Dancer*, 39; *Wellesley*, 56, 126; *UP II*, 509.
99. *Prose*, IX, 76. Appropriately, it was from the same essay as "Proper words in proper Places".
100. *Broadsides*, 1935, n.p.
101. *Wellesley*, 114, 115. See *Poems*, I, 216, 1. 43, and III, 870, 1. 93, as well as *A Tale of A Tub*, 80, 84–6, for Swift's references to gold-braid and lace, traditionally the marks of "Beaux" and military officers.
102. *Letters*, 891, to Oliver St. John Gogarty, postmarked 22 June, 1937.
103. *E&I*, 511, 517, 519.
104. King, *Swift in Ireland*, 93.
105. *Explorations*, 429.
106. Ibid., 431–2, 442. See *Correspondence*, IV, 51.
107. Ibid., 423.
108. Sheridan, 260–1.
109. Ibid., 272.

6 Swift's Poetry

1. I am again grateful for Professor Torchiana's permission to reprint a portion of Oliver Edwards's letter to him (c. August 1961) on Yeats and Swift: "Now, your query about when it was Yeats told me about himself and Swift's verse. He said (it was at 'Riversdale', his house in Rathfarnham, in 1934: I'm virtually certain it was 1934, tho' there's a bare chance it was 1935: those were the only two years I saw him in): 'I get my later manner from Swift.' And he proceeded to read . . . in, I think, a late 18th-cent. edition (by T. Sheridan, I think) he had of Swift, a Sir William Temple poem of Swift's – beginning (this is memory again, so subject to correction).
   'But [?] what does our proud ignorance learning call? and ending at the words '. . . and nauseate company.' ' "
2. F. Elrington Ball, *Swift's Verse: An Essay* (London: John Murray, 1929) 1–2. Archibald (180) has noted that Yeats had Ball's volume in his library.
3. *Wellesley*, 114, 23 Dec., 1936.
4. Swift, *Poems*, III, 812.
5. Ibid., II, 420. King, *Swift in Ireland*, 2.
6. *V. Poems*, 267, "All Things Can Tempt Me"; 506, "Remorse for Intemperate Speech"; 260, "The Fascination of What's Difficult".
7. *Poems*, I, 27. For Yeats's references to *Cadenus and Vanessa*, see *Explorations*, 281–5; for references to "The Progress of Beauty", see *A Vision*, 4n, and *Moore*, 148, 149–50. For his commendations of Swift's Sir William Temple

ode, see *Poems*, I, xlv, n., *Explorations*, 432, *Swift, or the Egotist*, 77, and Stephen Gwynn, *The Life and Frienships of Dean Swift* (New York: Holt, 1933) 27.

8. *Swift, or the Egotist*, 77.
9. *V. Poems*, 259. We cannot pinpoint the precise beginnings of a "later manner", nor can we establish when Yeats himself thought it began. A gradual development, evidence of the change was subtle, not radical.
10. Ibid., 262. See David R. Clark, *Lyric Resonance*, 255, for an amusing commentary on this epigram's history.
11. *Poems*, II, 651.
12. *V. Poems*, 287; *Poems*, III, 779.
13. *V. Poems*, 290–1; *Poems*, II, 506.
14. *V. Poems*, 292; *Poems*, II, 562. See Maurice Johnson, *The Sin of Wit* (Ann Arbor: Edwards Bros., 1950, rpt. 1966) 65.
15. *V. Poems*, 336; *Poems*, II, 505. The idea that the censure of fools and dunces was pleasurable praise to a wise man was frequently expounded by Swift in his letters and prose. See *Prose*, I, 242; *Correspondence*, I, 229; II, 126; III, 317; IV, 53, 125, 138.
16. *V. Poems*, 429; *Poems*, II, 364.
17. *Prose*, XI, 246–7.
18. *V. Poems*, 495; *Poems*, I, 230–1. Yeats never saw the poet as a hungry goose, but he always associated poetry and hunger: in "Ego Dominuus Tuus", Dante ate "that bitter bread", and Keats was a schoolboy with his nose pressed against a sweet-shop window. (*V. Poems*, 369–70.)
19. D.E.S. Maxwell, "Swift's Dark Grove: Yeats and the Anglo – Irish Tradition", rpt. in *W.B. Yeats: 1865–1965: Centenary Essays*, eds. D.E.S. Maxwell and S.B. Bushrui (Ibadan, Nigeria: Ibadan U.P., 1965) 28–9. *V. Poems*, 513.
20. *Poems*, II, 530; *V. Poems*, 510.
21. *V. Poems*, 565–6, 567; *Poems*, II, 419.
22. *V. Poems*, 630; *Poems*, I, 139.
23. See *Poems*, I, 139–40n.
24. *V. Poems*, 640; *Explorations*, 359. Yeats's source was "A Prayer for Stella", *Prose*, IX, 256.
25. *Correspondence*, IV, 52. We know Yeats read this because it contains the passage on the brave Catholic warriors he referred to in *On the Boiler*.

Appendix: Roger Casement: "They . . . blackened his good name"

1. Sir William Rothenstein, *Men and Memories* (New York: Tudor, 1937) II, 170–1. In *The Lives of Roger Casement* (New Haven: Yale U.P., 1976), B.L. Reid places the meetings of Yeats and Casement in Rothenstein's studio between mid-July and mid-August 1911 (142–3).
2. *Prodigal Father*, 424, JBY to Lily Yeats, 17 Aug., 1914.
3. B.L. Reid, *The Man From New York: John Quinn and his Friends* (New York: Oxford U.P., 1968) 187, AE to Quinn, 10 Dec., 1914.
4. *WBY I&R II*, 273; "Some New Letters from W.B. Yeats to Lady Gregory", between 24–5, Yeats to Eva Gore-Booth, 23 June [1916].
5. *V. Poems*, 395, 393, 394. Nancy Cardozo, *Lucky Eyes and A High Heart: The Life of Maud Gonne* (Indianapolis: Bobbs-Merrill, 1978) 309, Maud Gonne to

Quinn, 16 Aug., 1916.

6. Unterecker, *Yeats and Patrick McCartan*, 354, from Yeats to McCartan, 11 May, 1933. See also 357–8, 371, 372. For Shaw's views on Casement, see David R. Clark and Robin Skelton, eds., *The Irish Renaissance* (Dublin: Dolmen, 1975) 311–3, "The Roger Casement Trial", Dec. 1934.

7. William J. Maloney, *The Forged Casement Diaries* (Dublin: Talbot Press, 1936) 33, 48–51, 14, 87. "Nevinson" was Henry W. Nevinson, who had discussed politics with Yeats in 1901.

8. Ibid., 101.

9. See Maloney, 159–67, 175. The latter comment was from Ben S. Allen, of the Associated Press, who was shown the diaries in 1916, and believed that the typewritten extracts he was shown illustrated a degeneracy and madness not Casement's; his theory, held by many others, was that he had seen a diary copied by Casement during the Putumayo investigation.

10. Ibid., 216. The question of whether the diaries were forged excited sharply divided opinion before Maloney's book, and continues to do so, sometimes on national lines. Earlier studies, such as Denis Gwynn's *Traitor or Patriot: The Life and Death of Roger Casement* (New York: Jonathan Cape and Harrison Smith, 1931) and Alfred Noyes's *The Accusing Ghost of Roger Casement* (New York: Citadel Press, 1957) take the strong line, accusing the British of forgery. More recent studies, such as Brian Inglis's 1973 *Roger Casement* (London: Hodder & Stoughton), B.L. Reid's 1976 *The Lives of Roger Casement*, and George Dangerfield's 1976 study of Anglo–Irish relations, *The Damnable Question* (Boston: Little, Brown), all assert that the diaries were genuine. Yeats's "the lies of history", however, applied here; the most important thing was whether people believed, as did Yeats, that the diaries were forged.

11. *Letters*, 867, to Ethel Mannin, 15 Nov., 1936. One of the more unusual items Yeats might have found in the book was Casement's quotation of the final stanza of "The Lover tells of the Rose in his Heart" in a 1911 letter. (136)

12. *Wellesley*, 107–8, 28 Nov., 1936. Arra M. Garab, in "Yeats and *The Forged Casement Diaries*," *English Language Notes*, II (1965) 289–92, has identified both men whose names have been omitted as Alfred Noyes and Gilbert Murray, the latter of whom was associated with Oxford and the League of Nations.

13. *Letters*, 869, to Ethel Mannin, 30 Nov., 1936.

14. *Wellesley*, 108, Wellesley to Yeats, 1 Dec., 1936.

15. Ibid., 108–9, 4 Dec., 1936. Wherever possible, I have used her versions of these letters over Wade's because of their idosyncratic spelling and punctuation; Wade's version of this (*Letters*, 868–9) is edited. Unfortunately, we are denied Yeats's brief recapitulation of the Casement case in her edited version. When, also, did Yeats send her "the opening" of the ballad; her earlier letters do not specify. Was it sent without comment, or are we faced with more editing of these letters than is immediately apparent?

16. Ibid., 110, 7 Dec., 1936; 110–11, 9 Dec., 1936.

17. Ibid., 111, 10 Dec., 1936.

18. *Letters*, 873, to Ethel Mannin, postmarked 11 Dec., but obviously written prior to Yeats's 10 Dec. letter to Dorothy Wellesley.

19. *Wellesley*, 113, 21 Dec., 1936.

20. Ibid., 115, 23 Dec., 1936.

21. Ibid., 116, received 1 Jan., 1937.
22. Ibid., 121, on envelope, 21 Jan., 1937.
23. Ibid., 123, on envelope, 28 Jan., 1937.
24. *V. Poems*, 581-2.
25. Jeffares's *Commentary* (468) notes that the first line was, at one stage, "Come Gilbert Murray, Alfred Noyes", probably at the height of Yeats's specific rage against them, before his remorseful letter of 7 Dec. *V. Poems*, 582.
26. *Yeats*, 450n.
27. *Wellesley*, 126, 8 Feb., 1937.
28. *Letters*, 881-2, to Ethel Mannin, 11 Feb., 1937.
29. *Philadelphia Ledger*, 31 Aug., 1916, rpt. in Reid, *The Lives of Roger Casement*, 460-1. See Noyes's *The Accusing Ghost of Roger Casement*, 26-7 and *Two Worlds for Memory* (Philadelphia and New York: Lippincott, 1953) 126-43.
30. Noyes, *Two Worlds for Memory*, 132, 134.
31. *Letters*, 882-3, to the Editor of the *Irish Press*, published 13 Feb., 1937, also rpt. *V. Poems*, 838.
32. *Wellesley*, 128, 18 Feb., 1937. For Shaw's letter, see *The Matter With Ireland*, eds. Dan H. Laurence and David H. Greene (New York: Hill and Wang, 1962) 131-4; it also contains other Shaw items on Casement, from 1916 to 1937.
33. *Wellesley*, 127, Wellesley to Yeats, 19 Feb., 1937.
34. *Letters*, 884, to Ethel Mannin, 20 Feb., 1937.
35. Ibid., 885, to Ethel Mannin, 1 Mar., 1937.
36. *V. Poems*, 839-40. The banquet was held on 17 Aug.; see *Yeats and Georgian Ireland*, 339.
37. See Ellmann, *Identity of Yeats*, 293, and Jeffares, *Commentary*, 469, for dating.
38. *V. Poems*, 582n, 583-4.

Bibliography

Ball, Francis Elrington, *Swift's Verse: An Essay* (London: John Murray, 1929.)

Balliet, Conrad A., " 'The Dolls' of Yeats and the Birth of Christ'', *Research Studies*, 38 (1970) 54–7.

——, "Micheal MacLiammoir Recalls Maud Gonne MacBride", *Journal of Irish Literature*, 6 (1977) no. 2, 45–61.

Bax, Clifford, ed., *Florence Farr, Bernard Shaw and W.B. Yeats.* (Dublin: Cuala, 1941, rpt. Shannon: Irish U.P., 1971).

Beckson, Karl, ed., *Oscar Wilde: The Critical Heritage* (New York: Barnes & Noble, 1970).

Bornstein, George, "A Borrowing from Wilde in Yeats's *The King's Threshold*", *Notes and Queries*, 18 (1971) 421–2.

Bradford, Curtis, *Yeats at Work* (Carbondale, Illinois: Southern Illinois U.P., 1965).

Brèmont, Anna, Contesse de, *Oscar Wilde and His Mother* (London: Everett, 1911, rpt. New York: Haskell House, 1972).

Bridge, Ursula, ed., *W.B. Yeats and T. Sturge Moore: Their Correspondence 1901–1937* (New York: Oxford U.P., 1953).

Brown, Malcolm, *The Politics of Irish Literature: From Thomas Davis to W.B. Yeats* (Washington: U. of Washington Press, 1973).

Carden, Mary, "The Few and the Many: An Examination of W.B. Yeats's Politics". *Studies*, 58 (1969) no. 229, 57–62.

Cardozo, Nancy, *Lucky Eyes and A High Heart: The Life of Maud Gonne* (Indianapolis: Bobbs-Merrill, 1978).

Carpenter, Andrew, ed., *Place, Personality, and the Irish Writer* (New York: Barnes & Noble, 1977).

Clark, David R., *Lyric Resonance* (Amherst: U. of Massachusetts P., 1972).

——, *W.B. Yeats and the Theatre of Desolate Reality* (Chester Springs, Pa.: Dufour Editions, 1965).

Clarke, Austin, "Yeats and LeFanu". *Times Literary Supplement*, 12 Dec., 1968, 1409.

Coxhead, Elizabeth, *Lady Gregory: A Literary Portrait* (London: Secker & Warburg, 2d edn., 1966).

Cross, K.G.W. and T.R. Dunlop, *A Bibliography of Yeats Criticism 1887–1965* (New York: Macmillan, 1971).

Cullingford, Elizabeth, *Yeats, Ireland, and Fascism* (New York: NYU Press, 1981).

Dalsimer, Adele M., "Yeats's Unchanging Swift". *Eire – Ireland*, 9 (1974) no. 2, 65–89.

Dangerfield, George, *The Damnable Question: A Study in Anglo – Irish Relations* (Boston: Little, Brown, 1976).

Domville, Eric, *A Concordance to the Plays of W.B. Yeats* (Ithaca, N.Y.: Cornell U.P., 1972).

Donoghue, Denis, ed., *Jonathan Swift: A Critical Anthology* (Baltimore: Penguin, 1971).

Ellmann, Richard, *Eminent Domain: Yeats Among Wilde, Joyce, Pound, Eliot, and Auden* (New York: Oxford U.P., 1967).

——, *Golden Codgers: Biographical Speculations* (New York: Oxford U.P., 1973).

——, *The Identity of Yeats* (New York: Oxford U.P., 1954, rpt. 1968).

——, "Romantic Pantomime in Oscar Wilde", *Partisan Review*, 30 (1963) 342–55.

——, "The Uses of Decadence", Graduate School and University Center, The City University of New York. 14 Mar., 1980.

——, *Yeats: The Man and the Masks* (New York: Dutton, 1948).

——, ed. *The Artist as Critic: Critical Writings of Oscar Wilde* (New York: Random House, 1969).

Ensor, R.C.K., *England 1870–1914* (London: Oxford U.P., 1936).

Fearon, William Robert, *Parnell of Avondale* (Dublin: At The Sign of the Three Crosses Ltd, 1937).

Ferguson, Oliver W., *Jonathan Swift and Ireland* (Urbana, Indiana: U. of Indiana P., 1962).

Finneran, Richard J., ed., *Anglo – Irish Literature: A Review of Research* (New York: Modern Language Association, 1976).

Fischer, John Irwin, *On Swift's Poetry* (Gainesville, Florida: University Presses of Florida, 1978).

Fitzgerald, Mary, "Out of a medium's mouth: the Writing of *The Words upon the Window-Pane*," *Colby Library Quarterly*, XVII (1981) no. 2, 61–73.

Flanagan, Thomas, "A Discourse by Swift, A Play by Yeats", *University Review*, 5 (1968) 9–22.

——, "Yeats, Joyce, and the Matter of Ireland". *Critical Inquiry*, 2 (1975) 43–67.

Fletcher, Ian, ed., *The Complete Poems of Lionel Johnson* (London: Unicorn Press, 1953).

Friedman, Barton R., "Yeats, Johnson, and Ireland's Heroic Dead: Toward A Poetry of Politics", *Eire – Ireland*, 7 (1972) no. 4, 32–47.

Garab, Arra M., "Yeats and *The Forged Casement Diaries*". *English Language Notes*, 2 (1965) no. 4, 289–92.

Gide, André, *Oscar Wilde: In Memoriam (Reminiscences) De Profundis*, trans. Bernard Frechtman (New York: Philosophical Library, 1949).

Gilman, Richard, *Decadence: The Strange Life of an Epithet* (New York: Farrar, Straus & Giroux, 1979).

Gogarty, Oliver, *Wild Apples*, Preface by William Butler Yeats (Dublin: Cuala, 1930, rpt. Shannon: Irish U.P., 1971).

Greene, R.J., "Oscar Wilde's *Intentions:* An Early Modernist Manifesto", *British Journal of Aesthetics*, 13 (1973) 397–404.

Gregory, Horace, "William Butler Yeats and the Mask of Jonathan Swift", in *The Shield of Achilles* (New York: Harcourt, Brace, 1944), 136–55.

Gregory, Lady Isabella Augusta, *Coole* (Dublin: Cuala, 1931, rpt. Shannon: Irish U.P., 1971).

——, *Irish Folk-History Plays*, 2nd ser. (New York: G.P. Putnam's Sons, 1912).

——, *The Kiltartan Books: Combining the Kiltartan Poetry, History, and Wonder Books by Lady Gregory* (Gerrards Cross: Colin Smythe, 1971).

——, *Lady Gregory's Journals 1916–1930*, ed. Lennox Robinson (New York: Macmillan, 1947).

——, *Lady Gregory's Journals: Volume One (Books 1–29)*, ed. Daniel J. Murphy (New York: Oxford U.P., 1978).

——, *Our Irish Theatre: A Chapter of Autobiography* (New York: G.P. Putnam's Sons, 1912).

——, *Seventy Years: 1852–1922*, ed. Colin Smythe (New York: Macmillan, 1974).

——, ed., *Ideals in Ireland* (London: Unicorn, 1901, rpt. New York: Lemma Publishing Corp., 1973).

Gwynn, Denis, *Traitor or Patriot: The Life and Death of Roger Casement* (New York: Jonathan Cape & Harrison Smith, 1931).

Gwynn, Stephen, *The Life and Friendships of Dean Swift* (New York: Holt, 1933).

——, ed., *Scattering Branches: Tributes to the Memory of W.B. Yeats* (New York: Macmillan, 1940).

Harrison, Henry, *Parnell Vindicated: The Lifting of the Veil* (New York: Richard R. Smith, 1931).

Hart-Davis, Rupert, ed., *The Letters of Oscar Wilde* (London: Hart-Davis, 1962).

Hinkson, Katharine Tynan, *Twenty-Five Years: Reminiscences* (New York: Devin-Adair, 1913).

Hogan, Robert, and Michael J. O'Neill, eds, *Joseph Holloway's Abbey Theatre* (Carbondale, Illinois: Southern Illinois U.P., 1976).

——, eds, *Joseph Holloway's Irish Theatre*, 3 vols (Dixon, California: Proscenium Press, 1968–70).

Holland, Patrick, "From Parnell to O'Duffy: The Composition of Yeats's 'Parnell's Funeral' ". *Canadian Journal of Irish Studies*, 2 (1976) no. 1, 15–20.

Hone, Joseph M., *W.B. Yeats 1865–1939* (New York: Macmillan, 1943).

Hone, Joseph M. and Mario M. Rossi, *Bishop Berkeley* (New York: Macmillan, 1931).

Hyde, H. Montgomery, *Oscar Wilde: A Biography* (New York: Farrar, Straus & Giroux, 1975).

Inglis, Brian, *Roger Casement* (London: Hodder & Stoughton, 1973).

Irwin, W.R., "Swift the Verse Man", *Philological Quarterly*, 54 (1975) 222–38.

Jaffe, Nora Crow, *The Poet Swift* (Hanover, New Hampshire: The University Presses of New England, 1977).

Jeffares, A. Norman, *A Commentary on the Collected Poems of W.B. Yeats* (Stanford, California: Stanford U.P., 1968).

——, *W.B. Yeats: Man and Poet* (New Haven: Yale U.P., 1949).

——, ed., *Fair Liberty Was All His Cry: A Tercentenary Tribute to Jonathan Swift, 1667–1745* (New York: St. Martin's, 1967).

—— and K.G.W. Cross, eds, *In Excited Reverie: A Centenary Tribute to William Butler Yeats 1865–1939* (New York: Macmillan, 1969).

Jochum, K.P.S., *W.B. Yeats: A Classified Bibliography of Criticism* (Urbana, Illinois: U. of Illinois P., 1978).

Johnson, Maurice, *The Sin of Wit: Jonathan Swift As A Poet* (Syracuse: Syracuse U.P., 1950, rpt. Ann Arbor: Edwards Bros, Gordian Press, 1966).

——, "Swift's Poetry Reconsidered", in *English Writers of the Eighteenth Century*, ed. John H. Middendorf (New York: Columbia U.P., 1971, 223–48).

Johnson, Samuel, *The Lives of the Most Eminent English Poets*, vol. III (Chicago: Stone & Kimball, 1896).

Jullian, Philippe, *Oscar Wilde*, trans. Violet Wyndham (New York: Viking, 1969).

Kernahan, Coulson, *In Good Company: Some Personal Recollections of Swinburne, Lord Roberts Watts-Dunton, Oscar Wilde, Edward Whymper, S.J. Stone, Stephen Phillips.*

1917, rpt. Freeport, New York: Books for Libraries Press, 1968).

King, Richard Ashe, *Swift in Ireland* (London: T. Fisher Unwin, 1895).

Leslie, Shane, *The Skull of Swift* (London: Chatto & Windus, 1928).

Lyons, F.S.L., *Charles Stewart Parnell* (New York: Oxford U.P., 1977).

——, *The Fall of Parnell 1890–1891* (London: Routledge & Kegan Paul, 1960).

MacBride, Maud Gonne, *A Servant of the Queen* (London: Victor Gollancz, 1938).

MacMullan, D.H., "Yeats and O. Henry". *Times Literary Supplement*, 28 Nov., 1968, 1339.

Maloney, William J., *The Forged Casement Diaries* (Dublin: Talbot Press, 1936).

Marcus, Jane, "Salome: The Jewish Princess Was A New Woman", *Bulletin of the New York Public Library*, 78 (1974) 95–113.

Marlow, Joyce, *The Uncrowned Queen of Ireland: The Life of 'Kitty' O'Shea* (New York: Saturday Review Press: Dutton, 1975).

Maxwell, D.E.S. and S.B. Bushrui, eds, *W.B. Yeats 1865–1965: Centenary Essays on the Art of W.B. Yeats* (Ibadan, Nigeria: Ibadan U.P., 1965).

McHugh, Roger, ed., *Ah, Sweet Dancer: W.B. Yeats and Margot Ruddock* (New York: Macmillan, 1971).

——, ed., *W.B. Yeats's Letters to Katharine Tynan* (New York: McMullen Books, 1953).

McManus, Francis, ed., *The Yeats We Knew* (Cork: Mercier Press, 1965).

Mikhail, E.H., ed., *Oscar Wilde: Interviews and Recollections*, 2 vols (New York: Barnes & Noble, 1979).

——, ed., *W.B. Yeats: Interviews and Recollections,* 2 vols (New York: Barnes & Noble, 1977).

Miner, Earl Roy, "A Poem by Swift and W.B. Yeats's *Words upon the Window-Pane*", *Modern Language Notes*, 72 (1957) no. 4, 273–5.

Mitchell, Joan Towey, "Yeats, Pearse, and Cuchulain", *Eire – Ireland*, 11, (1976) no. 4, 51–65.

Morley, John, Viscount. *Recollections*, 2 vols (New York: Macmillan, 1917).

Murphy, Maureen, " 'What Stood in the Post Office / With Pearse and Connolly?': The Case for Robert Emmet", *Eire-Ireland*, 14 (1979) no. 3, 141–3.

Murphy, William Martin, *Prodigal Father: The Life of John Butler Yeats (1839–1922)* (Ithaca, New York: Cornell U.P., 1978).

Nassaar, Christopher S., "Vision of Evil: The Influence of Wilde's *Salome* on *Heart of Darkness* and *A Full Moon in March*". *Victorian Newsletter*, 33 (1978) 23–7.

Noyes, Alfred, *The Accusing Ghost of Roger Casement* New York: Citadel Press, 1957).

——, *Two Worlds for Memory* (Philadelphia & New York: Lippincott, 1953).

O'Brien, Conor Cruise, *Parnell and his Party.* (London: Oxford U.P., 1957).

O'Brien, R. Barry, *The Life of Charles Stewart Parnell,* 2 vols (1898, rpt. New York: Haskell House, 1968).

O'Connor, Frank, *My Father's Son* (New York: Knopf, 1969)

O'Driscoll, Robert, ed., *Theatre and Nationalism in Twentieth-Century Ireland* (Toronto: U. of Toronto Press, 1971).

—— and Lorna Reynolds, eds, *Yeats and the Theatre* (Niagara Falls: Maclean-Hunter, 1975).

Olney, James, "W.B. Yeats's Daimonic Memory". *Sewanee Review*, 85 (1977) 683–703.

O'Shea, Katharine, *Charles Stewart Parnell: His Love-Story and Political Life*, 2 vols (London: Cassell, 1914).

O'Sullivan, Vincent, *Aspects of Wilde* (New York: Holt, 1936).

Parrish, Stephen Maxfield, *A Concordance to the Poems of W.B. Yeats* (Ithaca, New York: Cornell U.P., 1963).

Pearce, Donald R., ed., *The Senate Speeches of W.B. Yeats* (Bloomington, Indiana: U. of Indiana P., 1960).

Pearson, Hesketh, *Oscar Wilde: His Life and Wit* (London: Methuen, 1954).

Power, Arthur. *The Drapier Letters and Her Ladyship – The Poet – and the Dog: Two One-Act Plays* (Dublin: Talbot Press, 1927).

Reid, B.L., *The Lives of Roger Casement* (New Haven: Yale U.P., 1976).

——, *The Man from New York: John Quinn and His Friends* (New York: Oxford U.P., 1968).

Ricketts, Charles S., *Self-Portrait: Taken from the Letters and Journals of Charles Ricketts, R.A.* Collected and compiled by T. Sturge Moore, ed. Cecil Lewis (London: Peter Davies, 1939).

Robinson, Lennox, *The Lost Leader* (Belfast: H.R. Carter, 1954).

Rogal, Samuel J., ''Keble's Hymn and Yeats's *Words Upon the Window-Pane*'', *Modern Drama*, 16 (1973) no. 1, 87–9.

Rose, Marilyn Gaddis, ''The Daughters of Herodias in *Herodiade, Salome*, and *A Full Moon in March*''. *Comparative Drama*, 1 (1967) no. 3, 172–81.

Rossi, Mario M. and Joseph M. Hone, *Swift, or the Egotist* (London: Victor Gollancz, 1934).

Rothenstein, Sir William, *Men and Memories*, 2 vols (New York: Tudor, 1937).

——, *Since Fifty: Men and Memories 1922–1938* (New York: Macmillan, 1940).

Russell, George William, *Letters from AE*, selected and ed. Alan Denson (London: Abelard-Schuman, 1961).

Schakel, Peter J., *The Poetry of Jonathan Swift* (Madison, Wisconsin: U. of Wisconsin P., 1978).

Schrickx, W., ''On Giordano Bruno, Wilde, and Yeats''. *English Studies*, 45, supp. presented to R.W. Zandvoort (1965) 257–64.

Shaw, George Bernard, *The Matter With Ireland*, eds. Dan H. Laurence and David H. Greene (New York: Hill & Wang, 1962).

Sheridan, Thomas, *The Life of the Rev. Dr. Jonathan Swift.* (London: C. Bathurst *et al.*, 1764, rpt. New York: Garland, 1974).

Shinagel, Michael, *A Concordance to the Poems of Jonathan Swift* (Ithaca, New York: Cornell U.P., 1972).

Singleton-Gates, Peter, and Maurice Girodias, *The Black Diaries of Roger Casement* (New York: Grove Press, 1959).

Sisson, C.H., ''Yeats and Swift'', *Agenda*, 9 (1971–2) no. 4–10, no. 1, 34–8.

Skelton, Robin and David R. Clark, eds, *The Irish Renaissance: A Gathering of Essays, Memoirs, and Letters from the Massachusetts Review* (Dublin: Dolmen, 1975).

Stamm, Rudolf, ''William Butler Yeats and *The Ballad of Reading Gaol* by Oscar Wilde'', in *The Shaping Powers at Work: Fifteen Essays on Poetic Transmutation (Heidelberg: Carl Winter Universitatsverlag, 1967, 210–19).

Stanford, W.B., ''Yeats in the Irish Senate''. *Review of English Literature*, 4 (1963) no. 3, 71–80.

Swift, Jonathan, *The Correspondence of Jonathan Swift*, ed. Harold Williams, 5 vols (London: Oxford U.P., 1963–5).

——, *Journal to Stella*, ed. Harold Williams, 2 vols (London: Oxford U.P., 1948).

——, *The Poems of Jonathan Swift*, ed. Harold Williams, 3 vols (London: Oxford U.P., 1958).

——, *The Prose Writings of Jonathan Swift*, ed. Herbert Davis *et al.*, 14 vols (London:

Blackwell, 1939–68).

——, *A Tale of A Tub*, eds.A.C. Guthkelch and D. Nichol Smith (London: Oxford U.P., 2nd ed., 1958).

Torchiana, Donald T., *W.B. Yeats and Georgian Ireland* (Evanston, Illinois: Northwestern U.P., 1966).

——, and Glenn O'Malley, eds "Some New Letters from W.B. Yeats to Lady Gregory", *Review of English Literature*, 4 (1963) no. 3, 9–47.

Unterecker, John, ed. *Yeats: A Collection of Critical Essays* (Engelwood Cliffs, N.J.: Prentice-Hall, 1963).

——, ed., *Yeats and Patrick McCartan: A Fenian Friendship* Dolmen Press Yeats Centenary Papers, no. 10 (Dublin: Dolmen, 1965).

Ure, Peter, "A Source for Yeats's 'Parnell's Funeral' ''. *English Studies*, 39 (1958), no. 6, 257–8.

Vozar, Lea B., "Yeats, Swift, Irish Patriotism, and 'Rationalistic Anti-Intellectualism' ''. *Massachusetts Studies in English*, 3 (1972) no. 4, 108–16.

Wade, Allan, ed., *A Bibliography of the Writings of W.B. Yeats* (London: Hart-Davis, 1951, 2nd edn., rev. 1958).

——, ed., *The Letters of W.B. Yeats* (New York: Macmillan, 1955).

Wilde, Oscar, *The Complete Works of Oscar Wilde*, 12 vols (Garden City, New York: Doubleday, 1923).

——, *De Profundis* (New York: Vintage, 1964).

——, *Essays and Lectures* (London: Methuen, 1909, rpt. New York: Garland, 1978).

——, *The Picture of Dorian Gray*, ed. Isobel Murray (London: Oxford U.P., 1974).

——, *The Soul of Man Under Socialism and Other Essays* (New York: Harper, 1970).

Wilson, F.A.C., " 'Parnell's Funeral', II''. *Explicator*, 27 (1969) no. 9, Item 72.

Yeats, John Butler, *Further Letters of John Butler Yeats*, selected by Lennox Robinson (Dublin: Cuala, 1920, rpt. Shannon: Irish U.P., 1971).

——, *Letters From Bedford Park: A Selection of the Correspondence (1890–1901) of John Butler Yeats*, ed. and introduced by William Martin Murphy (Dublin: Cuala, 1972).

——, *Letters to His Son W.B. Yeats and Others: 1869–1922*, ed. Joseph Hone (London: Faber & Faber, 2d edn., 1944).

——, *Passages From the Letters of John Butler Yeats*, selected by Ezra Pound (Dublin: Cuala, 1917, rpt. Shannon: Irish U.P., 1971).

Yeats, William Butler, *The Autobiography of William Butler Yeats* (New York: Collier, 1974).

——, *Essays and Introductions* (New York: Collier, 1961).

——, *Explorations*, selected by Mrs. W.B. Yeats (New York: Collier, 1973).

——, "Irish Drama: Interview With Mr. W.B. Yeats", *Observer*, 19 June 1910, 10.

——, *Letters on Poetry from W.B. Yeats to Dorothy Wellesley* (London: Oxford U.P., 1940, rpt. 1964).

——, *Letters to the New Island*, ed. Horace Reynolds (Cambridge: Harvard U.P., 1934, rpt. 1970).

——, *Memoirs*, ed. and transcribed by Denis Donoghue. (New York: Macmillan, 1973).

——, "Modern Ireland: An Address to American Audiences, 1932–1933'', ed. and transcribed by Curtis Bradford, *Massachusetts Reveiw*, 5 (1964) 256–88.

——, *Mythologies* (New York: Collier, 1969).

——, *On the Boiler* (Dublin: Cuala, n.d. [1939?], rpt. Shannon: Irish U.P., 1971).

——, *The Speckled Bird*, ed. William H. O'Donnell (Toronto: McClelland and

Stewart, 1967).

——, *Uncollected Prose: 1886–1896*, vol. I, ed. John P. Frayne (New York: Columbia U.P., 1970).

——, *Uncollected Prose: 1897–1939* vol. II, eds. John P. Frayne and Colton Johnson (New York: Columbia U.P., 1976).

——, *The Variorum Edition of the Plays of W.B. Yeats*, ed. Russell K. Alspach (New York: Macmillan, 1966).

——, *The Variorum Edition of the Poems of W.B. Yeats*, eds Peter Allt and Russell K. Alspach (New York: Macmillan, 1957).

——, *A Vision* (New York: Collier, 1966).

——, *A Vision: An Explanation of Life Founded upon the Writings of Giraldus and upon Certain Doctrines Attributed to Kusta Ben Luka* (London: privately printed by Werner Laurie, 1925, rpt. Ann Arbor: University Microfilms, n.d.).

——, ed., *A Book of Irish Verse*, 4th edn. (London: Methuen, 1920).

——, ed., *The Oxford Book of Modern Verse: 1892–1935* (New York: Oxford U.P., 1936, rpt. 1947).

——, ed., *Representative Irish Tales, First Series* (New York: Knickerbocker Press, G.P. Putnam's Sons, 1891).

——, ed., *Selections From The Writings of Lord Dunsany* (Dundrum, Churchtown: Cuala, 1912, rpt. Shannon: Irish U.P., 1971).

——, ed., *Twenty One Poems Written by Lionel Johnson* (Dundrum, Dun Emer, 1904, rpt. Shannon: Irish U.P., 1971).

——, and F.R. Higgins, eds, *Broadsides: A Collection of Old and New Songs* (Dublin: Cuala, 1935, rpt. Shannon: Irish U.P., 1971).

——, and Thomas Kinsella, *Davis, Mangan, Ferguson? Tradition and the Irish Writer* (Dublin: Dolmen, 1970).

——, and Dorothy Wellesley, eds, *Broadsides: A Collection of New Irish and English Songs* (Dublin: Cuala, 1937, rpt. Shannon: Irish U.P., 1971).

Index